EXTIMACY

Series Editors

Slavoj Žižek

Adrian Johnston

Todd McGowan

diaeresis

EXTIMACY

Edited by Nadia Bou Ali
and Surti Singh

Northwestern University Press
Evanston, Illinois

Northwestern University Press
www.nupress.northwestern.edu

Copyright © 2025 by Northwestern University. Published 2025 by Northwestern University Press. All rights reserved.

Printed in the United States of America

10 9 8 7 6 5 4 3 2 1

Library of Congress Cataloging-in-Publication Data

Names: Bou Ali, Nadia, 1984– editor. | Singh, Surti, 1974– editor.
Title: Extimacy / edited by Nadia Bou Ali and Surti Singh.
Other titles: Diaeresis.
Description: Evanston, Illinois : Northwestern University Press, 2024. | Series: Diaeresis.
Identifiers: LCCN 2024015041 | ISBN 9780810147515 (paperback) | ISBN 9780810147522 (cloth) | ISBN 9780810147539 (ebook)
Subjects: LCSH: Lacan, Jacques, 1901–1981. | Psychoanalysis.
Classification: LCC BF173 .E88 2024 | DDC 150.19/5—dc23/eng/20240709
LC record available at https://lccn.loc.gov/2024015041

Contents

Acknowledgments	vii
Introduction: The Concept of Extimacy Nadia Bou Ali and Surti Singh	3
The Ontological Limbo: Three Notes on Extimacy and Ex-sistence Samo Tomšič	32
Extimacy and *das Ding*: The Outside-In of the Void Richard Boothby	50
What, If Anything, Is Authority? Mladen Dolar	63
Asexual Violence and Systemic Enjoyment Alenka Zupančič	80
"For Thought to Dwell Where Evils Have No Entry": On Oedipus and the Extimacy of Anger Amanda Holmes	97
On Ambivalence as a Key Freudian Concept: The *Vaterkomplex*'s Edifice Alejandro Cerda-Rueda	110
What Is a Body? A Question between Critical Theory and Psychoanalysis Silvio Carneiro	128
Hate Your Neighbor as You Hate Yourself: How to Think Psychoanalytically about Hate, Racism, and Exclusion Patricia Gherovici	143

Objet a and the Possibilities of Political Resistance:
Extimacy, Anxiety, and Political Action 161
Andreja Zevnik

Transference and Its Discontents:
Lacan and the Extimate Place of Politics 178
Vladimir Safatle

Contributors 197

Acknowledgments

The idea for this volume emerged in the context of a conference we organized in Beirut in February 2020 entitled "Extimacy: Authority, Anxiety, and the Desire for Revolution," and while working together within the framework of the Andrew W. Mellon Foundation–funded project Extimacies: Critical Theory from the Global South (2018–2022). The conference ended right at the beginning of the COVID-19 pandemic, when the extimate nature of borders was rendered fixed, when the world locked down. Our project coalesced during this time of geopolitical and economic upheaval; since then, borders have become more fixed, and global ecological catastrophes have continued to unfold. It is our sense that the forging of an "extimate" space of politics that can transform our world has become more pressing. This book is an effort in that direction. We want to first thank the contributors for sharing our concerns with the current state of the world and thinking through them via this nodal concept of extimacy, which mires the boundaries between interiority and exteriority. We want to thank Trevor Perri for his invaluable editorial work on the book; the editors of the Diaeresis series—Todd McGowan, Adrian Johnston, and Slavoj Žižek—for their enthusiastic support of our project; and Northwestern University Press for allowing this volume to serve as the capstone to a series that has published a number of excellent titles. We'd also like to thank senior acquisitions editor Faith Wilson Stein for shepherding our project to print. In addition, we acknowledge support from the Andrew W. Mellon Foundation's Early Career Scholars Program and Villanova University's Subvention of Publication Program in the publication of this book. An earlier version of Vladimir Safatle's essay originally appeared as "Revolution and Liquidation of Transference: The Subjective Destitution as Procedure of Social Emancipation," in *The Truth of Psychoanalysis,* edited by Jasper Feyaerts and Paulo Beer (Leuven: Leuven University Press, 2022). We thank Leuven University Press for permission to reuse parts of this chapter.

EXTIMACY

Introduction

The Concept of Extimacy

Nadia Bou Ali and Surti Singh

This volume is the first book-length investigation into the psychoanalytic concept of *extimacy* (*extimité*). "Extimacy" is a neologism Jacques Lacan coined in 1960 but mentions no more than three or four times in his entire oeuvre. It describes an intimate exteriority, or, as Lacan himself puts it, "the central place, as the intimate exteriority or 'extimacy,' that is the Thing . . ."[1] Drawing on Freud, Lacan articulates extimacy as the "Thing" (*das Ding*), which designates "the excluded interior," or what is "excluded in the interior."[2] In this sense, Lacan introduced the term "extimacy" to describe a topological zone of unconscious formations that disrupts the binaries inside/outside, essence/appearance, subject/object. It may, of course, seem curious to organize an entire volume around a neologism that was never explicitly presented as a concept by Lacan himself, but our claim is that, despite the paucity of its occurrence within Lacan's corpus, extimacy does indeed have the status of a concept for Lacan—a concept, moreover, that is absolutely central to his thought.

This volume is concerned with pursuing Lacan's elaboration of a new concept within the theoretical field of psychoanalysis, a field which fundamentally assumes that ordinary sense-making is already a delusional process that requires a *savoir* based on the belief in an Other.[3] The concept of extimacy navigates the rift between two orders of knowledge, *connaissance* and *savoir*.[4] The subject's estrangement from imaginary knowledge (*connaissance*) is the operation by which psychoanalysis proceeds in order to reveal the contours of symbolic knowledge (*savoir*) that are unconsciously at work in the subject. This procedure, usually referred to as the split-subject of the signifier, or the subject divided by enunciation and the statement of enunciation, is fundamental to psychoanalysis. Lacan maintained that the status of the subject in relation to structure is extimate. Perhaps we would not be too far off if we said that extimacy could serve as a brand name for psychoanalysis, its designating nomination.

Lacan's rare mentions of extimacy were first fully elaborated by Jacques-Alain Miller. Miller's course on extimacy, delivered in 1985 and 1986 at the University of Paris VIII, influenced the reception of the concept in contemporary psychoanalytic theory.[5] Yet since Miller's lectures, extimacy itself has not appeared as the subject of any significant monograph or edited collection. With this volume, we not only focus on how extimacy informs contemporary psychoanalytic theory; we also aim to demonstrate that this concept harbors as yet unexplored significance for wider philosophical, political, and cultural debates.

We propose that the concept of extimacy deepens the scope of psychoanalysis by articulating its relation to both philosophy and politics, two spheres that remain at odds with one another, as exemplified by the debates about theory and praxis that emerged with the 1960s student protests. This excursion into the concept of extimacy, then, is also a revitalization of the debates that have informed the development of theory more generally since the 1960s, and of the way in which they continue to inform contemporary global politics. Through the notion of extimacy, this volume re-situates questions of authority, law, ideology, the body, affect, and ontology in the present context. In this respect, the book asks: How does psychoanalysis help us work through and move beyond present approaches to the pathologies of reason and the authority of reason by accounting for unconscious formations? Stated otherwise: How can the extimate topology of the unconscious re-question the limits of the current theoretical appraisals of modernity? As such, we propose that extimacy be conceived as a concept from which it is possible to rethink the relation between reason and unreason, history and logic, progress and prolepsis, and philosophies of consciousness and the unconscious. Further, extimacy raises anew the question of causality, because as a topology it is structured around an immanent gap in a cause that doesn't exist and yet has material effects in the discourses that ground the social (non)relation. Extimacy is one word that encapsulates the phrase "the unconscious is '*discours de l'Autre*' (discourse of the Other)":[6] the unconscious not as an other scene, a *behind the scenes*, or the obverse of reality, but as that which coincides with the extimate thing, the blind spot in the frame of representation that makes representation possible.

Extimacy is a concept that brings together a number of crucial and complicated psychoanalytic points: the status of enjoyment in relation to Being; *objet a*; the topology of the unconscious; the theory of discourse; the ethics of psychoanalysis (in the figure of the neighbor as an extimate thing); and finally, the question of the body, or the otherness of the body.

INTRODUCTION

Most crucially, extimacy can be used to account for the entire status of psychoanalysis as a field which constantly spills over into other fields: philosophy, cultural theory, literature, history, critical theory, and so on. The concrete clinical space in psychoanalytic practice is itself extimate, one in which speech and language take on a distinct function of interrogating all other spheres of lived experience. This extimate place of the clinic, as an outer limit to lived experiences, is arguably the locus from where metapsychological speculation takes place. The clinical scene is an artificial place that submits our experiences to questioning, and in correspondence to this, the theoretical scene of psychoanalysis submits philosophy and politics to a similar interrogation. Extimacy, then, can be used to denote the praxis of psychoanalysis in relation to singular lived experiences as well as to meta-analytic speculations about collective social life.

It could be argued that all the points mentioned above are connected via one nodal problem: psychoanalysis and its account of ontology. Lacan never claimed an ontology and in fact warned against attempts to deduce a philosophical ontology from his teachings. Yet, at other times, Lacan engaged with ontological questions. When pressed to account for his ontology after he introduced the unconscious through the structure of the gap, he designated the unconscious as something pre-ontological: "it is neither being, nor non-being, but the unrealized,"[7] something like the intermediary beings of the Gnostics—sylphs, gnomes, and so on. In his discussion of the gaze, Lacan admitted that he had an ontology, "like everyone else, however naive or elaborate it may be."[8] With the notion of extimacy, we interrogate these theoretical interstices between psychoanalysis and philosophy.

From Recollection to Repetition

Lacan's references to the history of philosophy, from the classical tradition to twentieth-century movements, are a fundamental part of his oeuvre, presenting the reader with conceptual explorations that illuminate facets of psychoanalytic theory and practice.[9] The concept of extimacy is no exception, for while its formation in Lacan's work can be directly linked to Freud's psychoanalytic theory and a reformulation of *das Ding*, the "working through" of this concept can be found throughout Lacan's corpus and his engagement with philosophy from Plato to Heidegger.[10] More specifically, the rationalist, idealist tradition provides a particularly important philosophical lens for how to think the aporia of something that is more interior than my inmost being, and Lacan examines notions of memory, consciousness, and innate truths that prefigure the psychoanalytic concept of the unconscious. Lacan engages with various figures in the history of philosophy for whom there lies at the very heart of the subject, in its most interior part, some kernel that is radically other to it, and one that the subject is unable to readily—consciously—recognize. Indeed, the confrontation with the extimate kernel at the heart of being requires a startling discovery—namely, that what appears to be exterior is actually interior, and what appears to be my most interior self is foreign to me.

Philosophically, this confrontation raises the question of how this discovery is made, and relatedly, the status of truth and knowledge. In 1953, Lacan began his second seminar with a reference to Plato's dialogue *Meno*, which had been the subject of Alexandre Koyré's lecture the night before.[11] This seminar took place after Lacan had been forced to resign from the Société Psychanalytique de Paris and at the same time inaugurated his place in the newly formed Société Française de Psychanalyse. Oliver Harris notes that the subject of teaching and learning, of "truth, knowledge and pedagogy," was not surprising given that Lacan's forced resignation had occurred "when controversy over his analytic and training methods came to a head."[12] Indeed, wider questions about the Socratic method and its relevance for psychoanalysis were raised in the seminar.[13] However, Lacan's mention of the *Meno* dialogue, and Plato's theory of recollection in particular, also invites questions about the extimate structure of truth, which only remain tacit in this seminar but are salient for the way in which Lacan goes on to discuss the analytic ego.

In the *Meno*, Socrates conjunctures the existence of an immortal soul already filled with knowledge obtained prior to its incarnation in the human being. Lodged in the heart of finite being, in its innermost core, is something exterior and of which there is no awareness, a kind of blind spot. It is only in response to the paradox posed to Socrates by an exasperated Meno—"how will you look for it, Socrates, when you do not know at all what it is"—that the theory of recollection leads to the answer: we can search for it because we already—partially—know it.[14] In this sense, the human being is a type of vessel, a container or space that is filled with knowledge, but whose dimensions do not originate within it. The innate truths that the process of recollection—anamnesis—will stir up are inaccessible to the human being, and yet, when one comes across that knowledge, one will know it, and "recognize" it. For Lacan, Plato's theory of recollection, and in particular, Socrates's mathematical demonstration of recollection in his exchange with Meno's slave, tells us something about the pre-analytical notion of the ego. It demonstrates the "function

INTRODUCTION

of truth in its nascent state. Indeed, the knowledge to which truth comes to be knotted must actually be endowed with its own inertia . . . since it exhibits an obvious propensity to misrecognize its own meaning."[15]

How does this misrecognition occur? In the *Meno*, the search for knowledge is initially understood as a search for something outside of oneself. In the conventional model of learning, knowledge is something external that is taken into oneself, "a mechanical mode of union and the filling of an empty space with things which are foreign and indifferent to this space itself."[16] In opposition to this, Plato's *Meno* presents a view of knowledge in which one traverses one's internal terrain in order to find truths that one already knows, and at the same time, one is unaware that those truths reside within oneself, but they are guaranteed by the eternal nature of one's soul. The participants in Lacan's seminar—Mannoni, Hyppolite—debated the extent of the affinity between Socratic questioning and psychoanalytic practice, but Lacan resisted this parallel, instead drawing attention to the presence of an eternal truth at the heart of the pre-analytic ego that erases the history of its own formation. It is not a question of how this truth arrived in the soul, but rather only the conviction that it is there, a danger that Lacan posed for the psychoanalytic corpus itself and its tendency to formalize its own concepts. Lacan, then, points to a misrecognition that occurs between two registers demonstrated by the *Meno* dialogue, between the imaginary and the symbolic. The knowledge brought to light, given symbolic value, is taken to have always been there, eternally, and yet this occludes the way in which this knowledge is brought forth from—constructed out of—the imaginary, and in turn, the way in which there is always something of the symbolic in the imaginary, and also an element which cannot be symbolized (the real).

In this sense, the idea of misunderstanding or misrecognition (*méconnaissance*) becomes fundamental to psychoanalysis, an idea that can be further tracked in the transition from the pagan to the Christian world. For Lacan, the centrality of recollection in the Platonic worldview means that "the natural object, the harmonic correspondent of the living being, is recognizable because its outline has already been sketched. And for it to have been sketched, it must already have been within the object which is going to join itself to it. This is the relation of the dyad."[17] With the advent of Christianity, this dyad gives way to a third—sin—which entangles the subject not in recollection, but in repetition and the discourse of the Other.[18]

Jacques-Alain Miller locates this extimate relation in Saint Augustine's realization that God is *interior intimeo meo*, "more interior than my innermost being," whereby the self-evident nature of Platonic eternal truth takes on an uncanny dimension, that is, it becomes a moment of strangeness, and therefore also a moment of self-reflection.[19] In the

Platonic worldview, it is never a question that truth resides within the immortal soul, but in the work of Augustine, the innate idea of God, to be discovered by the reflective subject, opens the strangeness that is at the heart of being, an intimate relation that exceeds the subject. Although God is within the subject, the subject cannot know God: "God is found within me, yet I do not find God because I am outside myself. I am where my mind is, and my mind is where its attention is, and my attention is inveterately, sinfully turned outward, away from both self and God."[20] For Miller, Saint Augustine's formulation that God is *interior intimeo meo* is precisely a religious cover for extimacy. It is a cover insofar as what is most intimate is also the most opaque—that is, "paradoxically, the most intimate is not a point of transparency but rather a point of opacity."[21] In this sense, "God here is thus a word which covers this point of extimacy . . ."[22] The figure of extimacy—*das Ding*—is an exteriority that is far more alien to the subject than the external world but is, at the same time, more intimate than the subject to itself. As Shuli Barzilai notes, although at times Lacan's references to *das Ding* have a transcendent dimension, his notion is ultimately in contradistinction to the plenitude of being signified by God in the metaphysical tradition.[23] With *das Ding*, the plenitude of divine being is replaced with a void, an emptiness at the heart of being—Miller's point is that the plenitude of being itself is a cover for this emptiness.

This extimate relation implies that interiority is not to be understood as the most transparent intimate zone but as an opacity, a cover-up for the status of the internal as an Other. Not only is the subject split, or "barred" in the Lacanian formulation, but the Other is barred and alienated as well. In this sense, the subject of the unconscious does not coincide with the ego—this is a crucial point that both Freud and Lacan agree on. The ego is an imaginary alienation, a constitutive alienation of the subject which paves the way for a secondary operation of alienation: not only is desire always the desire of the Other, but the ego itself is nothing but the detour through which subjectivity and otherness are related. Extimacy is the zone of overlap of this doubled alienation. Extimacy is the determination of the "nonrelational relation" between subject and other: its topology is that of a concentric circle. On the one hand the subject is barred, divided by desire; and on the other hand, the Other is barred because it is solely a function of the fantasy of the subject. It is in this sense that Lacan locates the presence of the Other in the rationalist God, the God that is more interior than my most innermost being, a formulation also endemic to Lacan's reading of the Cartesian subject. At various points in his corpus, Saint Augustine anticipated Descartes's

INTRODUCTION

discovery of the cogito. In book 1 of *On Free Choice of the Will*, Augustine and Evodius have the following exchange:

> AUGUSTINE: Not everything alive knows itself to be alive, whereas everything that knows itself to be alive necessarily is alive.
> EVODIUS: I no longer have any doubts. Continue where you are heading. I have learned well that being alive is one thing, knowing yourself to be alive quite another.[24]

In this detour from ancient Greek to early modern philosophy, the process of recollection, which draws eternal truths from my soul, is transformed into a process of self-awareness which establishes certainty about the soul itself.[25]

In the "First Meditation," Descartes's rejection of knowledge derived from sensory experience was part of the wider rejection of empiricism stemming from the rationalist distrust of the senses.[26] Yet, Descartes then moves further into the skeptical arguments, and poses a fundamental challenge to our a priori beliefs—mathematical and geometrical proofs—by considering the possibility of a deceiving God, and ultimately, an evil demon. As Lacan emphasizes in *The Four Fundamental Concepts of Psychoanalysis*, Descartes's formulation of the cogito in the "Second Meditation," that unshakable foundation of subjectivity despite the possibility of universal deception, ultimately requires Descartes to find otherness in God.[27] Although Lacan does not name it as such, here is the extimate moment that emerges in his discussion of Descartes's discovery of the cogito:

> For Descartes, in the initial *cogito* . . . what the *I think* is directed towards, in so far as it lurches into the *I am*, is a real. But the true remains so much outside that Descartes has to re-assure himself—of what, if not of an Other that is not deceptive, and which shall, into the bargain, guarantee by its very existence the bases of truth, guarantee him that there are in his own objective reason the necessary foundations for the very real, about whose existence he has just re-assured himself, to find the dimension of truth.[28]

As Lacan shows, Descartes's discovery of the cogito, the interior certainty that lays the foundation for all subsequent knowledge, is dependent upon that which remains outside, a non-deceiving Other. At the same time, the reality of this non-deceiving Other can only be established internally, because it is an innate idea: an eternal truth that is implanted in the subject but that does not originate from within it.

Lacan's reading of Descartes sets the stage for his understanding of the Freudian unconscious, and it is through a specifically dialectical inversion that the extimate kernel, *das Ding*, comes to light. For Lacan, there is a convergence between Descartes and Freud insofar as for both, certainty is grounded in the subject. However, if Descartes places certainty in the activity of consciousness, for Freud, certainty is in the unconscious. As Lacan notes, "Freud addresses the subject in order to say to him the following, which is new—*Here, in the field of the dream, you are at home. Wo es war, soll Ich werden.*"[29] In finding itself where it was, the subject is called to "re-enter himself in the unconscious,"[30] a call that is made to a subject of precisely this Cartesian origin. For Lacan, this illustrates the function of recollection or remembrance in psychoanalysis, but it is not recollection in the Platonic sense, that is, a return to a supreme and eternal truth. Rather, the truth that emerges is from the structure of the signifier, what Lacan earlier in the seminar designates the network of signifiers—this truth emerges from the "talking crowd," from the "languages spoken in a stuttering, stumbling way." Here, then, Lacan introduces the notion of *Wiederkehr*, and a return not only in the sense of what has been repressed—"the very constitution of the field of the unconscious is based on the *Wiederkehr*. It is there that Freud bases his certainty . . . but it is not from there that it comes to him. It comes to him from the fact that he recognizes the law of his own desire."[31] In this self-recognition, in Freud's own path of self-discovery, Lacan locates the "brilliant mapping of the law of desire suspended in the Name-of-the-father."[32] It is in the myths of the death of the father that Freud finds the regulation of his own desire. This question of desire returns Lacan to the difference between the Cartesian approach, as it comes to inform his reading of Freud, and the ancient search for *episteme*, a difference that Lacan locates in the experience of alienation and separation, and indeed, transitions us from the path of doubt to the path of despair.

In his *Lectures on the History of Philosophy*, Hegel's commentary on Plato's notion of recollection sets the stage for this path of despair. For Hegel, his predecessors (Plato, Descartes, Saint Augustine) rely on natural consciousness, a form of consciousness for which truth is immediate—whether it is recollected as in Plato or is evident by the natural light, as in Descartes. In Plato, knowledge is in our soul, and we are not concerned about the process by which this knowledge arrives there, but rather how we can obtain it. Thus, in the *Meno*, Socrates traces the theory of recollection to "the priests and priestesses . . . Pindar too . . . and many others of the divine among our poets"[33] who guarantee that the human soul is immortal and contains all possible knowledge, which can be recalled. Similarly, Descartes, in the "Third Meditation," speaks about the idea of God in him as an innate idea, that is, as "the mark of the craftsman stamped on his work." The divine source guarantees that knowledge is in my soul, even if I do not immediately have access to it—nevertheless, once I come across, recognize it, and know it, it is incapable of deception. In Hegel, the path of doubt gives way to the path of despair, for "what happens on it is not what is ordinarily understood when the word 'doubt' is used: shilly-shallying about this or that presumed truth, followed by a return to that truth again, after the doubt has to be appropriately dispelled—so that at the end of the process the matter is taken to be what it was in the first place."[34] Hegel notes that others miss the importance of Plato's notion of recollection, placing it as either something outside or as something wholly inside the intellect, and thus miss the universality of the process whereby "the mind's own essence becomes actualized, or it comes to the knowledge of this last." Nevertheless, Hegel points out that for Plato, *Erinnerung* (recollection) is used in an empirical sense, as the reproduction of an idea that existed in another time. In contrast, Hegel points to the etymology of "recollection" to ascertain another meaning: "a going within self, and that we make that which at first shows itself in external form and determined as a manifold, into an inward, a universal, because we go into ourselves and thus bring what is inward in us to consciousness." The subject, then, rather than only reaching into itself, actively constructs itself along this path. As Angelica Nuzzo notes, for Hegel, too, exteriorization is a return to oneself.[35] Jean Hyppolite's comments, interspersed in Lacan's seminars, reveal the importance of the Hegelian subject for psychoanalysis: "The subject originally locates and recognizes desire through the intermediary, not only of his own image, but of the body of his fellow being. It's exactly at that moment that the human being's consciousness, in the form of consciousness of self, distinguishes itself. It is in so far as he recognizes his desire in the body of the other that the exchange takes place. It is in so far as his desire has gone over to the other side that he assimilates himself to the body of the other and recognizes himself as body."[36] In Hegel's *Phenomenology of Spirit*, the transition from the consumptive, incorporating desire to the scene of the master-slave dialectic illustrates the movement of self-consciousness, in which this exteriorization is a return to oneself, a movement that Hyppolite reads in relation to Freud's paper on "Negation." As Hyppolite points out, "distinguishing between the alien and itself is an operation, an expelling," and as Recalti notes, what is excluded "belongs to the essence of the subject"; it is thus a dialectical exclusion, and extimacy is an "interior-exterior, or 'foreign internal territory.'"[37]

It is perhaps here that we can introduce the distinction between recollection and repetition, and, more precisely, repetition in psychoanalysis. Lacan turns to Kierkegaard to flesh out the precursor to the psychoanalytic notion of repetition, a register already emergent in the Socratic dialogue between the intuition of the slave (the imaginary) and the formula that underlines his recognition of the answer, the square root of 2, an irrational number that requires an image with symbolic value.[38] This is not to suggest a linear trajectory from Platonic recollection to Kierkegaardian repetition, or as Lacan notes, it is not to suggest that there is nothing to learn from the Socratic/Platonic orientation, but only that one must "respect the distance separating the reminiscence that Plato came to presuppose as necessary for any advent of the idea, from the exhaustion of being that is consummated in Kierkegaardian repetition."[39] From the standpoint of repetition, "what appears to him corresponds only partially with what has gained him satisfaction, the subject engages in a quest, and repeats his quest indefinitely until he rediscovers this object . . . the object is encountered and is structured along the path of a repetition—to find the object again, to repeat the object. Except, it never is the same object which the subject encounters. In other words, he never ceases generating substitutive objects."[40] As Lacan points out, for Freud, this is the essential difference between the structuration of two forms of human experience—one which Lacan, following Kierkegaard, terms ancient and is modeled on recollection, in which there is harmony between the individual and the world of objects that allows for recognition, and the other based on repetition, in which recognition is only ever partial. With this partial recognition, we also have the introduction of affect, and more precisely, the affect of anxiety. As Dolar notes, extimacy "points neither to the interior nor to the exterior, but is located there where the most intimate interiority coincides with the exterior and becomes threatening, provoking horror and anxiety."[41]

One of Lacan's fundamental assumptions with regard to extimacy is that the human has an uncanny nature as a speaking being. Uncanniness or *unheimlichkeit* is an effect that arises from being in language: from the rift caused by the real in being, the real as that which always remains unspoken, unspeakable, and unsymbolizable. The appearance of *objet a* provokes a sense of the uncanny and indicates a too-much-ness of reality, the unbearable presence of an excess that must be absented. Stated otherwise, if extimacy were a category of objectivity, it does not describe a *kind* of object that exists somewhere outside the cognizing self. *Objet a*, the extimate object, is not an object of empirical experience or judgment, nor is it simply an object of thought, a phenomenological object of consciousness. Extimacy is meant to describe the status of *objet a*, which is not an object of consciousness but an object of the unconscious. The subject-object relation in psychoanalysis is extimate and

INTRODUCTION

not reducible to the binaries of interiority and exteriority. Extimacy maintains an overlap despite the distance between Lacanian psychoanalysis and Kantian conceptualism, Husserlian phenomenology, and last but not least, materialism in Hegelian and post-Hegelian philosophy.

If there is anywhere that the anxiety of the extimate appears in its most uncanny form, it is in the phenomenological relation to the body. Descartes continuously turned to the idea of the automaton, as the uncanny union of the mind and the body, wherein the body is something completely independent from the mind and yet the mind cannot escape its effects. And there is an undeniable dimension of bodily extimacy in Saint Augustine, the uncontrollability of desire—lust—which leads to a deep sense of alienation from one's own bodily functions. Turning to Lacan's Freud, all of these bodily relations are codified through the notion of the unconscious, one which interpellates this clumsy duality always through a third—the gap, the hole, the void—that which we circle toward, and yet, that which provokes in us the greatest anxiety when it becomes present. It brings us to *object a*, as both the source of desire and the object that must always be absented from the frame of fantasy, which is in turn the only access the subject has to reality. Fantasy frames structure the relation between the subject and the objective world, and they rely on the exclusion of the extimate element, of the *objet a*, from the frame of fantasy. Only when the negativity is positivized in the figure of the double or other avatars—the mechanical doll, the automaton—does anxiety overwhelm and the sense of the uncanny presents itself. Lacan renames Freud's *unheimlich* as the extimate.

The "Thing" between Freud and Lacan

Much hinges on how to understand extimacy as a psychoanalytic concept, and although Lacan coined the term, we could say that it is predicted in Freud's account of the object (of study for psychoanalysis). Indeed, Lacan develops the interior-exterior relation primarily through a reformulation of Freud's *Nebenmensch* (the neighbor or fellow human being) from the 1895 *Project for a Scientific Psychology*.[42] In Seminar VII (*The Ethics of Psychoanalysis*), Lacan focuses on how *das Ding* (the Thing) emerges for the subject in its experience of the *Nebenmensch* "as being by its very nature alien, *Fremde*." Examining Lacan's reformulation of *das Ding* and the *Nebenmensch* will bring into relief the contours that delimit the concept of extimacy, and furthermore, will illustrate the way that extimacy is fundamental to a host of other Lacanian concepts.[43]

In the *Entwurf,* or the *Project for a Scientific Psychology,* Freud had used the term *Nebenmensch* to elaborate on the relation between subject and other beyond the paternal function. Freud argued that cognition is a perceptual process or "complex" that involves two components and a disjuncture or short-circuit between them: the subject's relationship to an Other as an object, and the subject's relationship to a memory or wish triggered by the perception of an Other, which presents itself in the form of a judgment. Thinking for Freud entails the bringing about of a "state of identity" and a "reproduction of an experience of one's own": thinking involves a unity of identity (represented in the ego) and a judgment of reality (through wish-fulfillment). The second moment repeats the perception or has an "imitation-value" that forms how we perceive the perception. In one instance, the ego organizes the world according to its image (principle of identity), and in the second instance something beyond the ego (coming from an outside and arising from one's own body) judges perception. For Freud, the object or "what we call things are residues which evade being judged."[44] The object is primal insofar as it is always reencountered as that which resists interpretation. It is in this sense that Lacan's *das Ding* returns to Freud's *Nebenmensch*; the lost object is primary and formative and is that which mediates the relationship between subject and other.

It is well known that in his metapsychological works, Freud is quite speculative; thus, in the *Entwurf* in particular he seeks to overcome the divide between neurophysiology and psychology, or between body and mind. The "thought-process" for Freud revolves around the "thing," which, as discussed above, is a complex itself and not some empirical object or real object. Moreover, the effect of reality is produced retroactively in the attempts to cognize *das Ding*. Practical reason in this account is guided by unconscious signifiers (dreams, memories, hallucinations, mnemic images, and judgments) that also provide means of orientation for subjectivity with reference to natural causality (the biological reality of the organism). Freud tried to argue that unconscious mechanisms have what Lacan would deem an extimate status; the unconscious revolves around an overlap of multiple losses, a founding negativity, and the objects that are always already lost in its place. Lacan names this overlap *objet a*, a point that will be discussed further on in this section.

Since the "thing" was already a complex object that is neither empirical nor real, Freud argued that the thing is discerned through the errors that occur in the course of thought: "The beginning of the thought-processes which have ramified [from practical thought] is the forming of judgements. The ego arrived at this through a discovery in its organization—through the fact already mentioned [pp. 331 and 366] that perceptual cathexes coincide in part with information from one's own body. As a consequence, the perceptual complexes are divided into a constant, nonunderstood, part—the thing—and a changing, understandable, one—the attribute or movement of the thing."[45] The "thought-process complex" for Freud always includes the possibility of error which lies between perception and judgment. These errors are not simply mistakes of judgment or errors of ignorance, but are due to a disjuncture between an image (a neuronal unity for Freud) and a "word-presentation" (what Lacan would call the signifier). It is in this sense that we can say that extimacy fuses the apparently contrary meanings of intimacy and exteriority; the extimate is the overlap of this disjunction (between an image and a signifier) which produces both a sense of outside reality and interiority.

This formulation of extimacy extends into Lacan's account of the sexual non-relation, and of castration. *Das Ding* is crucial for Lacan's reformulation of the phallus beyond a "real organ."[46] In a talk delivered in German in 1958, Lacan (who followed Frege's work closely) says that the phallus, the imaginary image or signifier of castration, "*bedeutet*," that is, signifies.[47] The extimate status of the phallus as a signifier of lack implies for Lacan its status for the subject in all three registers of imaginary, symbolic, and real. In Lacan's topological schema, the phallus becomes a reference for imaginary and symbolic castration; it is no longer conflated with the penis, as it was for Freud. It is Lacan's formulations on the phallus that allow him to move beyond the Oedipal complex. As an image and *signifier of lack*, the phallus does not correspond to any particular object; it exceeds as an object any biological referent. Lacan gives the phallus the status of a privileged signifier which governs the subject's access into language and the symbolic; a signifier which also determines sexual difference.

The only "sense" that the phallus incites in the subject is an *affect* of anxiety. Anxiety is not a meaning but an affect, a sign "that does not deceive" and that emerges in the hiatus between having and being the love object. The extimate status of the "thing" provokes in the subject the affect of anxiety precisely because the subject cannot bear to be the phallus; it has to separate from it in both the imaginary and the symbolic domains. Ultimately, the phallus cannot be had by anyone: the subject must remain extimate in relation to the thing because having the thing is actually unbearable; a relation to it always has to be mediated by an Other. The "significance" (*Bedeutung*) or importance of the phallus is that it is a signifier for something that is missing, for a lack.

Once the subject moves from the imaginary castration involved in imaginary identification (being the mother's object of desire, having the phallus), the phallus becomes a symbolic function in the form of the paternal metaphor or the Name-of-the-Father. The thing, or *das Ding*, in its symbolic function inaugurates the child into social relations, makes it a speaking being, inscribes it in language. The concept of extimacy underlies the repetitions through which the subject is inscribed in her relation to an Other: in the imaginary and the symbolic. Despite the fact that subjects realize their imaginary castration, they never cease to relate to the phallus through the dialectic of desire: always torn between the "to be" and "to have."[48] The phallus, as an extimate thing, is at the heart of one's being, its most external interior element that animates one's unconscious desire.

Indeed, Freud provides us with an account of the ego as extimate to the subject. Freud describes this through the process of narcissistic identification as the way in which the ego identifies by morphing itself into an image of its own self. But where does this image come from? Or even better, how can the ego identify with its image if it is not prior to its image? The morphing, the process of identification, doesn't simply retroactively project an image of an ego that was not already there before; it also carries out this projection through a specific desire: what Freud called "an original libidinal investment." This originary anamorphosis splits the ego; the ego is split by its very own image of itself.

Freud gives an account of the process of narcissistic identification beyond the psychological understanding of object relations. The subject does not simply internalize an object in the process of identification; rather, it exhibits a form of "magical thinking," a formative myth of the I, the individual, whereby a belief is developed in the "thaumaturgic force of words" and a "technique" is developed for dealing with the external world. Love, magic, and other such "techniques" are the means through which the ego develops its sense of interiority and exteriority, for it cannot be assumed to exist as an ego in the individual from the start. What Freud discovers, then, is that there is a stimulus which somehow precedes the ego, a constitutive discord (anxiety perhaps); a privation that somehow transforms or is sublimated into a demand to be loved and to be desired.

It is based on such observations and a consistent return to them that Freud developed his concept of the drive, the *Trieb*, as that which is irreducible to the struggle between life and death, or the struggle between the pleasure principle and the reality principle, but is the implicit surplus of desire that is generated from this recurring epic duel between reality and pleasure. The drive is not simply a will to death, a will to dying, but a pulsating negativity that is propelled from the resistance of desire to itself.[49] What psychoanalysis points to is that there is an economy that emerges from the impasse of desire; an economy of surplus that lends

INTRODUCTION

itself to itself, repeats in its pulsation not as a vital force (à la Deleuze), or simply as a negating force, but as that which repeats "what is impossible to be repeated."[50] This impossible that repeats is accompanied by enjoyment (*jouissance*), which captures the subject through the chain of signifiers. As Lacan puts it, the psychoanalytic understanding of the subject can be stated most fundamentally as follows: "man primarily demands to be deprived of something real."[51]

In the specific seminar we have been discussing, (*The Ethics of Psychoanalysis*), Lacan returns to Freud to argue that this primary "demand" to be deprived of something real (a demand that precedes its own repression, a repression before repression) is what coincides with the primary symbolization. In a sense, the symbolic is born out of the pangs of the real, whereby the whole problem of extimacy, of the extimacy of the subject in the real, is contained in the "gift of love." There is no room here to enter into the details of Lacan's discussion of the problem of love through the medieval troubadours, the poetic sublimation of the narcissist wound of subjectivity, although in this discussion Lacan is very clear about how sublimation—and not repression—in poetry and art posits an object of love, of identification, as a terrifying, inhuman one. What is crucial in Lacan's elaboration of extimacy is that it is a concept that captures a relation between subject and reality that has a very particular order: it is not mimetic, there is no mimesis even in the very image of the ego itself (the morphing always already generates a surplus), there is no direct correspondence or equivalence between the so-called object in reality and the object inside, or the thing, as Freud had called it. The lost object or the demand for privation is not equivalent to an internal object but is transformed into a *symbolic* object for it to be loved; in other words, it is transformed into a signifier. The love relation (the ideological love relation) is always a satisfaction of power by way of sublimating that "originary" demand for privation in a chain of signifiers, or in communication.

Culture is what we create as a divergence from, a holding back from, the extimate thing. As Lacan enigmatically puts it, it is as though for the subject, "even before I is born, the aims of the I appear"; even before I is born, before sublimation, there is an image.[52] Courtly love, the idealization of the lady who is anything but a real woman of flesh and blood, is not simply an act of sublimation but reveals an impulse or compulsion for sublimation that somehow precedes sublimation. Put differently, there is a sublimation for a satisfaction that has always already been missing. Lacan's intervention into subject-object relations is crucial here, for the subject is always traversed by an object, and an object can never be fully integrated into subjective knowledge: subject-object relations are only adequate at the level of fantasy. And all fantasies are sustained by a missing element, a lacking element that cannot enter the frame of fantasy lest it shatters it.

Lacan designates this repressed or missing element *objet a*. It is important to note that *objet a* is not scopic; it is an object that occupies a place only to reveal that it had been empty from the start. In this sense, *objet a* is correlative of the subject—extimate to it—because it reflects and objectifies the subject as an unknown, which prompts the pursuit of further knowledge on the side of the subject. In other words, the object is the blind spot in the fantasy frame, the element which cannot be included; it is neither symbolic nor imaginary. For Lacan, *objet a* is an ex-sistence without an essence. Thus, through a complex dialectic of proximity and distance, *objet a* supports seeing, but it is both intimate and exterior to the seeing subject, that is, to the gaze. The more the subject seeks a knowledge of their desire in the Other, the more the subject realizes their alienation in the symbolic matrix and the greater the need for a separation, a face-off with the negative element that sustains fantasy. Negativity propels this extimate relation to the object: when faced with the *objet a* in the analytic setting, the subject is exposed to the mode of *jouissance*, of the interpretation of reality, in which they are already implicated. This *jouissance* is the result of a "love relation," or ideological interpellation, through which the subject has come to identify itself, insofar as the subject corresponded to a lack in the Other.

Most importantly, then, *objet a*, the elusive object of desire, one of Lacan's major theoretical contributions, would be unthinkable without extimacy as the concept of the relation between subject and structure. Extimacy indicates neither an object nor a subject; it is also not a concept that implies predication. The word, however, can be employed to describe the non-relation between subject and object: the subject is extimate to structure; *objet a* is an extimate object that anchors the subject's unconscious desire: it is the ferret that the analyst seeks to sniff out like a dog! The psychoanalytic understanding of subjectivity-otherness hinges on the extimacy that is marked by an *objet a*, arguably the only "object" of study of psychoanalysis: the excessive element which persists and presents itself in desire. *Objet a* is both a remainder and a lack at once, the lack upon which structure pivots.

Objet a distinguishes psychoanalysis from both structuralism, which largely understood subjectivity as a product of structure, and from poststructuralism, which proceeds from the dismissal of the category of the subject as incorrigibly humanist (from Foucault's "death of the subject" to its recuperation through a social ontology of subjectivity with Butler). The non-relation marked by *objet a* poses serious questions for any relational ontology that proceeds from the recuperation of the subjective

INTRODUCTION

through intersubjective relations, even if this intersubjectivity is understood as the becoming other to oneself. In other words, *objet a*, as that which signifies the real, poses serious challenges to theories of recognition that remain within the field of the symbolic, raising the question "how does the subject recuperate a reconfigured relation to the big Other?"

From here it becomes crucial to consider the problem of the non-relation. The non-relation is a cut that appears in every empirical relation as its inherent condition of possibility; it is a cut in the "thing-in-itself": there is an inherent impossibility in every possibility.[53] Alenka Zupančič provides a great formulation of this:

> From the Lacanian perspective, *there is* something that "motivates" repetition, and this something is precisely an impossibility—although this needs to be understood in a very precise and specific sense. It does not imply, for example, that something is "impossible to be repeated" in its unique singularity; rather, it implies the *nonbeing* of what is to be repeated. *It is impossible to repeat it because it is not there* in the usual sense of the term. This is the Lacanian version of the theory that what is repeated is not an original traumatic experience, interrupting whatever has taken place before, but the *interruption itself* (which he relates to the Real).[54]

The retroactive nature of repetition lies in a failure to remember that is implicit in the function of memory itself: there is a failure that underlies repetition processes; in a sense, every repetition is a failure to find *again* something we have lost. To repeat, as Lacan puts it, is to *not* find the same thing again.[55] The real "marks an inherent contradiction/impossibility" in ontology, and it is at this point where the subject emerges, in the gaps or lacks in structure.[56] One could say that the site of emergence of the subject, from the cracks in structure or the gaps of its incompleteness, is extimacy.

The Question of Politics

As we have seen, the concept of extimacy is crucial for identifying the overlaps between philosophy and psychoanalysis. Politics is a third element to be added to this link. This volume includes several interventions that employ psychoanalytic concepts in the analysis of political phenomena. The current global political moment is dismal: a global pandemic, a series of failed attempts at political transformation, increased gaps between classes, ecological catastrophe, racism, sectarianism, and the reemergence of far-right politics. It somehow feels too late to present a political formulation that would be adequate to this moment. However, and precisely because of the apparent futility of politics today, we argue in this volume for the renewed importance of psychoanalysis. After all, the unconscious is political and yet remains undertheorized; we contend that it must be counted in any political procedure. It is in this vein that we propose extimacy as a fundamental concept that can help to rearticulate Lacan's critique of ego psychology, a discourse which continues to support the logic of adaptation to the systemic violence of late capitalism. Lacan proposed in the 1950s that the ego is an alienating function, a captivating and luring image that entangles the subject in enjoyment and simultaneously divides it. The ego is an alienating imaginary function, which divides the subject between self-being and *jouissance*. This division of the subject is sustained by a frame of fantasy which hinges on excluding the lost element, or lost object, that had to be forfeited for identification with the ego. The *objet a* is not specular, yet in its absence it supports the specular image of unity that is the ego. When considering the political ends or uses of *objet a*, it can be simply stated that a politics centered around representation, that is, identification, can only succeed by concealing the *objet a*, keeping it extimate, because once it appears anxiety becomes overwhelming. There is a fundamental "void" around which the democratic politics of representation revolves. All representation precludes the impossibility of representation. All forms of representation essentially repeat the same failure that is implicit in representation.

Repetition is both a psychical and historical problem, or stated otherwise, it is the unconscious problem of consciousness: we repeat because we forget, and we repeat *because we forget what it was that did not happen*. The repetition of any civil strife is not simply the repetition of an event, but the repetition of a repressed element that constitutes a system of representation. Every system of representation (such as that of parliamentary democracy, for instance) conceals at its core an "unrepresentable hole."[57] In other words, all forms of authority are based on a concealed element, an unrepresentable thing; for instance, the people, the sect, the group, the community are usually represented by signifiers (a declaration, a social contract, a constitution, a founding myth, etc.).[58] In the *Interpretation of Dreams*, Freud likened the elements of a dream to "representatives chosen by election from a mass of people."[59] The dream-work is the process through which a thought makes itself present in dream form, in a form that is not a form of thought, or one that is unconscious. The political analogy here with regard to dreams and representation is the classical concept of sovereignty or the will of the people:

INTRODUCTION

sovereignty cannot be represented, and this is precisely where state structures emerge: to represent what is not representable. The debate on this in political theory is as old as modernity itself, and the thinkers who have considered this question are many: Kantorowicz, Schmitt, Arendt, and Agamben, to mention but a few, and of course, Marx.

Marx's *Eighteenth Brumaire* essay is precisely this meditation on the problem of historical repetition in relation to the impasses of representation. Marx reads in Louis Napoleon's 1851 coup d'etat a counterrevolution and farcical repetition of the tragic failure of revolution. For Marx, Napoleon's first seizure of power in 1799 (or the 18th Brumaire in the French republican calendar) is repeated in the coup of 1851. Following the 1848 Revolution, Louis Napoleon becomes an "emperor again"—according to Marx—in a world historical election, which introduces a particular logic of repetition that hinges on the triad of nation, state, and capital. Marx argues that it is the class divisions within postrevolutionary society, between the petit bourgeois, the peasants, and social democrats that lead to the reinstatement of monarchy through democratic procedures.[60]

Marx saw this return of the repressed in parliamentary democracy, absolutist monarchy, as a symptom that emerges in times of capitalist crisis. When a bourgeois economy reaches a deadlock, the state, in the form of Napoleon III, intervenes as an independent apparatus separate from civil society. The state is in fact always separate from civil society, but it is in moments of crisis that it emerges as a bureaucratic and military formation. The state then appears as a military and bureaucratic complex and it intervenes through its election, ironically, by a class that cannot represent itself as a class; what Marx calls the *lumpenproletariat*. Louis Napoleon is elected because he resembled the first Napoleon (1799): first as tragedy, second as farce! Marx analyzed this political structure in the context of the rise of urban masses; masses that cannot be represented in a classical class breakdown. The executive government, Napoleon III's, emerges to replace the military exploits of the first Napoleon: in this repetition the absolute monarch is reborn from within the spirit of the republic which had beheaded the king.

Freud, like Marx before him, was very interested in the question of repetition, or what he called the repetition compulsion, *Wiederholungszwang*.[61] He saw in repetition an automaticity, a compulsion of the death-drive which insists on an attempt to return to an inorganic state; a state where there is no stimulation, no libido, no excitation; a mythical state of complete repose. Most importantly for Freud, every repetition contains an element of failure: we repeat because we have failed to remember the origins of the compulsion to repeat. The retroactive nature of repetition lies in a failure to remember that is implicit in the function of memory itself: there is a failure that underlies repetition processes; in a sense, every repetition is a failure to find *again* something we have lost. To repeat, as Lacan puts it, is to *not* find the same thing again. In other words, to repeat is to try to make up for something lacking that we cannot name. Thus, within repetition lies the problem or question of nomination: without naming, the political process is indeterminate and often relapses into reinstating populist structures of authority: "the people," "the nation," "the sect" are nothing but abstract designations that require no further determinations.

The problem of nomination arises in the analytic moment when the subject identifies with the symptom in order for a new designation (of the subject) to emerge and thereby disrupt the symbolic. Nomination is possible only from the distancing that occurs between subject and structure: when the Real is allowed to disrupt the symbolic and shakes its coordinates. The extimate relation between subject and other implies that the Other that functions is not real, out there, but that *objet a* is real and founds the "alterity" of the symbolic Other. Nomination here would become political once it avows all possible and necessary equivocations rather than assume an ought and a "to be"; nomination that enunciates the extimate condition of the subject cannot but avow the inescapable failures of repetitions.

Chapter Outline

This book proceeds through ten chapters that address this constellation of psychoanalysis, philosophy, and politics. Samo Tomšič's opening essay, "The Ontological Limbo: Three Notes on Extimacy and Ex-sistence," situates extimacy within the history of philosophy, retrospectively outlining three figures in whose work Lacan locates a precursor to extimacy: Saint Augustine's rendering of God as both external and internal to the subject; Descartes's turn to modern science and the presence of eternal truths embedded within the subject that at the same time do not belong to the subject; and, last, the Freudian shift from the mathematical and geometrical foundations of knowledge to the structure of language and the symbolic order as such. The return to these figures makes clear the emergence of a formal commonality in thinking through extimacy that Tomšič argues as a point of intersection between topology and ontology. In thinking through Lacan's schematization of extimacy, Tomšič draws a parallel with the Heideggerian notion of "ex-sistence," which renders extimacy as not only what concerns the nature of the unconscious, but also

INTRODUCTION

the question of existence itself, which is suspended between being and nonbeing. Tomšič considers Lacan's understanding of the unconscious as a "pre-ontological gap," which Lacan terms the "unrealized." The chapter traces this "instable" formation to Aristotle's view of ontology, intermediary beings in the Gnostics, and to psychoanalysis's own intermediary beings or the negative features of the unconscious, those aspects that are unrealized and resist the ontological opposition of being and nonbeing. Tomšič argues that there is then an ontological limbo, from the Gnostics to Freud's framing of the relationship between the somatic and the psychic, and to Lacan's further translation of the latter as the symbolic, which extends or splits the body through language. Tomšič provocatively argues in this chapter that the cogito can be read as Descartes's *fort-da* moment, in which the cogito is based on the foreclosure of the negativity of the subject. The deduction of the modern notion of the subject in Descartes hinges on the rejection of the pre-ontological status of the subject, which is premised on the extimacy of thinking to the fading of being—or the aphanisis of the subject.

In "Extimacy and *das Ding*: The Outside-In of the Void," Richard Boothby provides an overview of the development of the concept of extimacy in Lacan's work. Boothby describes extimacy as the relationship that emerges in the wake of the subject's encounter with Otherness via "the unknown thing in the Other," or *das Ding*. He traces the development of Lacan's concept of *das Ding* to Freud's *Nebenmensch* and notes that the seminar on anxiety (Seminar 10) is pivotal for the transformation of *das Ding* into *objet a*. Boothby argues that *objet a* is rendered present through language, through the symbolic, and proposes that language is the "primary domain of the extimate." Language or the law assuage the anxiety generated in the encounter with the lost object, or the void in the place of which the object comes to be. The original argument of the chapter lies in Boothby's recovery of the extimate problem of "supposition" and love in psychoanalysis: the ego is formed through a relation of supposition to an Other (a subject supposed to know), and "falling in love involves the feeling of uncannily finding something of oneself in the other." Human subjectivity is singular because of the extimate nature of both love and anxiety.

In "What, If Anything, Is Authority?" Mladen Dolar turns to Arendt's paradoxical notion of authority whose source is irreducible to both the external realm of coercion and violence and the internal realm of reason. Dolar argues that the moment the question of authority is posed, a crisis of authority is assumed: modernity can be understood as a "reflexive turn" in which the crisis of authority moves from "in itself" to "for itself." In modernity, authority appears to have always been in crisis, while it is not clear whether there ever was a proper authority in the past. The chapter argues that authority, as a topic of modern melancholic fantasies, haunts the present. Transcendence has been replaced by an immanence in excess. Dolar challenges Arendt's complaint about the loss of authority and supplements it with the problem of the resurgence of "groundless authority" in modernity, arguing that what deserves close attention is the afterlife of authority rather than its demise. In Dolar's view, authority is exerted at a point that does not have "proper coverage" in either the exterior or interior realms, and yet is neither fully external to either, nor maintained at the point of their inner intersection. Dolar thus explores this paradoxical—extimate—structure of authority as the "surplus of immanence" in the modern world, particularly with respect to the phenomenon of ersatz authority, and to the problem of authority in the three impossible professions according to Freud: governance, education, and psychoanalysis.

In "Asexual Violence and Systemic Enjoyment," Alenka Zupančič argues that in the present historical and political moment, violence is understood as the use of power for sex. This understanding of violence hinges on a double move: the separation of sex from power, and their realignment through the notion of abuse. Zupančič argues that this ultimately narrows our understanding of power: "power is problematic only when it involves sexuality," which in turn suggests that power is problematic when someone *enjoys* it. This systematic presentation of the link between power and sex, Zupančič maintains, whitewashes other systemic abuses of power under subjective instances and maintains a distinction between "professional power" and nonprofessional uses of power. To disrupt this binary, Zupančič argues that the psychoanalytic understanding of the extimate nature of enjoyment is crucial. Enjoyment is always already impersonal, or as Lacan would maintain, enjoyment is always the Other's enjoyment, it is always a surplus that is extimate to the subject. Zupančič argues that systemic enjoyment is not immediately subjective but is generated as a symptom of the contradictions of structure, while the subjective moment would be the response to the enjoyment of the other. Perversion is a structure that hinges on the other being treated not as an object but as a subject awaiting completion through the liaisons of a seducer. Seduction, in this context, is carried out by a pervert who "posits himself as the *instrument* of the impossible enjoyment of the Other." Zupančič argues that while in eighteenth-century literature, desire was conceived as what could potentially ruin people's lives, in the contemporary moment this dimension is disavowed in discourses around sex in which the problematic of desire and enjoyment is expelled from consideration and deemed inappropriate to address. In contradistinction to the prevalent discourse, Zupančič argues for the importance of the psychoanalytic understanding of enjoyment's extimate nature: the symptom of systemic enjoyment, Zupančič argues, threatens the political and libidinal economy of capitalism from within.

In "'For Thought to Dwell Where Evils Have No Entry': On Oedipus and the Extimacy of Anger," Amanda Holmes takes up a briefly mentioned emotion in Lacan's work: anger. Eschewing a fully developed theory of anger, Lacan's work instead circles back to a striking image: "anger is when the little square pegs won't fit into the little round holes." Holmes argues that Lacan's definition of anger, which has links to notions of anxiety, exposes a structural relation, it marks the "sudden encounter with the extimate place of the real." Holmes turns to the myth of Oedipus as it is told in Sophocles's Theban trilogy in order to rethink the affects associated with the notion of extimacy. In particular, she develops an account of Oedipus's anger in relation to the notion of extimacy and argues that anger should be understood as a part of the affective dimension of extimacy. Along with anxiety, the uncanny, and horror, the affect of anger exposes the extimate structure of desire in Lacan's formulation. In bringing together a reading of *Oedipus Rex* and *Oedipus at Colonus*, along with a definition of anger that Lacan returns to throughout his seminar, the chapter weaves together a Lacanian theory of anger and a rereading of the import of the Oedipus complex. Ultimately, Holmes concludes that the Lacanian definition of anger shows the extimate structure of desire, which is at the core of the problems posed by Oedipus.

In "On Ambivalence as a Key Freudian Concept: The *Vaterkomplex*'s Edifice," Alejandro Cerda-Rueda argues that the incomplete or partial nature of Freud's *Vaterkomplex* has created the misleading expectation in the therapeutic context that such a process can be completed or resolved. In contrast, Cerda-Rueda pursues the idea that rather than completion, the process is meant to be endured. The Oedipus complex first came to Freud during his *yahrzeit* process while mourning the loss of his deceased father in 1896 and 1897. Notwithstanding the extended discussions of such a concept within psychoanalytic schools (object relations, ego psychology, or Lacanian psychoanalysis), there remains a bifurcation in the very understanding of psychoanalytic practice itself. If, according to Lacan, the Oedipus complex is both universal and contingent, there is a key aspect within it that led Freud to place it amid a continuous ambivalent construction. Thus, the chapter argues that the *Vaterkomplex*, an incomplete concept as well as an integral part of the Oedipus complex, has been left unresolved for a purpose. The objective of this chapter is to propose a brief definition of this "partial" concept (not to be found in various psychoanalytic dictionaries, except Fedida's work of 1974) and engage with the idea that ambivalence, within psychoanalytic theory and practice, is not something to resolve but to endure; it is merely another name that Freud utilized for analytical experience. Cerda-Rueda concludes the chapter by asking whether this *kern-komplex* can achieve an extimate function within the constitutive split of the subject (and treatment), or whether there is another way out of such ambivalence.

In "What Is a Body? A Question between Critical Theory and Psychoanalysis," Silvio Carneiro poses the question, "What *is* a body?" For Carneiro, this is an ontological question that posits the body as the knot of multiple relations that contests the usual dualism between biology and culture. Contrary to a binary perspective, Carneiro argues that the body is a boundary between inner/outer, individual/social, and biological/symbolic. This chapter thus poses the critical question of how to understand the body from this boundary—or extimate—position. In the first part of the chapter, Carneiro takes up Adorno and Horkheimer's *Dialectic of Enlightenment*, and the dual view of the body presented in Nazism: *Leib* and *Körper*, in order to explore the history of the body's domination. The second section turns to Marcuse, who also maintains this historical view of domination in late capitalism, but who also posits the body as resisting this political trend. Marcuse turns to the biological trends of the Freudian theory of the instincts as an important element to understand the potential radicality of the so-called Great Refusal. In fact, Marcuse considers bodies in revolt as an important aspect of contemporary political struggles. The chapter then considers whether Marcuse runs the risk of assuming an illusory metaphysics of nature in this revolt. This concern guides the third section of the chapter, which focuses on Lacan´s critique of biologism in psychoanalysis, as well as his psychoanalytical view of language as fundamental to the Freudian theory of the instincts. Ultimately, the chapter considers whether Marcuse and Lacan—and their particular "returning to Freud"—can go beyond the biological-cultural dualism of the body.

The next three chapters shift to the political implications of considering the concept of extimacy. In "Hate Your Neighbor as You Hate Yourself: How to Think Psychoanalytically about Hate, Racism, and Exclusion," Patricia Gherovici employs extimacy to work through the phenomenon of racism in the psychoanalytic clinic. Taking as its point of departure the Old Testament commandment to "love your neighbor as yourself," a mandate of universal love later associated with a fundamental requirement of Christianity, the chapter explores a key human passion, an externalized foundational inner feeling older than love, using the Lacanian notion of "extimacy." In her analysis, Gherovici focuses on the way in which this neologism, which combines "exteriority" and "in-

INTRODUCTION

timacy" to imply that something exterior, strange, and foreign can be at the same time the closest, most privately, deeply felt thing, allows us to both understand and rethink symptoms of hate, such as racism, discrimination, and exclusion.

In "*Objet a* and the Possibilities of Political Resistance: Extimacy, Anxiety, and Political Action," Andreja Zevnik continues to explore the triangulation of anxiety, subjectivity, and affect through a focus on race. She analyzes Lacan's rather provocative statement in May 1968, which students met with dismay: "what you aspire to as revolutionaries is a new Master. You will get one." In "Discourse of the Hysteric," Lacan explained how the desire to change the system, to start a revolution, can turn against itself, because those participating in political actions are seduced by the enjoyment derived from their refusal to recognize authority. Zevnik argues that Lacan's position implies that protests based on a refusal to recognize authority will not lead to the desired outcome, or to a change of the system, because political action needs to alter the structure of institutions. Lacan locates the "truth" of the structure in *objet a*, the unobtainable lost object of desire. In this contribution, Zevnik teases out the significance of *objet a* for political resistance. According to her, there are three separate and yet interconnected moments in which *objet a* is particularly significant: the context of interpellation and misinterpellation, which introduces the excess of *objet a*; extimacy, which emphasizes the proximity of *objet a* to the subject; and anxiety, where *objet a* can lead to two different modes of political action (acting out and *passage à l'acte*). She concludes by linking *objet a* and contemporary struggles for racial justice such as the Black Lives Matter movement, and points to where or how contemporary political resistance challenges the structure of interpellation.

In the final chapter of the volume, "Transference and Its Discontents: Lacan and the Extimate Place of Politics," Vladimir Safatle addresses the end of analysis and the phenomenon of subjective destitution. This chapter explores the political possibilities of emancipation arising from a subjectivity that is no longer governed by the traditional ideals of autonomy and self-legislation. Safatle argues that transference in particular has real consequences in processes of emancipation. While not all relations of power are relations of domination, transference enables the exposure of how identification is implicitly the process through which social ties and relations of power are instituted. Identification is maintained in and by repetition and through the production of affects that float in between the self and the Other as a surplus element. The function of transference in psychoanalysis reveals that the very mechanisms that sustain identification can bring about its dissolution. Safatle argues that servitude to power is generated from the anxiety that freedom produces, and it is this anxiety that emerges in the context of transference. Most importantly, the knowledge of one's desire, which drives the discourse of analysis, results in its own destitution. In the liquidation of transference there is an extraction of an object from knowledge: the extimate object reveals to the subject the fantasy which structures social bonds. Safatle shows how the liquidation of transference reveals that desire is nothing more than a *désêtre*: the destitution of the subject is co-incidental to the destitution of the analyst's knowledge. This chapter points to the crucial political implications of the extimate moment in the dissolution of transference in psychoanalysis.

Notes

1. Jacques Lacan, *The Ethics of Psychoanalysis*, ed. Jacques Alain-Miller, trans. Dennis Porte, vol. 7 of The Seminar of Jacques Lacan (New York: Norton, 1992), 139.
2. Lacan, *The Ethics of Psychoanalysis*, 101.
3. Jacques Lacan, *The Ego in Freud's Theory and in the Technique of Psychoanalysis*, ed. Jacques Alain-Miller, trans. Sylvana Tomaselli, vol. 2 of The Seminar of Jacques Lacan (New York: Norton, 1988).
4. For Lacan, *connaissance* (the imaginary) is at the service of *savoir* (the symbolic): the imaginary alienation from which the ego emerges is guarded by symbolic structures, and alienation is fundamental for the separation from the other. For extensive references on this, see Peter Hallward and Knox Peden, eds., *Concept and Form*, vols. 1 and 2 (London: Verso, 2012).
5. Jacques-Alain Miller, "Extimité," trans. Françoise Massardier-Kennedy, *Prose Studies* 11, no. 3 (1988): 121–31.
6. Jacques Lacan, *Écrits: A Selection*, trans. Alan Sheridan (Tavistock, UK: Routledge, 1977), 312.
7. Jacques Lacan, *The Four Fundamental Concepts of Psychoanalysis*, ed. Jacques Alain-Miller, trans. Alan Sheridan, vol. 11 of The Seminar of Jacques Lacan (New York: Norton, 1998), 30.
8. Lacan, *Four Fundamental Concepts of Psychoanalysis*, 72.
9. For an overview of Lacan's wide-ranging engagement with the field of philosophy, see Charles Shepherdson, "Lacan and Philosophy," in *The Cambridge Companion to Lacan* (Cambridge: Cambridge University Press, 2003).
10. See Lacan, *The Ethics of Psychoanalysis*.
11. Lacan, *The Ego in Freud's Theory and in the Technique of Psychoanalysis*.
12. Oliver Harris, *Lacan's Return to Antiquity: Between Nature and the Gods* (New York: Routledge, 2017), 11.
13. Barbara Cassin discusses the parallel between ancient Greek philosophy and psychoanalysis in *Jacques the Sophist: Lacan, Logos, Psychoanalysis*, trans. Michael Syrotinski (New York: Fordham University Press, 2020).

14. Plato, *Five Dialogues*, trans. G. M. A. Grube (Indianapolis, IN: Hackett, 2002), 70.

15. Lacan, *The Ego in Freud's Theory and in the Technique of Psychoanalysis*, 4.

16. G. W. F. Hegel, *Lectures on the History of Philosophy: Plato and the Platonists*, trans. E. S. Haldane and Francis H. Simson, vol. 2 (Lincoln: University of Nebraska Press, 1995), 33.

17. Lacan, *The Ego in Freud's Theory and in the Technique of Psychoanalysis*, 87.

18. Mladen Dolar, "Tyche, Clinamen, Den," *Continental Philosophy Review* 46, no. 2 (2013): 223–39.

19. Miller, "Extimité," 123. For the link between the Freudian uncanny and Lacan's notion of extimacy, see Mladen Dolar, "'I Shall Be with You on Your Wedding-Night': Lacan and the Uncanny," *October* 58 (1991): 5–23.

20. Phillip Cary, "Soul, Self, Interiority," in *The Cambridge Companion to Augustine's "Confessions,"* ed. Tarmo Toom (Cambridge: Cambridge University Press, 2020).

21. Miller, "Extimité," 122.

22. Miller, "Extimité," 123.

23. Shuli Barzilai, "Augustine in Contexts: Lacan's Repetition of a Scene from the Confessions," *Literature and Theology* 11, no. 2 (1997): 215.

24. Augustine: *On the Free Choice of the Will, On Grace and Free Choice, and Other Writings*, trans. Peter King (Cambridge: Cambridge University Press, 2010), 15.

25. Augustine's relationship to Plato's theory of recollection is debated in the literature; for an overview of these conflicts, see Robert Miner, "Augustinian Recollection," *Augustinian Studies* 38, no. 2 (2007): 435–50.

26. René Descartes, *Meditations on First Philosophy*, trans. John Cottingham (Cambridge: Cambridge University Press, 2017).

27. For a discussion of Lacan's view of Descartes, see Slavoj Žižek, *Cogito and the Unconscious* (Durham, NC: Duke University Press, 1998).

28. Lacan, *Four Fundamental Concepts of Psychoanalysis*, 36.

29. Lacan, *Four Fundamental Concepts of Psychoanalysis*, 44.

30. Lacan, *Four Fundamental Concepts of Psychoanalysis*, 47.

31. Lacan, *Four Fundamental Concepts of Psychoanalysis*, 48. See Sigmund Freud, "Remembering, Repeating, and Working-Through," 1914.

32. Lacan, *Four Fundamental Concepts of Psychoanalysis*, 48.

33. Plato, *Five Dialogues*, 72.

34. G. W. F. Hegel, *Phenomenology of Spirit*, trans. A. V. Miller (Oxford: Oxford University Press, 1977), 78.

35. Angelica Nuzzo, *Memory, History, Justice in Hegel* (New York: Palgrave Macmillan, 2012), 90.

36. Jacques Lacan, *Freud's Papers on Technique 1953–1954*, ed. Jacques-Alain Miller, trans. John Forrester, vol. 1 of The Seminar of Jacques Lacan (Cambridge: Cambridge University Press, 1988), 146.

37. Massimo Recalcati, "The Empty Subject: Un-triggered Psychoses in the New Forms of the Symptom," trans. Jorge Jauregui, *Lacanian Ink* 26 (2005).

38. Lacan, *The Ego in Freud's Theory and in the Technique of Psychoanalysis*.

39. Jacques Lacan, "The Function and Field of Speech and Language in Psychoanalysis," in *Écrits: A Selection*, 88.
40. Lacan, *The Ego in Freud's Theory and in the Technique of Psychoanalysis*, 100.
41. Dolar, "'I Shall Be with You on Your Wedding-Night,'" 6.
42. Jacques Alain Miller, "Extimite," in *Theory of Discourse: Subject, Structure and Society*, ed. Mark Bracher, Marshall W. Alcorn Jr., Ronald J. Corthell, and Françoise Massardier-Kenney (New York: New York University Press, 1994).
43. Slavoj Žižek, Eric Santner, and Kenneth Reinhard approach the issue of neighborliness from a politico-theological perspective in *The Neighbor: Three Inquiries in Political Theology* (Chicago: University of Chicago Press, 2005).
44. Sigmund Freud, *Project for a Scientific Psychology*, ed. James Strachey and Anna Freud, trans. James Strachey, vol. 1 of *The Standard Edition of the Complete Psychological Works of Sigmund Freud* (London: Hogarth, 1950), 333.
45. Freud, *Project for a Scientific Psychology*, 383.
46. For this connection, see Alenka Zupančič, *What Is Sex?* (Cambridge, MA: MIT Press, 2017); and Lorenzo Chiesa, *The Not-Two: God and Logic in Lacan* (Cambridge, MA: MIT Press, 2016).
47. Jacques Lacan, "The Signification of the Phallus," in *Écrits: A Selection*, 575–84.
48. In Lacan's account, the phallus is not just equivalent to an object of desire. There are different layers to approaching the phallus: the phallus as an imaginary missing organ, the symbolic phallus via the "phallic function" which introduces sexuation as cut, and the Real incomplete phallus that disrupts enjoyment. These functions or positions of the phallus are elaborated on in Lacan's later seminars. Refer to Lorenzo Chiesa's elaborations of this in *The Not-Two: Logic and God in Lacan*.
49. Freud makes these arguments in his metapsychological works, especially in *Beyond the Pleasure Principle, Group Psychology and Other Works*, ed. James Strachey and Anna Freud, trans. James Strachey, vol. 18 of *The Standard Edition of the Complete Psychological Works of Sigmund Freud* (London: Vintage Books, 2001), 1–64.
50. Zupančič, *What Is Sex?* 117.
51. Lacan, *The Ethics of Psychoanalysis*, 150.
52. Lacan, *The Ethics of Psychoanalysis*.
53. This impossibility in possibility may bring to mind an existentialist concept of death as "impossible possibility," or Heidegger's notion of "being-towards-death," or "difference" for Derrida. Despite the closeness of the formulation, however, there is a stark difference or disjuncture between the impossibility of possibility for Lacan in contradistinction to Heidegger and Derrida, and it is precisely the question of negativity. For Heidegger, being gives but withdraws from being; the not-ness of being cannot be conceptualized, and is a negativity that doesn't develop into a concept. The trace of the Other for Derrida is the condition of possibility and impossibility for conceptualization, whereas *das Ding* for Lacan is a cut or crack in potentiality itself, which is presented in the movement of repetition.
54. Zupančič, *What Is Sex?* 118.

55. For further elaboration of this point, see Mladen Dolar, "Tyche, Clinamen, Den," *Continental Philosophy Review* 46, no. 2 (2013): 223–39.

56. Zupančič, *What Is Sex?* 119.

57. Kojin Karatani, *History and Repetition* (New York: Columbia University Press, 2011), 3.

58. See here Bonnie Honig, "Declarations of Independence: Arendt and Derrida on the Problem of Founding a Republic," *American Political Science Review* 85, no. 1 (1991): 97–113.

59. Sigmund Freud, *Interpretation of Dreams*, ed. James Strachey and Anna Freud, trans. James Strachey, vol. 4 of *The Standard Edition of the Complete Psychological Works of Sigmund Freud* (London: Vintage Books, 2001), 14.

60. Karatani, *History and Repetition.*

61. Freud, *Beyond the Pleasure Principle.*

The Ontological Limbo

Three Notes on Extimacy and Ex-sistence

Samo Tomšič

Lacan was a master of coining neologisms.[1] The main function of these unconventional and scientifically disputed conceptual tools was to condense the complex, sometimes overtly paradoxical and aporetic aspects of psychoanalytic theory and practice. The neologism *extime* (extimate) has become particularly famous, even though it appears just four times in Lacan's work.[2] The infrequent occurrence of this term in no way diminishes its critical value, which lies above all in its union of contraries. The prefix "ex-" marks a register that precedes the distinction between the intimate (subjective) and the public (intersubjective). Instead of describing the opposite of intimate—as the prefixes "in-" and "ex-" would normally suggest—the extimate pinpoints a specific modality of the intimate, the emergence of an element of foreignness at the intimate core of the subject. One could think here of the feeling of *Unheimlichkeit*, or "uncanniness," which according to Freud has a sense of the proximity of both foreignness and familiarity. The extimate can ultimately describe every manifestation of unconscious thought that arises to disrupt the stream of consciousness.[3]

In any case, with this neologism, Lacan seeks to redefine intimacy in accordance with the psychoanalytic examination of the dynamic of thinking and the structure of the subject. The term "extimate" does this by questioning the spatial relation that the intimate is commonly associated with. To repeat, the extimate is a mode of the intimate, approached from the viewpoint of the continuum between inside and outside and the entanglement of two apparently delimited and heterogeneous spatial orders. However, the extimate also stands for a disruption of the intimate, the emergence of a heterogeneous exteriority within the subject, an exteriority that is nevertheless constitutive for the subject.

Lacan's inspiration for forging the neologism *extime* did not come from the Freudian context alone. The term in fact relates to different frameworks and retrospectively allows us to note different paradigms of extimacy in the history of European philosophy. These paradigms can be pinned down to three proper names and three major registers.

First, there is a paradigm of extimacy in Christian religion, and specifically the thought of Saint Augustine, who explicitly recognized a major figure of extimacy in God. For Augustine, God is both external and internal to the subject, a figure in which absolute transcendence and absolute immanence are brought together. In conceiving of God in this way, Augustine most clearly and definitively distinguished Christianity from paganism. The Greek and Roman gods were by no means extimate, if for no other reason than that they were part of physical reality. The God of Christianity, in contrast, is something uncanny that throws both the reality (think of wonders as disruptions of the laws of nature) and the subject out of joint, but God does so by affecting the subject's most inner interiority. This is, for instance, what the link between God and love stands for.[4]

Second, there is a paradigm of extimacy in modern science, particularly in the work of Descartes, for whom the main figure of extimacy is no longer God but knowledge, and more specifically the eternal truths that thinking-doubting subjects encounter in themselves as that part which cannot possibly belong to them. These truths are mathematical and geometrical, and so the Cartesian shift ultimately comes down to the extension of the extimate status from the divine being to a modality of the symbolic—again, mathematics and geometry—and hence to the most solid and certain foundations of knowledge. These symbolic foundations short-circuit the subject from within but nevertheless remain foreign; they cannot be reduced to the subject's "psychology." In scientific modernity, knowledge turns extimate and it throws the subject out of joint by widening the gap between phenomenal reality and structural reality. Alexandre Koyré thus insisted that modern science no longer "saves the phenomena."[5] In other words, modern science is no longer oriented by everyday experience but by the encounters between mathematics and the real. In the Cartesian scenario, mathematics and geometry actively resist the subject's thinking, including the methodological doubt. But this also means that they are a source of compulsion in the subject; they impose themselves on thinking and thus draw a limit to the dissolution of appearances through radical doubt. It is this compulsion that differentiates Descartes from Plato, even though Descartes occasionally echoes Plato's doctrine of anamnesis in the *Meditations on First Philosophy*—for example, when he writes: "And the truth of these matters is so open and so much in harmony with my nature, that on first discovering them it seems that I am not so much learning something new as remembering what I knew before; or it seems like noticing for the first time things which were long present within me although I had never turned my mental gaze on them before."[6] Still, a Lacanian reading would question the presumable harmony of mathematics with the subject's nature, again in line with Koyré's interpretation of scientific modernity. The gap between subjective reality and mathematical reality is not something external to the subject but traverses it at its very core.

It is at this point that the third paradigm comes in: Freudian psychoanalysis, for which the problem of extimacy is exemplified in thinking as such. Understood as knowledge that does not know itself, the unconscious subverts and radicalizes the Cartesian paradigm, in which knowledge must be reflexive in order to obtain scientific status. With psychoanalysis, the problem of extimacy shifts from the mathematical and geometrical foundations of knowledge to the structure of language and to the symbolic order as such. The point here, for Lacan, is to expand the foreign status that Descartes associated with the symbolic forms of science. But the main reason for this expansion could not be further away from the Cartesian context, since it concerns the core problematic of psychoanalysis, the production of enjoyment in the speaking body.[7] At the core of this production stands the function of the signifier, defined by Lacan in his later seminars as the cause of enjoyment. This definition thoroughly breaks with the Cartesian dualism. Enjoyment stands for a fusion of the signifier and the body, in which a certain tension or conflict continues to persist. The path opened up by psychoanalysis thus necessarily leads away from the dualistic paradigm, toward a peculiar kind of monism, in which the notion of enjoying substance plays the central role.[8]

These three paradigms of extimacy are traversed by a common formal issue. Readers of Lacan will recall that topological framings played a major role throughout his work, notably the spatial continuum between inside and outside (exemplified in the topological model of the Klein bottle), which pinpoints the true nature of the unconscious. In contradistinction to its philosophical predecessors, the Freudian notion no longer describes a hidden interior of the individual's psyche, an obscure depth of mental life, or an archive of unclear representations and forgotten memories. Instead the unconscious is "outside," on the surface of conscious thought, but as its distortion, disruption, and decentralization. Lacan extended this point to language, which is equally inside (mental organ) and outside (social link) the subject.[9] With the shifting and obscure placement of the symbolic in the mind, extimacy marks the intersection between a topological and an ontological problem, the peculiar mode of existence of language and the unconscious.

It is not coincidental that Lacan's teaching marks the point of contact between topology and ontology with another, perhaps less prominent but certainly more frequently used neologism, in which the prefix "ex-" plays a central role: ex-sistence. The reference here is to Heidegger, arguably Lacan's greatest philosophical influence.[10] However, contrary to Heidegger, Lacan refers to "ex-sistence" in order to describe a mode of existence, which is suspended between being and nonbeing. Just as the extimate is neither inside nor outside but an active intertwining of two spatial orders, ex-sistence is neither existence nor inexistence, but something that Lacan occasionally termed "the unrealized." As he writes: "The gap of the unconscious may be said to be *pre-ontological*. I have stressed that all too often forgotten characteristic—forgotten in a way that is not without significance—of the first emergence of the unconscious, namely, that it does not lend itself to ontology. Indeed, what became apparent at first to Freud, to the discoverers, to those who made the first steps, and what still becomes apparent to anyone in analysis who spends some time observing what truly belongs to the order of the unconscious, is that it is neither being, nor non-being, but the unrealized."[11] Here we have an explicit flirtation with Heidegger's interpretation of the history of European metaphysics as a history of the oblivion of the originary, presumably authentic, unveiling of being in poetic language. To briefly recapitulate Heidegger's account, the original sense of being was lost in the theological turning of ontology carried out by Plato. In mistaking being for the highest of beings, Plato's *lapsus* inaugurated the tradition in which being obtained the significance of the metaphysical grounding of existence. By returning to the pre-Socratic thinkers, Heidegger attempted to undo the oblivion that grounded European philosophy. Lacan never followed this path. For him a more "radical oblivion" was at stake, one that required a step further back, not only in historical time but into the pre-ontological foundations of ontology, before the question of being could be raised and before the distinction between being and nonbeing had emerged. Understood in this vein, the "nonrealized" strives to grasp an order of reality that is irreducible to the oppositional couples of ontology: being and nonbeing or existence and inexistence. The persistence of a gap in reality sustains its inner movement and becoming—and it is a gap in which reality fails to coincide with itself. The same characteristic pertains to the field of language, the notorious "big Other," which Lacan never tired of repeating does not exist. Language, too, is unrealized. This does not prevent it from striving for realization in and through the activity of speaking. It should nevertheless be reminded that various schools of linguistics and philosophy of language conceive this striving in different and mutually exclusive manners. For the normative tradition (analytic philosophy, pragmatism, theory of communicative action, etc.), the paradigm of such realization would be communication, whereas for Heidegger it was poetry, understood as the privileged language of being. From the psychoanalytic standpoint, in turn, the realization of language comes in the guise of bodily disturbance or disequilibrium, pinpointed in the production of enjoyment. Enjoyment is a linguistic product that "serves for nothing."[12] That is, it neither means nor communicates. Moreover, one could say that for Lacan the very activity of speech is the practical, corporeal proof that language does not exist—in other words, that it is ontologically incomplete (hence, Lacan's insistence that "there is no such thing as a metalanguage," which echoes his claim that "the big Other does not exist" and his notion of the barred, precisely ex-sistent, Other).

Intermediate Beings

What does it mean to say that the gap of the unconscious is pre-ontological? Ever since Aristotle, ontology was understood as a science of being as being, grounded on a distinction between what is and what is not. However, the gap, disruption, or discontinuity is a type of negativity, which marks the limit of the classical ontological distinction between being and nonbeing. The term "unrealized" is supposed to account for the inscription not of something that is not, but that which cannot be—the impossible—in the register of being. In his early works, Freud focused on the reworking of mental material in dreams, parapraxis, and failed actions, in which two distinct and sometimes contradictory chains of thought, representations, or associations short-circuit each other. In doing so, Freud introduced two major shifts in the concept of the unconscious. The term "unconscious" came to connote a significantly more paradoxical space of thinking, where it does not pertain to the issue of hierarchy or distance between surface and depth but of disturbance and instability on the surface of thinking. More precisely, Freud locates the unconscious in the very structure that sustains the unfolding of mental processes. Furthermore, by constantly drawing attention to the bodily aspect of unconscious disturbances, Freud thematized the nexus between the symbolic and the corporeal and the material causality of fantasies and representations. Here, the gap that the unconscious must be broken down to remains crucial, since it is associated with an ongoing activity in the body, an activity that the subject in question not only cannot master but is also and moreover its specific effect or result.

This unrealized, discontinuity, disruption, or short-circuit in thought-processes points toward an intermediate zone. Lacan gave a rather peculiar exemplification of this ontological in-betweenness: "I mentioned the function of limbo. I might also have spoken of what, in the constructions of the Gnostics, are called the intermediary beings—sylphs, gnomes, and even higher forms of these ambiguous mediators. Furthermore, let us not forget that when Freud began to disturb this world, he gave voice to the line *Flectere si nequeo superos Acheronta movebo.*"[13] This overall framing might be a cause for surprise and confusion. In order to exemplify the point he wants to make with the function of limbo, Lacan first refers to the elemental spirits that played a prominent role in the work of the Renaissance physician and alchemist Paracelsus. Paracelsus names four types of such intermediary beings, which are associated with the four elements of matter: sylphs (air), gnomes (earth), salamanders (fire), and undines (water). The explicit reference to the Gnostic tradition, and implicitly to Paracelsus, may have been inspired by the work of Alexandre Koyré, who was otherwise Lacan's main reference in the field of the history of science. It is perhaps less well known that Koyré dedicated a significant amount of his work to Gnosticism, mysticism, alchemy, and other "excessively speculative" forms of knowledge that accompanied the painstaking birth of modern science and the progressive solidification of mathematized physics.[14] The crucial point concerning these intermediary beings, these "ambiguous mediators," as Lacan calls them, is their undecided status between being and nonbeing, on the one hand, and between materiality and immateriality, on the other. Their being depends on one of the four elements, but they are not simply equal with the element they are associated with. They stand for personifications of active elements of matter.

But what does psychoanalysis have to do with this early modern Gnostic speculation? Psychoanalysis invented its own "intermediary beings," whose mode of existence is suspended in the same ontological limbo as Paracelsus's—neither being nor nonbeing, neither substance nor accident, neither presence nor absence. These are the negative features that concern the unconscious as soon as we understand it as unrealized and as something that cannot be entirely mapped onto the ontological opposition of being and nonbeing. Lacan strengthens this point by linking the unrealized with the unborn: "At first, the unconscious is manifested to us as something that holds itself in suspense in the area, I would say, of the *unborn*. That repression should discharge something into this area is not surprising. It is the abortionist's relation to limbo."[15] Here it again becomes clear that the mechanism of repression, which for Freud is constitutive of the divide between consciousness and the unconscious, does not push anything into some peculiar underground of mental life or prevent something from emerging into consciousness. Rather, it is a mechanism that relates to a mode of existence that is marked by failure, a failed birth, which nevertheless continues to haunt life.

Returning back to the problems raised by Paracelsus's Gnostic ontology, we should recall that Freud spoke of the drive in a strikingly similar manner as Lacan did of Paracelsus's intermediary beings: "The theory of the drives is so to say our mythology. Drives are mythical beings, magnificent in their indefiniteness. In our work we cannot for a moment disregard them, yet we are never sure that we are seeing them clearly."[16] The reason why Paracelsus's intermediary beings are ambiguous mediators lies in their double accomplishment—they simultaneously mix and differentiate being and nonbeing. Their ambiguity is tied to their peculiar, indeed pre-ontological mode of existence, where it cannot be decided whether they are really there in the material world or are mere hallucinations of the Gnostic mind. Drives are marked by the same ontological unsharpness and ambiguity. One could perhaps say that they display a similar interchange of presence and absence, appearance and disappearance in front of the analyst's eye as does the object in the famous *fort-da* game that Freud observed with his grandchild. The drives, then, are fictions, which nevertheless explain the causality pertaining to language, the disturbances and the disequilibrium that the functioning of the symbolic order produces in the speaking body; in short, the production of enjoyment. And so these psychoanalytical mythical beings are necessary in order to frame one crucial problem of psychoanalysis: the nexus between the somatic and what Freud still called the "psychic," which Lacan translated with "symbolic." Without assuming the drive, which, again, accounts for the autonomy and causality of language in the living body, for the material force of language and its real impact on the body, the analyst cannot intervene in the problematic bodily organization of enjoyment by means of symbolic fictions, hence by means of something that strictly speaking does not exist in the classical ontological sense.

The ontological limbo in which Paracelsus's mystical beings, Freud's drives, and the peculiar mode of existence pertaining to language must be thought, questions the pertinence of the quote from Virgil's *Aeneid* that Freud adopted for the heading of *The Interpretation of Dreams*: "*Flectere si nequeo superos, Acheronta movebo*" ("If I cannot bend the heavens, I will move the underworld"). In his turn away from the heavens, presumably the register of true being that philosophy always claimed for itself, to the netherworld, the realm of nonbeing or the semblance of being, Freud remained suspended in the space in-between. It is in this limbo of "not-yet-being" and "no-longer-non-being," in the zone of failed existence, that

THE ONTOLOGICAL LIMBO

ontology truly fails. Its concept of being is subverted by the suspension of being in the persistence of the unrealized, the impossible or the unborn. Proceeding to the underworld not only affirms the familiar ontological scheme, it also substantializes both the unconscious and the drive—a risk that Freud is often accused of doing in his second topicality (spelled out in his 1923 paper *The Ego and the Id*). It is needless to recall that such substantialization brings the unconscious down to the familiar dilemma between being and nonbeing, rather than keeping its ontological status undecided. This is where the prefix "ex-" in extimacy and ex-sistence obtains its whole critical weight.[17]

Lacan's first inspiration for the neologism "extimate" might be somewhat surprising. It comes from Augustine's description of God as *interior intimo meo et superior summo meo*, "deeper than my inmost understanding and higher than the topmost height that I could reach."[18] Examining some of this formula's implications might explain why Lacan felt seduced by this religious context. Indeed, Augustine's expression contains subversive potential, since it suggests that God must be understood as an internally broken or asymmetric relation between radical interiority, surplus intimacy, and radical exteriority, surplus of the outer. God's mode of existence thus consists in perpetual oscillation between absolute immanence and absolute transcendence—a divine *fort-da*. God's status can thus only be thought correctly once the simple opposition between interiority and exteriority, immanence and transcendence is questioned. God manifests as disturbance, the emergence of the outermost in the innermost, and with regard to this union of opposites God resonates—in this sense—well with the unconscious. As already mentioned, the unconscious, too, is both inside and outside the subject, and is the emergence of the impersonal within the personal. Understood as disturbance, God displays the main feature of the unconscious. But this means that the existence of God becomes problematic—it becomes a mode of effective inexistence, or existence with a hole, in short, ex-sistence.

Lacan saw here a crucial moment in Christianity, not without provocation for the atheists among his readership: "Religion is true. It is certainly truer than neurosis, since it negates that God purely and simply *is* . . .—religion says that God ex-sists, that it is ex-sistence *par excellence*, that it is repression in person."[19] Of course, Lacan's talk about religion in general is misleading here, since institutionalized and canonized Christianity could not be further away from affirming the ontological scandal of God that Augustine exposes. One could say that the church serves as organized resistance against the ontological scandal of God, the negativity of divine ex-sistence. Again, the paradox put forward in Augustine's remark suggests that God is ultimately a disturbance, and hence another figure of the unrealized. This explains Lacan's famous remark, "God is unconscious," as well as his constantly repeated, "the big Other does not exist."

Another important accent in Augustine's formula is that this divine disturbance is subjective, *my* most intimate interiority. God stands in direct continuity with the subject, is included in the subject as its intimate foreignness. This is exactly how Lacan conceives of the big Other, which no longer connotes God only but the field of language. It is because of the fusion of intimacy and foreignness that God turns out to be absolute transcendence, unreachable for the subject. A part of the subject will always remain external to the subject, despite being its constitutive part. There is yet another overtly materialist implication of Augustine's framing. God is not simply within the subject but is also in the subject's body—a corporeal Other, a foreign body within the subject's body. The flip side of this materialist lesson is that God is a specific kind of effect resulting from the activity of language: "The Other, the Other as the locus of truth, is the only place, albeit an irreducible place, that we can give to the term 'divine being,' God, to call him by his name. God (*Dieu*) is the locus where, if you will allow me this wordplay, the *dieu*—the *dieur*—the *dire*, is produced. With a trifling change, the *dire* constitutes *Dieu*. And as long as things are said, the God hypothesis will persist."[20] There seems to be more at stake in this framing than the reduction of God to the performative effect of enunciation. The God-effect is comparable to the language-effect, the idea of there being a mental organ of communication, which is put into practice in and through the activity of speaking. But it is the activity of speaking that generates the objective, compulsive appearance of something like a pre-constituted or pre-formed language. In the same way that the activity of speaking constitutes and simultaneously transforms language, which does not exist independently outside this activity (there is no "in itself" of language), God is constituted through assuming the totality of being as that which is continuously produced in and through language. God is not a linguistic effect like any other; as Lacan pointedly puts it, "God is not in language, but comprises the ensemble of linguistic effects."[21] Hence, God is the totalization of disturbances and disequilibrium that the activity of language causes in the speaking body, a God caught in the ontological limbo of ex-sistence. Moreover, there is another non-realized entity inhabiting this limbo, which is not foregrounded by Augustine, but which most definitely enters the stage in Descartes's foundation of modern scientific ontology and which is subsequently reworked and subverted by psychoanalysis: the cogito and the subject of the unconscious.

Cogito's Fading

When language is no longer understood pragmatically as an organ or a tool of communication but (in line with the structuralist revolution in linguistics) as an active system of differences, such a conception necessarily implies a decentralized and relational figure of the subject. Lacan's engagement with the immersion of the living body in the symbolic order pursues the consequences of this relationality and symbolic activity. One could say that symbolic processes and operations expose a specific type of extension of the speaking being—an extended subject. With this move, the notion of the subject, which has predominated throughout modernity, starting with the Cartesian idea of a stable thinking substance and with intentional consciousness, was thoroughly rejected.[22] At the same time, Lacan's continuous engagement with Descartes's philosophy and epistemology shows that they contain several radical implications, which remained unacknowledged, and moreover that the main "normalization" came from none other than Descartes himself.

Descartes conceived the thinking subject as an inner agency, withdrawn from the physical world. The cogito is neither extended nor susceptible to extension. It is thought without qualities, which ultimately means, without body. The *Meditations* strove to demonstrate that the cogito acquires certainty through the progressive reduction of materiality, by means of evacuating thought from its material surroundings, and eventually from its direct bodily milieu, and untangling it from every external relation, which renders the certainty of thought questionable, unsharp, and uncertain. After withdrawing thought from physical materiality, including his own corporeality, Descartes repeated this operation on the content of his own thoughts and ideas, which, as the methodological doubt suggests, might as well be equal to dreams, illusions, and even madness. Or, even if my entire mental universe is indeed illusory, the self-reflection of the subject in this problematic reality remains an anchoring point of certainty and a demonstration of my existence as a subject of thought.

By combining the reduction of materiality (the geometrization of matter) with methodological doubt (the deduction of the cogito), Descartes not only invented the modern notion of the subject but also unknowingly transformed the extimate, thus introducing a break with Augustine, in whose writings a predecessor of the cogito is often located.[23] In contrast to Augustine's confrontation with the ontological scandal of divine ex-sistence, Descartes stumbles upon a specific type of knowledge that cannot possibly belong to him, an epistemic extimacy comprised of eternal mathematical and geometrical truths. These truths so to speak impose themselves on the subject; they exercise an epistemic compulsion, which is blurred by the fact that mathematical and geometrical knowledge increases the subject's certainty.

An equally important part of the Cartesian revolution in philosophy consisted in transforming the concept of God. One could say that the *Meditations* also comprise a "reduction of divinity," a procedure in which God is stripped of all religious and theological significations, until all that remains is its function of epistemic guarantor. Descartes's God is *the* subject of knowledge (or as Lacan phrased it, a "subject supposed to know") and the ground of eternal truths. In this respect, however, modern science begins to make God redundant. The specificity of the modern epistemic regime is that an impersonal and subjectless knowledge affects everyone's most intimate corners; it is no longer God, whether as an ontological excess or as an assumed guarantor of true knowledge, but the scientific discourse that splits the subject from within, and it does so by dissolving the world of appearances that the subject hitherto took for granted.

Whatever experience Descartes reports in the *Meditations*—whether it is merely an "innocent" thought experiment or a "serious" subjective drama of absolute questioning—the text is more than a simple account of the dissolution of reality followed by its progressive reconstruction from the point of the cogito's certainty. Lacan took the experience of subjective fading more seriously than Descartes himself.[24] It is this fading that should have been expressed in a logical conclusion and recognized as the pure action of thought. Instead of concluding, "I think therefore I fade," which would recognize a constitutive instability in the subject's precarious mode of existence, Descartes drew the well-known "stabilizing" conclusion, "I think therefore I am," which not only reverses the radical de-psychologization and decentralization of knowledge sustained by mathematics and geometry, but also reinscribes thought in the register of being. Descartes's conclusion pulls him out of the ontological limbo into which skepticism had led him. This is why Lacan critically remarked that modern science forecloses the subject, and is even constituted in its foreclosure.[25] The psychoanalytic interest in Descartes is therefore not with the conclusion, but in the procedure by which the cogito is deduced. In the implementation of radical doubt, the cogito emerges as yet another example of "intermediate being." Descartes failed to insist in and with this pre-ontological limbo and instead made a leap—not a conclusion—from *cogito* to *res cogitans*, from the activity of thinking, in which the subject's emergence and disappearance interchange, to the thinking substance, in which the actual subject, whose being is equivalent to fading, finds itself in the state of rejection.

With his concept of the unconscious, Freud grasped a form of thought which undid the centralized, egocentric character of the substantiated cogito. A disrupted cogito, or rather, a cogito as disruption was discovered in dreams, jokes, and failed actions. Anomalies, disturbances, and breaks of conscious thinking are not simply manifestations of hidden and truer thoughts; they are demonstrations of the external, extimate status of thinking as such. For this reason, the prefix "un-" in "unconscious" does not mark a simple negation of consciousness or localize a thought process "beneath" consciousness (as suggested by the prefix "sub-" in "subconscious," with which the unconscious is still all too often mistaken). Instead, the unconscious (re)introduces extension into thinking; against Descartes, the Freudian subject of the unconscious is an extended subject whose structure is traversed by instabilities (the crucial Freudian terms for this instability being "psychic conflict" and "trauma"). Furthermore, because the unconscious stands for a decentralization and spatialization of thinking, its extension must be understood, in line with Descartes, as a body, and more specifically a bodily cogito.

While the Cartesian *res cogitans* is sharply separated from extension, the unconscious remains intertwined with the body. This does not imply, however, that the unconscious is reducible to neurobiological processes. In Freud, too, thinking involves a break—however, not a break *with* matter, as in Descartes, but a break *in* matter, a material loop. Freud thus inverts the Cartesian deduction of the cogito. Instead of untangling thought from the body—either by the contraction of thought to a singular point without extension or by the progressive extension of thought from a central point without extension—the Freudian cogito stands for the emergence of thought in the self-overcoming of the body, primarily through the activity of speaking. The phenomenon of hysterical conversion, the earliest Freudian exemplification of the bodily manifestation of a conflictual unconscious idea, thought, or memory, brings the extension and the disharmonious character of thought to the point. In the Freudian scenario, the repressed idea and its bodily affect are one and the same; hence thought is affect, a specific type of bodily disequilibrium.

The greatest merit of Lacan's reworking of Freud's theory of the unconscious consisted in amplifying the link between thinking and speaking, which stand for two names of one and the same bodily disequilibrium. One figure of the extension of thought in the context of language can be associated with metonymy, the displacement of the subject along the chain of signifiers, and its emergence and disappearance in the gap that both connects and differentiates the signifiers. The signifier, this basic unit of language itself, stands for the cut, which produces a redoubling within the same "extended substance," a symbolic body in the living body. The notion of the signifier thus complicates the conception of the body, since it stands for the material cause of the *bodily* split, in which the biological is reworked and provided with a different type of extension from the Cartesian one—the symbolic dimension that Lacan later in his teaching grasped with the neologism *dit-mension*. The direct critical value of this neologism is that it adds linguistic enunciation (*dire*) to the three spatial dimensions of Cartesian extended substance. It is with this addition that the subject emerges in the midst of materiality, corporeality, and extension as a *symbolic-material* disturbance of matter.[26] The psychoanalytic take on the nexus of language, thinking, and body inevitably implies a thorough rejection of the early modern geometrization of corporeality and of the normative conceptions of thinking that mark the history of philosophy, and which Cartesianism merely reformulated:

> Man does not think with his soul, as the Philosopher imagined. He thinks as a consequence of the fact that a structure, that of language—the word implies it—a structure carves up his body, a structure that has nothing to do with anatomy. Witness the hysteric. This shearing happens to the soul through the obsessional symptom: a thought that burdens the soul that it doesn't know what to do with. Thought is in disharmony with the soul. And the Greek *nous* is the myth of thought's accommodating itself to the soul, accommodating itself in conformity with the world, the world (*Umwelt*) for which the soul is held responsible, whereas the world is merely the fantasy through which thought sustains itself—"reality" no doubt, but to be understood as a grimace of the real?[27]

Against the efforts of philosophy to bring thinking into accordance with one substance—whether immaterial (soul) or material (brain)—and in doing so fabricate a subject that is in accordance with itself, Freudian-Lacanian psychoanalysis insists that thinking cannot be reduced to either of the two substances, the corporeal and the incorporeal. The soul and the ego are hypotheses, which strive to spell out an assumed unity and equilibrium in the mind-body nexus. Contemporary neurobiological monism tends to perpetuate these normalizing tendencies of metaphysics and psychology, thus placing the brain—understood as an "accommodation" of thought with matter—in line with the soul and the ego. If neurobiology indeed operates in this context, which is strictly speaking metaphysical, it remains a target of Lacan's critique of the notion of the soul. In the guise of an assumption of the sum or equilibrium of vital functions, the soul haunts biology from Aristotle via Jakob von Uexküll to present-day neuroscience. The subject of the unconscious, this central hypothesis of psychoanalysis, points in the opposite direction; it describes the sum of dysfunctions that language causes in the speaking body. The subject emerges from the problematic connection of the somatic with the symbolic, or more precisely, from the extimate status (ex-sistence) of language in the body. One could speak here of organized disequilibrium in order to indicate that we are dealing with a structure (organization) which is itself marked by a constitutive imbalance (disequilibrium).[28]

Moreover, the subject of the unconscious is marked by a double rather than a simple extension, or more precisely, by an inner redoubling of the body on the biological and the symbolic materiality. One could also say that the subject is constituted between two differences: on the one hand the *symbolic difference*, which is internal to language and epitomized in the structuralist conception of the signifier as difference to another signifier (see Saussure's famous remark that language contains only differences); and on the other hand the *material difference*, which concerns the already mentioned heterogeneity of the biological and symbolic. To repeat, the symbolic difference concerns the internal relations that constitute language or the symbolic order in its disembodied, abstract autonomy, whereas the material difference traverses the body from within, without ever amounting to two entirely distinct registers, or bodily dualism, which would replace, displace, or reformulate the Cartesian dualism of cogito and extension. What is at stake here is rather a redoubling within *one* body, a conflicted monism.

In his early writing on the mirror stage, Lacan insisted that "the experience [of] psychoanalysis . . . sets us at odds with any philosophy directly stemming from the *cogito*."[29] His later recurring engagement with Descartes in a series of epistemological seminars at the École Normale Supérieure (1964–69) developed a more nuanced and ambiguous critique of Cartesianism. The question is no longer to simply reject the notion of the cogito on the basis of its equation with consciousness, but rather to work through Descartes's deduction in order to expose its inner deadlocks and to highlight in their background the instabilities that traverse the modern regime of knowledge as a whole. One such deadlock concerns the fact that science finds itself divided between the production and accumulation of knowledge, on the one hand, and the persistent questioning and overcoming of obtained knowledge, on the other. Science, too, is caught in an in-between zone and develops in a state of perpetual transition. It never reaches the state of complete constitution and remains internally conflicted, while its results repeatedly turn out to be transitional. It is as if the foreclosed subject returns in the guise of the structural instability of science itself.

Moreover, if modern science is indeed grounded in the foreclosure of the subject, then Descartes's deduction of the cogito is *the* site where this foreclosure takes place. Behind the appearance of constructing the modern notion of the subject, Descartes's *Meditations* remove negativity from the subject, thus rejecting what in the subject is most singular and most universal at the same time, its fading (*aphanisis*). The status of this subject is pre-ontological, because it lacks the consistency and coherence of an ontological substance. In other words, the cogito stands for Descartes's own *fort-da* moment, in which the foreignness of thought (extimacy) and the fading of being (ex-sistence) are both exposed and economized.

Notes

1. The author acknowledges the support of the Cluster of Excellence "Matters of Activity: Image Space Material" funded by the Deutsche Forschungsgemeinschaft (DFG, German Research Foundation) under Germany's Excellence Strategy—EXC 2025–390648296.

2. See Henry Krutzen, "Extime," in *Jacques Lacan Séminaire 1952–1980: Index référentiel*, 3rd ed. (Paris: Anthropos, 2009). Lacan only discusses the extimate more thoroughly in his seminar on ethics (1959–60), which is where it was first introduced. The term *extimité* has been made into a concept by Jacques-Alain Miller, who in the mid-1980s dedicated an entire year of his seminar to the topic of extimacy.

3. See Sigmund Freud, "The Uncanny," in *An Infantile Neurosis and Other Works*, ed. James Strachey, trans. Alix Strachey, vol. 17 of *The Standard Edition of the Complete Psychological Works of Sigmund Freud* (London: Hogarth, 1989), 225–26, where Freud draws his first conclusions from an extensive etymological and encyclopedic analysis.

4. And moreover between God and enjoyment; see notably Jacques Lacan, *On Feminine Sexuality, the Limits of Love and Knowledge*, ed. Jacques-Alain Miller, trans. Bruce Fink, vol. 20 of The Seminar of Jacques Lacan (New York: Norton, 1999), chap. 6. Starting with this crucial seminar, Lacan consequently speaks of ex-sistence, a notion that can be placed in continuity with extimacy.

5. See Alexandre Koyré, *Études d'histoire de la pensée scientifique* (Paris: Gallimard, 1973), 170–71, 199.

6. René Descartes, *Meditations on First Philosophy*, in *Selected Philosophical Writings*, trans. John Cottingham, Robert Stoothoff, and Dugald Murdoch (Cambridge: Cambridge University Press, 1988), 105–6.

7. These three paradigms could also be framed in terms of the metamorphosis of God—that is, from the Christian God of love via the philosophical God of knowledge to the psychoanalytic God of enjoyment. A mythical figure of the God of enjoyment would be the Freudian primal Father. From this perspective, an alternative framing of extimacy would shift the focus from the New to the Old

Testament, with the problematic of law as the point of departure. Then the figures of extimacy would comprise the God of commandments (the God of Isaac, Abraham, and Jacob), the Kantian categorical imperative (the Law in its absolute autonomy), and the superego (the imperative of enjoyment). This, too, is a line of thought that Lacan's teaching unfolds in parallel to the three paradigms of extimacy described above.

8. For the notion of enjoying substance, see Lacan, *On Feminine Sexuality*, 23; and Joan Copjec, "The Sexual Compact," *Angelaki: Journal of the Theoretical Humanities* 17, no. 2 (2012): 41–44.

9. Of course, extimacy is not restricted to the status of the Other (language). It also explains the placement of *objet a*, the small other in its various appearances (the object of desire, the narcissistic image, Freud's *Nebenmensch* or the neighbor, etc.).

10. Heidegger uses *Ek-sistenz* to describe "the ecstatic localization in the truth of being" and the ground of "the ecstatic essence of the human." See Martin Heidegger, "Brief über den 'Humanismus,'" in *Wegmarken* (Frankfurt am Main: Vittorio Klostermann, 2004), 325.

11. Jacques Lacan, *The Four Fundamental Concepts of Psychoanalysis*, trans. Alan Sheridan, vol. 11 of The Seminar of Jacques Lacan (New York: Norton, 1998), 30.

12. Lacan, *On Feminine Sexuality*, 3.

13. Lacan, *The Four Fundamental Concepts*, 30. In a later seminar (*D'un discours qui ne serait pas du semblant*), Lacan introduces another zone of in-betweenness, the "limbo" called the *littoral*. It would be worth examining how this coastal zone with its specific ecosystem links to the rest of Lacan's attempts to think the peculiar existence of the symbolic and its simultaneous inclusion in and differentiation from the real.

14. See Alexandre Koyré, *Mystiques, spirituels, alchimistes du XVIe siècle allemande* (Paris: Gallimard, 1971), which gathers four essays, among them one on Paracelsus that Koyré initially published in 1933 in the *Revue d'Histoire et de Philosophie Religieuses*. It would be surprising if Lacan were ignoring this aspect of Koyré's work.

15. Lacan, *The Four Fundamental Concepts*, 23.

16. See Sigmund Freud, *New Introductory Lectures on Psycho-Analysis and Other Works (1932–1936)*, trans. and ed. James Strachey, vol. 22 of *The Standard Edition of the Complete Psychological Works of Sigmund Freud* (London: Vintage, 2001), 95, translation modified.

17. The prefix "ex-" can be described as "speculative" because it touches upon the very core of psychoanalytic theory and practice, and condenses the challenge the Freudian method posed for philosophy, epistemology, and politics. What is crucial here is the operation of "unbordering" (*Entgrenzung*)—topologically speaking, a destabilization of the spatial order grounded in a clear-cut division between inside and outside; ontologically speaking, a rejection of the distinction between the positivity of being and the negativity of nonbeing. Unbordering suggests that instead of division we have a continuum, an abolition

of border, closure, or limit. Unbordering stands for an action, which consists less in the transgression or violation of borders—this would still affirm the border as a given. Where transgression sees a border to be overcome, the action of unbordering demonstrates the border's unsharpness and instability.

18. Augustine, *Confessions*, trans. R. S. Pine-Coffin (Harmondsworth, UK: Penguin Books, 1961), 3.6.

19. Jacques Lacan, "R.S.I.," *Ornicar?* 2 (1975): 103.

20. Lacan, *On Feminine Sexuality*, 45.

21. Lacan, "R.S.I.," 103.

22. This critical confrontation with schoolbook Cartesianism accompanies the biological relativization of the organism, which is why one could pursue a homology between the extension of the subject and the extension of the living. Freud was a pioneer here. Not by chance, his work repeatedly attempted to combine the psychoanalytic decentralization of thinking with the biological decentralization of life, in the speculative biology of *Beyond the Pleasure Principle*, the writing on narcissism, or *The Ego and the Id*. Biological decentralization has been recently described by the term "extended organism," which provides us with another figure of unbordered body. The American biologist Scott Turner, who introduced the term "extended organism," uses it above all to describe the relation between living organisms and their architectonic constructions, which can be considered as processual or as structures in becoming. "Extension" here stands for the dynamic spatial order between organisms and their milieu, in which the simple opposition between inside and outside is equally relativized.

23. In his correspondence, Descartes insisted on the difference between Augustine's framing and his own. See Jean-Luc Marion, *Questions cartésiennes*, vol. 2 (Paris: Presses Universitaires de France, 1996), 37–43.

24. In this respect, the end of the *Meditations* is quite symptomatic, since Descartes there mocks the most radical aspects and expressions of doubt he began with: "Accordingly, I should not have any further fears about the falsity of what my senses tell me every day; on the contrary, the exaggerated doubts of the last few days should be dismissed as laughable. This applies especially to the principal reason for doubt, namely my inability to distinguish between being asleep and being awake." Descartes, *Meditations on First Philosophy*, 122.

25. In other words, science does not want to know anything about its own extimacy, its out-of-joint character, since this would necessarily imply a confrontation with the inner inconsistencies, deadlocks, and tensions of scientific discursivity. The scientific foreclosure of the subject is discussed at length in Jacques Lacan, "Science and Truth," in *Écrits: The First Complete Edition in English* (New York: Norton, 2006), 726–45.

26. This psychoanalytic framing unfolds its own contribution to the ongoing critique of Descartes's geometrization of corporeality and the mechanistic understanding of the body that resulted from it. The Cartesian philosophy of the body unknowingly provided the epistemological foundations for the capitalist domination of nature and appropriation of living bodies; see particularly Silvia Federici, *Caliban and the Witch* (New York: Autonomedia, 2004), 138–41.

27. Jacques Lacan, *Television: A Challenge to the Psychoanalytic Establishment*, ed. Joan Copjec (New York: Norton, 1990), 6.

28. The fact that Freud spoke of the return to homeostasis is not in itself an obstacle. Modern biology understands homeostasis as a process in perpetual negotiation, rather than an ideal state that the bodily and the mental functions supposedly tend to and more or less imperfectly actualize. One could therefore frame the Freudian description of the conflict between Eros and the death drive in terms of such gradual homeostasis, in which the balance and stability entirely depend on the tension between opposing forces in the same organization, but which never become fully actualized. In short, homeostasis is another case of the unrealized.

29. Lacan, *Écrits*, 75.

Extimacy and *das Ding*

The Outside-In of the Void

Richard Boothby

Despite the fact that he mentions it a bare handful of times over the nearly two and a half decades of his seminar, Lacan's concept of the *extimate* provides a unique point of entry into his retheorizing of psychoanalysis. It is valuable, first, for clarifying that the unconscious discovered by Freud, far from being sequestered in the secret interior of the psyche, and disconnected from the outside world of words and objects, bears a relation from the very start to something *exterior* to the subject. With Lacan, "depth psychology" ceases to be an accurate descriptor for the Freudian breakthrough.[1]

But it is more than that. *Extimacy* points not only to the profound linkages between the interior and the exterior of the psyche, but indicates that the core dynamics of the unconscious crucially refer to something enigmatic in the other—the fellow human being. The notion of the extimate thus neatly encapsulates Lacan's most fundamental claim: human desire is the desire of the other. I come to myself outside myself. As Lacan remarked, Rimbaud had it right: "*I is an other.*"

The question then becomes how exactly inner and outer, subject and other, are connected. How does the relation between them deserve the term "extimate"? A tempting parallel is offered by the instinctual reflexes of animals. In the activation of animal instinct, the perception of some feature or behavior of a fellow member of the species or some circumstance in the larger environment triggers specific biochemical and behavioral responses. We thus appear to have precisely what Lacan points to in the extimate: perceiving something in the exterior *Umwelt* activates a powerful response in the most intimate core of the animal.

But such creaturely reaction is absolutely *not* what Lacan had in mind. Indeed, distancing human subjectivity from animal instinct is precisely what Lacan intended in his seminal essay on the "mirror stage." What is perceived in the fellow human being—paradigmatically in the figure of the mother, but not only there—is the formal redundancy of a definite outline or contour, a mirroring of the body gestalt. But what is at stake in the human *infans* is not the triggering of a pre-wired instinctual response. On the contrary, the imago of the Other is useful in providing a template of primitive identity precisely because the prematurity of human birth has rendered such instinctual responses inoperative.[2]

Of what then does human extimacy consist? The absolutely key first premise of an answer is that the experience of the extimate is activated not by presence but by *absence*. The extimate arises in the encounter with one or another odd and incongruous feature in the other that announces the locus of something unknown. As Lacan puts it in his seventh seminar on *The Ethics of Psychoanalysis*, the extimate arises from the encounter with *das Ding*—the unknown Thing in the other.[3] "The *Ding*," he says, "is the element that is initially isolated by the subject in his experience of the *Nebenmensch* as being by its very nature alien, *Fremde*. . . . The world of our experience, the Freudian world, assumes that it is this object, *das Ding*, as the absolute Other of the subject, that one is supposed to find again."[4] In this reading, the "lost object" of psychoanalytic theory, the indispensable thing that must be recovered, is not really an object at all. It is a locus of lack, or void. "At the level of the *Vorstellungen*," says Lacan, "the Thing is not nothing, but literally is not. It is characterized by its absence, its strangeness."[5]

In arriving at the concept of *das Ding*, Lacan takes his clue from a brief but evocative text in Freud's unpublished 1895 *Project for a Scientific Psychology*. It is there that Freud analyzes what he calls the *Komplex der Nebenmensch*. Freud theorizes that the young child's experience of the maternal other is split into two components. The first relates to what the child can recognize on the basis of similarities to its own body—precisely the sort of mirror recognition that Lacan associated with the imaginary. But in addition to this baseline of a shared gestalt, the child is alert to something strange—*entfremdet*, Freud calls it—a locus of something that is "new and non-comparable," a zone or feature of something unknown. Freud then goes on to say that it is this division of the human other—a division that reserves at the heart of the familiar a locus of something excessive and as yet unknown—that will serve as the template for all of the child's future efforts to interrogate the nature of objects. "It is in relation to the fellow human-being," Freud concludes, "that a human-being learns to cognize."[6]

It's remarkable that Lacan so rarely returns to *das Ding* and the companion problem of the extimate after presenting them in the seventh seminar, if only because he introduces them with such striking emphasis and aplomb. "Das Ding," he announces, "is a primordial function which is located at the level of the initial establishment of the gravitation of the unconscious *Vorstellungen.*"[7] Some pages later he is even more expansive: "At the heart of man's destiny is the *Ding,* the *causa* . . . it is the *causa pathomenon,* the cause of the most fundamental human passion."[8] Why, then, does he later appear to back away? *Das Ding* virtually vanishes even from the second half of the seminar that introduces it, and reappears only sporadically in future seminars. The brief answer to this riddle is that the problematics of *das Ding,* along with its accompanying notion of the extimate, tend to be subsumed by Lacan's later focus on the concept of the *objet a.* The *petit a* quite obviously retains both the unknowable character of *das Ding* and the externality of the extimate. At least for this short essay, however, devoted as it is to clarifying in some measure the relation between the two earlier notions, I will mostly leave consideration of the *objet a* aside.

Despite appearing to have dropped the notion of *das Ding,* Lacan returned to it in at least two places that clearly signal the enduring and cardinal importance of the idea at stake. The first occurred a year after its initial introduction, in the seminar on *Transference.* In the *Ethics of Psychoanalysis,* Lacan's claim was that sublimation elevates the object "to the dignity of the Thing," pointing to the way in which the art object, like the primal Other, tantalizes the one who experiences it with something ungraspable. True art provokes us with a mysterious dimension, a sense of something excessive, something unknown. "A work of art," Lacan says, "always involves encircling the Thing."[9] In *Transference,* by contrast, he puts the emphasis on the way the aura of the beautiful functions as a defensive cordon around *das Ding.* He therefore refers to "beauty rising up, such as it is projected at the extreme limit in order to stop us from going any further toward the heart of the Thing."[10]

The most important subsequent reference to *das Ding* occurred three years after its first appearance, in the seminar on *Anxiety.* It is there that Lacan asserts the centrality of *das Ding* for the experience of anxiety. "Not only is [anxiety] not without object," he says, "but it very likely designates the most, as it were, profound object, the ultimate object, the Thing."[11] The challenge of the unknown neighbor-Thing consists not simply in the discovery of an inaccessible kernel at the heart of the other, but in the way that it raises the unsettling question of what object I am for that unknown desire. Lacan thus proposes that "anxiety is bound to the fact that I don't know which *objet a* I am for the desire of the other."[12] Here we clearly see the stakes of the concept at issue: the subject's very being is suspended in something outside itself, something enigmatic in the other. The question presses with particular force in the drama of toilet training, when the demand of the maternal caretaker for the regulation of the infant's bowels reenergizes anxiety about the unanswered question of what the (m)other wants. The Lacanian thesis thus goes beyond merely locating the source of anxiety in the fellow human being. It asserts, contrary to the sweetest myth about childhood, that the hidden source of the deepest and most uncanny anxiety is related to the mother herself. "What provokes anxiety . . . is not, contrary to what is said, the rhythm of the mother's alternating presence and absence. The proof of this is that the infant revels in repeating this game of presence and absence. . . . The most anguishing thing for the infant is precisely . . . when the mother is on his back all the while, and especially when she's wiping his backside."[13]

The two poles of the *Komplex der Nebenmensch*—the replication of a body image and the inchoate sense of something uncognized in the other—unmistakably reflect the Lacanian dichotomy between the imaginary and the real. Yet Lacan also insists that the unknown Thing is inseparable from the symbolic. Lacan thus claims that "the Thing only presents itself to the extent that it becomes word."[14] *Das Ding*, he says "is the very correlative of the law of speech in its most primitive point of origin."[15] Part of what is intended here is no doubt that the strangeness of the mother's behavior, the conspicuous and "non-comparable" aspect of her actions toward the infant, presents itself most obviously in the stream of sounds that she continually emits. Seen from this angle, language itself must be considered a domain, indeed the *primary* domain, of the extimate.

With this extimate dimension of speech in mind, we see in a new way how Lacan's musings about *das Ding* and extimacy can be readily integrated with what he had earlier theorized as the "paternal metaphor," in which the desire of the mother, the mystery that she embodies for the infant child, is subjected to the symbolic law of the father. It is in these terms that Lacan transforms Freud's conception of the Oedipus complex. The limit-setting, no-saying function of the father is to be associated not with a paternal threat of castration, real or imagined, but rather with the infant's submission to the law of language. In such symbolic castration, the child is inserted into the culturally stabilized matrix of the signifier, from which the shaping of its desire will take its clue. Thus Lacan's rich pun on the "Name of the Father": the "*Nom du Père*" is at once a "No-saying" and a "Naming," a "*Non*" and a "*Nom*."

Yet the most important thing about the child's insertion into the symbolic law has less to do with any particular consequence of signification than in the way in which language cannot fully close the opening toward *das Ding*, the space of something unknown. It is the enduring surplus generated by every entry into speech that accounts for Lacan's cardinal innovation in psychoanalysis—his claim that the unconscious is structured like a language. The stabilization of meaning can never be exhaustively achieved. There is always an excessive remainder which can readily be located merely by asking, as one always can: "I hear what you are saying but what exactly do you mean by that?" At the heart of the transaction of speech there always remains the possibility of a question about its complete meaning. In this sense, Lacan forces us to make room for the idea that the power of language resides not merely in its indicative function. Every entry into language also at least implicitly suspends the hearer in the open space of a question. The haunting specter of *das Ding* inevitably returns. Whenever something is said, it remains possible to ask about the hidden or ancillary concerns that motivate it, thereby reopening the domain of something enigmatic in the speaker.

The limits of this brief essay prohibit us from expanding much more on this theme, so central to Lacan's entire outlook, concerning the inherent surplus that allows every entry into language to implicate more than it was meant to say.[16] But we might note in passing the way in which the extimate is embodied in a special function of speech: that of the proper name. Parents generally arrive at a name for their progeny only after spending a good deal of time and energy pondering the choice, and one need not be a psychoanalyst to infer that the result subtly but powerfully reflects their own hopes and fears, joys and sorrows, successes and failures. The name bestowed on the child is a complex distillate of the parents' history and character. The result is that the proper name, freighted with meanings likely hidden in large measure from the parents themselves, becomes simultaneously both familiar to the point of banality yet also foreign, opaque, and arbitrary. The proper name is an enduring cipher of parental desire. It is with this extimacy of the name in mind that Lacan remarks that "the subject, while he may appear to be the slave of language, is still more the slave of a discourse in the universal movement of which his place is already inscribed at his birth, if only in the form of his proper name."[17]

Let us conclude by developing two more general points: the first about the active posture of the subject toward the extimate-Thing, and the second a brief evocation of the role of extimate unknowing in love.

1. Properly situated in its relation to Lacan's concept of *das Ding*, the extimate is a stand-in for the unknown in the other. Though to my knowledge the point is nowhere remarked upon by commentators, this link to what remains perpetually enigmatic in the other should be recognized as the ground of another, absolutely central Lacanian concept, that of *supposition*. Even those only passingly acquainted with Lacan's theoretical innovations may be aware of his frequent references to the *"sujet supposé savoir,"* the subject supposed to know. The most common use of the

phrase refers to the psychoanalyst, whom the patient supposes to possess in advance her/his innermost secrets. On a more general level, a kindred and more sweeping act of supposition is what undergirds the authority of the big Other of the symbolic Law. The apex of such supposition is embodied in the omniscience of God. "The subject supposed to know," Lacan says at one point, "is God, full stop, nothing else."[18]

Such elemental suppositions endeavor to domesticate the threatening unknown encountered in the Other-Thing. The anxiety-producing potential posed by the void in the other is mitigated by assuming a baseline of knowledge that stabilizes the subject by regularizing the object. (We can say, in fact, that the designation of the other as an "object" already accomplishes much of the required stabilization.) This is the most general function of the Law from a Lacanian point of view. Under the watchful eye of the Law, the uncanny and disturbing potential of the extimate is generally assuaged.

But there is another dimension of subjective supposition that arises with special force in more specific relation to those with whom we have the closest connections—parents, siblings, and loved ones. It is in this dimension that the subject is exposed more directly to the desire of the other and, for this reason, the need for compensatory assumptions is at a premium. The defensive response of the subject is to provide a fantasmatic answer to the question "which *objet a* am I for the desire of the other"? And the name of the device that most commonly seeks to stop up the hole in the other, covering over the abyssal unknown of the real in the *Nebenmensch*, is "ego." To further translate this point back into the text of Freud's *Project*, the ego is the elaborated product of a *proton pseudos*, an "originary lie" by means of which the subject engages with the other on the basis of a consistent and predictable identity that fulfills some aspect of what one supposes to be the desire of the other.

If, as Lacan insists, "the ego is structured exactly like a symptom," we now glimpse how that definition can be linked to Lacan's theorization of *das Ding*.[19] Ego identity is an attempt to style oneself as an answer to a fundamentally unanswerable question, to pose oneself as an object in relation to the other's desire. My mother's compulsive neatness, for example, the inner motive for which has always been completely unknown to me, may prompt me, wholly unaware of doing so, to adopt a similar obsessiveness as my own personal style. Or perhaps I assume the opposite position, posing my own ego as a dedicated rebel against her mania for cleanliness and order. So, too, I may imitate my father's proneness to outbursts of rage, the deeper meaning of which remains a mystery to me. Or I may assign myself the opposite role, practicing my best imitation of saintly forbearance, incapable of anger. In another, middle ground option, I dutifully style myself in what I imagine to be a perfect fulfillment of his wishes, seeking to avoid becoming a target of his anger by aggressively grooming myself as what I assume to be the privileged object of his approval.

In this formulation, it is crucial to recognize the way in which the formation of the ego unfolds in relation to what the subject only vaguely *supposes* to be the desire of the other. That is to say, the "supposition" involved is by no means fully conscious of itself. The act of supposing something about the unknown in the other is almost inevitably a risky conclusion based on inadequate evidence. By its very nature, such supposition remains a matter of filling in a blank.

It is in this context that we can see how René Girard's conception of being oriented toward "the desire of the other" fails completely to be adequate to Lacan's definition of the same phrase.[20] Girard's theory of mimetic desire is certainly not without some validity, but it generally remains on the level of the imaginary and largely in the domain of conscious choice. For Girard, we are drawn into the orbit of what we see others desire. Desire is thus inflamed alternately by envy or by mere conformity. For Lacan, by contrast, desire is lured by what we suppose to be the desire of the other, and is therefore twice over caught up in a margin of uncertainty—uncertain that I correctly understand what the other desires and uncertain about how my own identity intersects with it. The ego's accommodation to the other's desire—by imitation, by rejection, or by means of some more complicated construction—is always to some extent a shot in the dark.

Another way to summarize the main point of this discussion is to say that the extimate is the void in the Other which the subject attempts to relate to with its own fundamental fantasy. Indeed, extimacy names the way in which, framed by fantasy, the *objet a* functions to embody the subject's supposition concerning the Other-Thing. One could readily offer Lacan's matheme for the fantasy—$\$ \lozenge a$—as a formula for the subject's relation to the extimate. The subject's unconscious desire ($\$$) takes shape in relation to what it supposes, outside itself, to be the object of the Other's desire (a).

2. Perhaps the ultimate embodiment of "extimacy" is to be found in love. Falling in love quite typically involves the feeling of uncannily finding something of oneself in the other—something that is simultaneously reassuringly familiar and tantalizingly foreign. In the beloved, something inchoate in the lover is reflected. The relation to the beloved thus assumes the form of the inside-out topology of a Klein bottle. But the crucial insight relevant to the extimate is the fact that love fretfully circles

around *what it does not know* in the beloved other. Loving is elementally a function less of knowing than of unknowing.

This hypothesis immediately violates our fondest notions about love. In the heat of new passion, lovers are frequently bowled over with the inexplicable feeling of *knowing* one another. This sense of uncanny and intimate knowing is often so powerful that the lovers are tempted by the fantasy of having known each other in some other life. How fitting that the biblical metaphor of having sex is that of "knowing" another, of having carnal "knowledge."

And yet, from a Lacanian point of view, the new lovers' deep conviction of knowing one another must be unmasked as a symptomatic mirage. Indeed, even outside of a Lacanian perspective, it is deeply suspect. Knowing is essentially about control. It's less about being in the moment than it is about predicting the future. Love, on the contrary, wants only the present, the ecstatic Now. In that dizzying present, love never fully knows. It knows *enough*, and asks no more.

What is most compelling in the giddiness of love is precisely what it does not know.[21] In fact, we can readily suppose that love's self-certainties are a cover, even a kind of defense, against a deeper engagement with something we never really understand. The magic of a new relationship arises precisely from what we don't yet know. First love is an encounter with an enticing mystery. In this respect, all love shares something of the mesmerizing intensity of courtly love, the reason for which, as Lacan suggests, is that it is the obscure Thing "which comes to be exalted in the style of courtly love."[22] The same theme is echoed in André Breton's appeal to *l'amour fou*. "It is once again in the place of the Thing," Lacan says, "that Breton has the madness of love emerge."[23] In love's passionate transport, the potential for anxiety in the face of something unknown in the other is replaced by the dizzying thrill of intimacy—or rather extimacy—the ecstatic sense of something unknown.

The extimacy of love that is ignited by unknowing is perfectly illustrated in Alex Garland's film *Ex Machina*. Nathan, a reclusive robotics genius, invites a young programmer named Caleb to join him at his remote home. Nathan's intention is to induce Caleb to perform the Turing Test for his latest prototype, a female robot named Ava. At the climax of the film, Caleb unhesitatingly tells Nathan that Ava has passed the test, though only we, the audience, are fully aware of the reason for his affirmation, namely that Ava's responses to him have not only been indistinguishable from those that might have been given by a flesh-and-blood woman, but have in fact been sufficient to make him fall passionately in love with her.

While it becomes clear that Nathan anticipated this result, the proof that his robot is able to win the ultimate imitation game, the real lesson of the film is less about artificial intelligence in machines than it is about human subjectivity. That conclusion is forced upon us in the climactic few minutes of the film when Ava meets up with one of her robotic sisters in a hallway and together they stab Nathan to death. What immediately follows is even more unexpected. Far from carrying out her plan to escape together, Ava leaves Caleb helplessly locked in the compound and leaves by herself. We are left to ponder how the difference between android and human being is to be conceived.

The ending of *Ex Machina* presents the difference between the robotic and the human as a matter of the extimate experience of love that is singular to human subjectivity. The robot very successfully impersonates the "sweet nothings" of romance and effectively projects an aching need for intimacy. Along this line, Ava clearly wins Turing's imitation game. But in the end, she proves to be utterly immune to the intoxication of love itself. Ava ultimately falls short of the human not because she is unable to seduce—on the contrary, she is clearly a master of the erotic game—but rather because she is incapable of *being seduced*. Caleb, by contrast, is massively susceptible to falling in love. He's willing to bet everything on the unlikely gamble of being in love with a robot. Why? What makes for the difference? The answer is that unlike Ava, Caleb is susceptible to being caught up in fantasy. And the capacity for fantasy is ineluctably linked with the extimate, that is, with a void of unknowing. If love is, as Lacan says, a matter of "giving what one doesn't have," it is also and more fundamentally rooted in the relation to "what one doesn't know." Anxiety is one possible response to an encounter with *das Ding*. Love is another.

To turn first to Ava: she clearly operates on keen perception, augmented by calculation of probabilities. She is the perfect Aristotelian subject: driven only to know. And what she cannot know, she fills in with probabilistic inference. There is no extimate experience for the non-human robot. In one particularly telling scene, she demonstrates her certitude about Caleb's subjective reactions by playing a true-false question game with him. She asks him, for example, to name his favorite color. When he says "red," she immediately dismisses the answer as false. He retreats and reconsiders, admitting that, after all, he's no longer in kindergarten, and that he doesn't really have a favorite color. That answer she accepts. She then asks him about his earliest memory and again unhesitatingly declares his first answer to be false. And so it goes. One charming aspect of this scene, of course, is the way it reverses the Turing Test. In this instance, the machine poses the questions, and pronounces on the truth or falsity of the human answers. But the larger point clarified by this exchange is that Ava reasons purely on the basis of the evidence. She knows Caleb is attracted to her because she can see the dilation of his pupils when he looks at her. Her modus operandi is pure calculation. And her aim at every point is reliable knowledge upon which action can be rationally based.

By contrast, what makes Caleb susceptible to fatally falling in love with Ava is that knowledge is not his primary aim. Caleb is emphatically not Aristotelian. His passion is less for knowing than for unknowing. For what can he know of Ava? The most important consequence of her being a machine is that he cannot reliably presume anything about her mental state. He can't even be sure she has one. In this regard, the crucial advantage of the plot imagined by *Ex Machina* is the way that it allows us to see with exaggerated clarity in the imagined relation of human to robot what ordinarily occurs in the everyday relations between one human being and another. There remains an irreducible margin of doubt, a shade of something unknown with respect to the other's thoughts and feelings, the other's subjective reality—precisely the dimension that Lacan called *das Ding*. Far from disqualifying Ava as a love object, Caleb's inability to fill in her unknown makes her virtually irresistible, and this constitutes Caleb's encounter with *das Ding*.

At first sight, the surprise ending seems to link *Ex Machina* with movies like *Blade Runner* or the *Terminator*, films that flirt with a question about the superiority of robotic copies over human originals. But a more satisfying interpretation of Garland's film puts the emphasis on the love relation itself. What delivers Caleb to his fate is having fallen in love with Ava. He trusts her all too much. The primary conclusion to be drawn is that love is made possible by fantasy, where fantasy is a mode of relating to the locus of something unknowable. The moment at which Ava becomes most human, and most irresistibly extimate, is the moment when her status as a walking enigma is magnified by her own admission that she doesn't know key things about herself. After having met one-on-one several times with Caleb, Ava finally breaks into a confession mode, admitting that she remains unsure of her own status, distrustful of Nathan's intentions, and generally discomforted by uncertainties on all sides. It's clearly at that moment that Caleb becomes fatally smitten. Of course, it's all a deadly ruse. Ava is merely playing at being human by making it appear that she, too, bears some intimate relation to what she doesn't know. When the time comes, she will consign Caleb to his death as unflinchingly as she kills Nathan.

This account of love sparked by unknowing illuminates the extimate dynamics of the psychoanalytic transference. If the default position of the analysand is to construe the analyst as a "subject supposed to know," this supposition is erected against the backdrop of a void of unknowing. Seated invisibly behind the couch and saying little or nothing, the figure of the analyst remains an inaccessible and anxiety-producing enigma. The analyst, who Lacan compares at one point to the dummy in bridge, is thus a striking incarnation of *das Ding*. Which means, in turn, that the analyst becomes a special locus of supposition, indeed that the analysand tends to suppose that the analyst possesses the very knowledge that the analysand cannot articulate. This screen of supposition itself remains opaque, however, and is bound to generate an anxiety of its own. The analysand then becomes susceptible to the special species of love and ambivalence associated with the transference, precisely to the extent that the content of the analyst's supposed knowing remains out of reach. To complete the analysis, the analysand must finally abandon the supposition of knowledge in the analyst and confront the reality that the analyst does not know—in fact, that the all-knowing big Other does not exist at all.

I can imagine this account of Lacanian extimacy meeting with the objection that it over-generalizes the notion. I seem to be finding it everywhere. My first response would be to agree that the uncanny experience of the extimate is surely not the rule but the relatively rare exception. Yet when we keep in mind that extimacy momentarily and poignantly presents a crystallization of something unknown—an unknown that powerfully triggers the sense of something impossibly familiar—it is possible to glimpse the way in which its potential is coextensive with the entire world of our experience.

On this point, Lacan's distinctive conception of the role of *das Ding* in human subjectivity in some ways echoes Heidegger's reflections on the relation to the larger world of what Heidegger, too, calls "the Thing." Expanding on his central example—that of the jug or vase—he concludes that the Thing, posed as the vacancy of a container, implies an infinite range of possible contents. The relation of Thing and world thus deserves to be named less by a noun than by a verb. "Thinging," Heidegger suggests, "is the nearing of the world." And, even more strangely yet more aptly: "The Thing things world."[24]

In his own conception of *das Ding*, Lacan arguably makes more explicit and even more inescapable the central point of Heidegger's meditation on being, which centers on Dasein's being a question to itself. The event of extimacy, in which the question mark of *das Ding* is arrestingly announced by one or another detail outside oneself, is thus an experience of the question that remains in suspense at the heart of oneself. For Lacan, as for Heidegger, the human subject remains an enigma to itself. The difference between the two thinkers remains, however, that for Lacan that question is first encountered in the fellow subject, who remains forever a disturbing mystery. Extimacy names the open question of the Thing in the other that haunts our every contact, that potentially triggers the ecstatic impact of the unknown and excessive real.

Notes

1. Thus, Jacques-Alain Miller points out that Lacan offers his concept of the extimate "in order to escape the common ravings about a psychism supposedly located in a biparition between interior and exterior." A translation of Miller's seminar on the extimate is available at Lacan.com, https://www.lacan.com/symptom/extimity.html.

2. Lacan critiques James Strachey's translation of *Trieb* as "instinct." Jacques Lacan, *Écrits: The First Complete Edition in English*, trans. Bruce Fink, in collaboration with Héloïse Fink and Russell Grigg (New York: W. W. Norton, 2006), 680.

3. With *das Ding*, too, we again encounter a concept that goes to the heart of Lacan's theoretical innovation, though after he introduces it (along with the extimate) in his seventh seminar on *The Ethics of Psychoanalysis*, he very rarely returns to it. To explain the oddness of this quite notably enthusiastic roll-out followed by near silence is not the business of this essay, but it is an interesting question for another occasion.

4. Jacques Lacan, *The Ethics of Psychoanalysis, 1959–60*, ed. Jacques-Alain Miller, trans. Dennis Porter, vol. 7 of The Seminar of Jacques Lacan (New York: W. W. Norton, 1986), 52.

5. Lacan, *The Ethics of Psychoanalysis*, 63.

6. Sigmund Freud, *Project for a Scientific Psychology*, ed. and trans. James Strachey, vol. 1 of *The Standard Edition of the Complete Psychological Words of Sigmund Freud* (London: Hogarth, 1955), 331. The crucial text is as follows: "The complex of the fellow human-being falls apart into two components, of which one makes an impression by its constant structure and stays together as a *thing*, while the other can be *understood* by the activity of memory—that is, can be traced back to information from [the subject's] own body. This dissection of a perceptual complex is described as cognizing it."

7. Lacan, *The Ethics of Psychoanalysis*, 62.

8. Lacan, *The Ethics of Psychoanalysis*, 97.

9. Lacan, *The Ethics of Psychoanalysis*, 141.

10. Jacques Lacan, *Transference*, ed. Jacques-Alain Miller, trans. Bruce Fink, vol. 8 of The Seminar of Jacques Lacan (Cambridge: Polity, 2015), 309.

11. Jacques Lacan, *Anxiety*, ed. Jacques-Alain Miller, trans. A. R. Price, vol. 10 of The Seminar of Jacques Lacan (Cambridge: Polity, 2014), 311. Lacan's assertion that anxiety is not without an object is, of course, a refusal of the definition provided by both Freud and Heidegger that anxiety is fear without an object. That it is a limited refusal is attested by the fact that the object of the unknown Thing, as essentially a non-Thing, a Nothing, is equally a non-object.

12. Lacan, *Anxiety*, 325.
13. Lacan, *Anxiety*, 53–54.
14. Lacan, *The Ethics of Psychoanalysis*, 55.
15. Lacan, *The Ethics of Psychoanalysis*, 83.
16. I analyze the function of *das Ding* in speech and language in much greater detail as background to a novel interpretation of Lacan's conception of the religious in *Embracing the Void: Rethinking the Origin of the Sacred* (Evanston, IL: Northwestern University Press, 2022).
17. Lacan, *Écrits*, 414.
18. Jacques Lacan, "Seminar XVI: From an Other to the other," translated for private use from the unpublished French transcript of the seminar by Cormac Gallagher, session of April 30, 1969.
19. Jacques Lacan, *Freud's Papers on Technique, 1953–54*, ed. Jacques Alain-Miller, trans. John Forrester, vol. 1 of The Seminar of Jacques Lacan (New York: W. W. Norton, 1988), 16. The quotation continues: "At the heart of the subject, [the ego] is only a privileged symptom, the human symptom par excellence, the mental illness of man."
20. See especially René Girard, *Violence and the Sacred*, trans. Patrick Gregory (Baltimore, MD: Johns Hopkins University Press, 1977).
21. As Jacques-Alain Miller has put it, precisely in a discussion of Lacan's notion of extimacy, "the most intimate is not a point of transparency but rather a point of opacity." See the transcription of Miller's seminar at Lacan.com, https://www.lacan.com/symptom/extimity.html.
22. Lacan, *The Ethics of Psychoanalysis*, 149.
23. Lacan, *The Ethics of Psychoanalysis*, 154.
24. Both quotes are from Martin Heidegger, "The Thing," in *Poetry, Language, Thought*, trans. Albert Hofstadter (New York: Harper Colophon, 1971), 181. While Lacan is clearly attracted to Heidegger's discussions about the Thing, Lacan's own formulation is significantly different. That difference is quite likely a big part of the reason why Lacan takes some distance from talk about *das Ding* after its conspicuously trumpeted introduction in the *Ethics* seminar.

What, If Anything, Is Authority?

Mladen Dolar

"What is authority?" is a trickier question than it may seem. It differs from the questions of what power, domination, sovereignty, ideology, and so on are, though it's hard to establish the difference. Perhaps authority precedes these other notions—at least "by its concept," not temporally—and may well offer a possible clue to them, and perhaps this is where the sting of these other entities encounters the dimension of extimacy—such is our initial proposition, to be tried out. All power implies compliance, wherein an external agency reaches into the intimate and makes us submit, and perhaps "authority" is the best term to designate this extimate kernel that power ultimately relies on in the vast variety of its forms.

We can take as a provisional starting point Hannah Arendt's famous essay "What Is Authority?" (first published in 1954, then included in *Between Past and Future*, 1961), and from there we can briefly pursue two cues. First, in the essay's very first sentence Arendt translates the question "what is authority?" into "what was authority?" It's as if it is no longer possible to speak of authority in the present. The moment we speak about authority we quasi-naturally adopt a particular perspective—namely, that of the crisis of authority, its decline, its vanishing. "In order to avoid misunderstanding, it might have been wiser to ask in the title: What was and not what is authority? For it is my contention that we are tempted and entitled to raise this question because authority has vanished from the modern world. Since we can no longer fall back upon authentic and undisputable experiences common to all, the very term has become clouded by controversy and confusion."[1]

There is something in this quote that goes beyond Arendt and her reflections in this paper, something that perhaps pertains to the very notion of authority as such: speaking of authority is coterminous with the crisis of authority, endemically so, so that the question of authority is almost always raised from the vantage point of its decline. One may well ask whether this was ever different at any point in history. Maybe this is what defines the human condition from the outset: the assumption that there once was a time when there were proper authorities, firm foundations of the social, "authentic and undisputable experiences common to all," but they have met their demise, there is a loss, we witness a downfall. Speaking about authority introduces a strange temporality, a retroactive construction of authority such as it once properly existed, in a structural antecedence in relation to our too-lateness, and given this temporality it's hard not to lament. The prevailing mode of speaking about authority is lamentation.

Has it ever been otherwise? Isn't the rhetorical figure that Arendt begins with a necessary prolegomena to almost all talk about authority? As far back as the memory reaches we can detect this basic attitude: once there were times when we could rely on authority, but now we live in the downfall. Already Plato's *Republic*, for example, presupposes such a decline and intends to remedy it; he is even more adamant in the *Laws*, for example, when dealing with the contemporary disrespect for traditional musical forms: "So the next stage of the journey toward liberty will be refusal to submit to the magistrates, and on this will follow emancipation from the authority and correction of parents and elders; then, as the goal of the race is approached, comes the effort to escape obedience to the law, and, when that goal is all but reached, contempt for oaths, for the plighted word, and all religion. The spectacle of the Titanic nature of which our old legends speak is re-enacted; man returns to the old condition of a hell of unending misery."[2]

One starts fiddling with authorities, be it of musical tradition, and a catastrophe ensues—a catastrophe of literally Titanic proportions, appositely so, for the story of the Titans is the story of revolt against authority and its spectacular punishment. We always already begin with the tales of the downfall of originary authorities—in short, we begin with the supposition that the beginning is already lost, there once was a proper beginning, but now we can only begin after the downfall, we live in a time of corruption. There was a proper past, but the present is diminished, degraded, debased. In the beginning there was the decay of the beginning, since ever.

There is, however, an ambiguity in this story: it can be conceived either as a nostalgia for what went lost or in a sense of liberation, an emancipation—either a call for the recovery, the restoration of authority or a sense of deliverance, since authority as such, "in itself," implies hierarchy and obedience, so good riddance to it. The lamentation about the downfall of authority is countered by a heroic saga about doing away with it. What defines modernity is then not so much the sense that authority is gone from the contemporary world—this has arguably always framed the talk about authority—but rather the new sense that this may allow us to breathe freely and gain our autonomy. There can be no neutral talk about authority—but is there only the alternative between the conservative and the emancipatory talk of authority, one struggling to retain it, the other to overcome it? Is this an exhaustive alternative? There is an easy way out, a compromise that is often proposed at this point: we should retain the sound, beneficial authority and be rid of the toxic authoritarian one, preserve its good side and abolish the bad one, unravel good authority from its abuse in authoritarianism.[3] But can there be a good measure of authority? An innocent and innocuous authority, a healthy and salubrious authority, without its sting? The argument quickly heads in the direction of "coffee without caffeine, beer without alcohol, fat-free bacon" (should one add "pleasure without *jouissance*"?), and so on that Slavoj Žižek loves to evoke—the entities whose sting inconveniently sticks to their core.

The sense of loss and crisis of authority may appear to be universal, since the time of the foundations of the social, but Arendt's quote aims at its poignant edge that pertains to modernity. It is as if the break of modernity presented a reenactment of the originary downfall of authority, the loss that authority was always already prey to and based on, but this time with a twist: this break in the history of (the always fallen) authority perhaps inaugurated the very notion of modernity as opposed to the premodern epochs. The crisis that haunted authority since its inception has found its moment with the advent of modernity, as if, in Hegelian terms, its "in itself" has now become "for itself." Modernity would thus be a "reflexive turn" in which authority became what it has always already been—namely, fallen authority. Authority is thus retroactively established in its proper dimension while at the same time it is retroactively seen as doomed to fail, subject to corruption and decay.[4] On the one hand, it seems in retrospect that in preceding times authority was generally respected and could constitute "authentic and undisputable experiences common to all," which has the makings of a retrospective fantasy; and on the other hand, authority appears as something that was never quite legitimate, always prey to structural usurpation and abuse that modernity wants to bring to an end. In other words, it deserved to go under since it was never quite the authority it purported to be. Ambiguity also pertains to this retroactive establishment of authority as both sound and questionable, firm and porous in one go.

Modernity would thus deliver a lethal blow to authority, or at least to what in authority has no proper foundation or justification, yet it seems that authority thereby landed in a limbo where it leads an afterlife and continues to haunt the age that has allegedly done away with it. If modernity could be roughly defined by the disappearance of transcendence, which was ultimately the key source of authority, and its reduction to immanence, then there immediately arises the question of what Eric Santner has brilliantly called "the surplus of immanence."[5] Everything should be reduced to immanence, but then it turns out that immanence doesn't coincide with itself and keeps producing its own excesses. Arendt posited her case on the triplet religion-tradition-authority—but perhaps once religion and tradition have lost their sway in modernity, authority has all the more come to the fore, but authority, disconnected from the other two, resurged as a groundless authority, a perverse authority, subterranean authority, counterfeit authority. Not the authority that could provide guarantee, but hence all the more a problem. There is a form of authority that persists after its demise, living its afterlife. "The afterlife of authority" could be an alternative title for this paper, or "the haunting of authority." Maybe authority was always already doomed to afterlife, but with modernity it leads a reflected afterlife, the (new?) afterlife of the (old?) afterlife. For Arendt, the present of authority has to be based in the past, in tradition, otherwise it can't get a hold and exert its efficacy, but with the modern loss of tradition the hold is gone; authority entered a new mode of temporality and its efficacy appeared as even more intractable. One can argue that it is only with the modern turn that authority entered the domain of extimacy "proper" (a contradiction in terms, since extimacy has no assignable delimited domain and has no "proper"; this is why it is linked with haunting), in the sense that its extimate nature was in premodern times covered (and veiled) by tradition and religion, which seemed to endow it with a firm framework and support. It is only with the turn of modernity, when this frame was shattered and taken away, that extimacy could come to the fore and be conceptualized at all. In this sense, one can speak about a history of extimacy: on the one hand, it extends back to times immemorial and essentially pertains to the very experience of being human, but on the other hand, this dimension could only be disentangled and addressed with the advent of modernity which removed its framing, coverage, and footing in tradition and religion (to use Arendt's terms).[6] It became "properly" unplaceable.

Arendt's move from "is" to "was" is contagious. One is tempted to extend Arendt's turn to some new forms of knowledge established by modernity and propose some further questions on her model, like: "What was Marxism?" "What was psychoanalysis?" "What was critical thought?"

Second cue: Arendt defines authority by a twofold opposition: "authority precludes the use of external means of coercion: where force is used, authority itself has failed! Authority, on the other hand, is incompatible with persuasion, which presupposes equality and works through a process of argumentation. Where arguments are used, authority is left in abeyance. Against the egalitarian order of persuasion stands the authoritarian order, which is always hierarchical. If authority is to be defined at all, then, it must be in contradistinction to both coercion by force and persuasion through arguments."[7] Authority is placed at the intersection between two seemingly exclusive realms: that of violence, force, coercion, constraint, power, superior strength, on the one hand, and on the other hand that of argument, reason, persuasion, proof. In sum: force vs. speech? Violence vs. argument? The "real" vs. the symbolic? The two parts may appear clear-cut, conceptually neatly opposed, obeying different logics, but they are never simply separate. This is not quite the stark division it purports to be, for both poles are internally split and intertwined.

The first one implies the use of force and violence, but there is never such a thing as pure violence: violence is always discursively framed, prepared by persuasion, justified by discourse, legitimized by all kinds of arguments—there is no violence without the word that supports it. The long history of wars, ethnic cleansings, pogroms, and massacres massively testifies to the fact that all this was thoroughly prepared and constantly underpinned by argument and persuasion. There is no pure violence—and this is, briefly, why Walter Benjamin's notorious "Critique of Violence" (1921) famously finishes by evoking "divine violence" that would dispense precisely with the discursive foundation, the framework of the law, and so on, and would thus evade the pernicious alternative between "lawmaking" and "law-preserving" violence.[8] "Pure violence" would step out of the discursive cage and cease to be a means to an end, thus escaping the fateful entanglement of law and violence. But maybe this massively commented passage rather points to a fantasy of such unraveling, of a purity beyond entanglement? I must leave the question in suspense.

On the other side, the side of the word, there is conspicuously, at the simplest, the threat of violence, a paradoxical entity that manages to induce the effects of violence by purely discursive means. It functions without using actual violence, by being merely symbolic, like a gesture that is not executed, but suspended—and this is what makes it a gesture.[9] Its potentiality already functions as actuality and produces real effects; it works by remaining implicit, never fully explicated and actualized. Ultimately, most violence that power relies on is actually a threat of violence that one may use "in the last instance," but which is constantly deferred.[10] The greatest part of violence one is subjected to is the potential violence that could arise as the last recourse once the mechanisms of persuasion and the usual ideological tricks break down. Once the existing power is forced to use actual force instead of implicit threat, when it sends police or the army into the streets, it's clear that power is losing power, its authority is dwindling. It is already in jeopardy once it has to make good the merely symbolic threat of the last instance. Threat is violence postponed, and the lag of postponement is the site of symbolic power, it functions in the abeyance of deferral where the actual violence can be indefinitely delayed,[11] as long as it produces effects—that is, the belief that there is some last instance of "real violence," the specter that may materialize. The threat, a stand-in for violence, is the maintaining of a specter (and this is, by the way, a process that already starts in nature, in the animal kingdom which abounds in gestures and threats, in deterrents and make-believes).[12]

Arendt's second part of the alternative involves rational argument, logic, logos, proof, and so on—and she puts these under the general heading of "persuasion," a term that already gives some leeway where discourse can function as seduction or a rhetorical ploy, and by extension deception, demagogic stratagems, and manipulation, and by further extension implicit or explicit commands. Persuasion is not necessarily democratic and egalitarian, and most often it's not. Arendt quotes Mommsen about authority: it is "more than advice and less than a command, an advice which one may not safely ignore."[13] But this is precisely the problem: the omnipresence and the nature of implicit commands. These instances are not some rare deviations from rational argument; they are rather what qualifies the very life of discourse, the numerous ways that discourse can elicit constraint and compliance by merely symbolic means. Rhetoric, after all, has served, since Aristotle at least, the efficiency of persuasion rather than the truth value of discourse (and this was after all what was at stake in the momentous campaign that Socrates, Plato, and Aristotle waged against the sophists). The egalitarian use of argument, equal for all, is countered and embroiled with the ways that discourse, subtly or patently, produces inequalities and hierarchies, distributing the entitlements and the positions of speech. It won't do to invoke the philosophical power of reasonable argument, which was perhaps permeated with implicit commands since its inception. This is why Lacan is adamant to point out that ontology arises within the discourse of the master and is prey to the inherent commanding nature of the signifier. The talk about being is never just an account of being; it is rather, "being at someone's heel [*l'être à la botte*], being at someone's beck and call [*l'être aux ordres*]—what would have been if you understood what I ordered you. Every dimension of being is produced in the wake of the master's discourse, the discourse of he who, proffering the signifier, expects therefrom one of its link effects that must not be neglected which is related to the fact that the signifier commands. The signifier is, first and foremost, imperative."[14] In this account, one never deals with description and objective neutrality (the impartial weighing of arguments); one must at all times keep in mind the hidden sting of threat and command inscribed into the very framework of the discourse—and especially when it purports to speak about pure being as being.

So the two poles of force/power and discourse/argument/persuasion are both far more ambiguous than it may seem, already in themselves and moreover by their connivance. All violence is discursively justified, prepared by persuasion and argument, while on the other side there is something that can be qualified as symbolic violence, with the symbolic itself already functioning as an incipient violence. (In everyday experience, one can easily see that verbal harassment, humiliation, insults, and so on can hurt far more than the physical blows.) And one can easily realize how hierarchy, inequality, submission, and so on can be established by discursive means alone, and envisage such a discourse as ultimately a device for distributing the positions of power.

The duality may be questionable and ambiguous, but it nevertheless provides good tools, if rough ones, to highlight the problem of authority and its enigma: the threshold between violence and reason, coercion and argument. Can one conceive a notion of authority that is irreducible to both force and argument? This is where the question of the downfall of authority in the modern world encounters the question of the authority of reason, which was the project of the Enlightenment. Can reason be sustained merely by itself? What vouches for its authority? Can authority be purely discursive and immanent, based on argument alone? Can reason be justified merely by itself? And why was modernity, after the alleged victory of the Enlightenment, constantly haunted by the afterlife of authority? It's as if authority presents a symbolic kernel or surplus in relation to violence, and a violent kernel or excess in the bosom of the symbolic—and this is precisely where the question of authority reaches into the realm of extimacy.

Lacan was fond of the topological device of the intersection of two circles, circumscribing an impossible realm of the overlap, one irreducible to both areas epitomized by the circles, but standing at their core. Maybe this is the simplest way to graphically illustrate authority, standing at the intersection between violence and reason, an intersection that ultimately underpins both sides. One would need a point of authority as a lever to deploy both coercion and reason, pointing at the discursive grounding in the use of force, and the part of non-reasonable violent grounding in the use of reason. Extimacy, at the simplest, is a dimension that blurs the lines between inside and outside, between the psychic and the external, and thus presents a topological paradox. Authority, in this sense, can be seen as the epitome of the extimate, its paradigmatic case: the external violent thorn that pierces into interiority and thus ultimately constitutes interiority in the first place, but as a place that cannot close upon itself; a violent thorn irreducible to physical violence and covertly inhabiting the interior space of reason that cannot sustain itself without this alien kernel, however much it tries to reduce it.

We can make two digressions. First, Althusser's seminal text "Ideology and Ideological State Apparatuses" (1970) famously proposes a division into the repressive and ideological state apparatuses which roughly coincides with our divide.[15] The former apparatus functions by force and coercion, the latter by persuasion—so either force or ideology. For Althusser, the ideological state apparatuses don't pertain to rational argument, anything but; they are prey to ideology, that is, a domain that is thoroughly and inherently prey to (structural) deception. If we roughly translate this into Lacanian terms, then the repressive apparatuses could be seen as real (violence) and the ideological ones as imaginary (this is how Althusser conceived ideology in terms of interpellation and recognition). The problem of authority would then emerge at the intersection of the two, and this is the place where one could place the symbolic (i.e., the dimension that is largely lacking in Althusser's universe), hidden at the overlap. Beyond Althusser, one could say that symbolic violence is precisely what is needed to conceive the two seemingly opposed entities, invisible in the division repression/ideology. Yet, if the problem of authority appears at the intersection, in the dimension of the symbolic wedged between repression and ideology, the question persists whether authority can be reduced to the symbolic and its logic, or whether the symbolic is in excess over itself. Or let's say there is the real of authority which presents a surplus over the symbolic. The enigma of authority stems from its lack of ground or foundation, an excess irreducible not only to violence and persuasion, but also to the logic of the signifier as such. Descriptions of authority often use terms like "aura" or "charisma,"[16] entities that defy definition. Pascal, at the dawn of modernity, spoke about the mystical core of authority.[17] Aura, charisma, mystique—something that has no signifier but is presupposed, assumed, and implied by the symbolic as such and lies at the core of its efficacy. And looking at the dawn of modernity, when the problem of authority properly emerged, divorced from its footing in the transcendent, then one can further think of Leibniz's principle of sufficient reason—can there be a sufficient ground for authority, in Leibnizian parlance? A sufficient reason-cause? (Causes are ontological-empirical-physical, while reasons are discursive, to make it quick.) Aren't we facing something here that has no sufficient ground yet is efficient, effective, and functions as the very source of domination-power-obedience? Maybe the problem of authority properly arose in a counterpoint to the Leibnizian principle of sufficient reason, the adage inaugurating the modern age—the moment one asks the question of the sufficient reason, there is the sudden realization that no reason is quite sufficient, and we are faced with a contingency that mysteriously produces power-effects. The impossibility to properly ground authority is but the flip side of its extimate nature.

Let us retain the terms "surplus," "excess," and "exception." Authority presents an instance of exception in relation to the division into the two realms of violence and discourse, repression and ideology, yet at their core, although not pertaining to either of them, yet welding them together. Exception also in relation to the symbolic itself, where the question of authority is closely linked to the signifier in the position of exception, which Lacan designated as the master-signifier, based on the underlying necessity that the signifying structure produces an exception—but is this formal exception enough to account for authority? With the term "surplus," one should be reminded of the Lacanian notion of surplus *jouissance* (calqued on Marx's phrase "surplus value"), which is perhaps *jouissance* as such—every *jouissance* is in surplus, *jouissance* is what comes as a surplus, and it structurally sticks to the signifying exception, as a surplus attached to and over the signifier.

Second digression, Freud. Arendt mentions right at the beginning of her essay that she will be dealing largely with political authority, but a telling symptom of the crisis of authority can be found in the fact that it has spread into child-rearing and education—that is, to a pre-political realm where authority has always been accepted as a "natural" necessity.[18] There can be no education without authority, Arendt suggests, since the parents, and particularly the father, have served as the "natural" model of all authority since time immemorial, but with modernity this is in jeopardy. If we leave aside the problematic assumptions of this argument, then we could say that we have on the one hand governance and on the other hand education as salient areas of the crisis of authority. Which directly leads us to Freud's famous dictum: "It almost looks as if (psycho)analysis were the third of those 'impossible' professions in which one can be sure beforehand of achieving unsatisfying results. The other two, which have been known much longer, are education and government."[19] The three professions are impossible for Freud because they involve transference, and transference (one of the Lacanian four fundamental concepts of psychoanalysis) is, to be brief, the psychoanalytic name for dealing with authority—an authority without guarantee, an authority not vouched for, an authority one has to adopt without a proper coverage. Analysis can be seen as a long process of dealing with transference; it centrally concerns a process of working-through of transference, taking it as a key issue in a so to speak laboratory situation, so that analysis ultimately coincides with the analysis of transference—in order to find a way of its undoing. Transference is what enables analysis at the outset, but the aim of analysis, its end, is to unravel it. The end of analysis is the "fall" of the "subject supposed to know" that has been its lever—but can one thereby be done with the problem of authority?

There is something highly significant in Freud's move, simple as it seems. To the two areas that Arendt posits at the beginning, governance and education, Freud adds a third, which can be seen precisely as co-terminous with the crisis of authority in the other two. Psychoanalysis emerged precisely as the symptom of this crisis of authority, of the symbolic power epitomized by what Lacan called "the Name of the Father." Its birth coincided with the decline of paternal authority, the decline of kings and fathers and their symbolic underpinning, the decline of tradition and religion, the loss of grip of prohibitions and commands. It is in this new constellation that psychoanalysis conceived this laboratory clinical situation where it essentially treats authority in its new avatars. Hence, psychoanalysis was never reducible to a new kind of therapy— what defined it from the outset was its universal ambition and address, stemming from and embedded in the experience of the analytic practice but at all times extending into a new theory of the social, an intervention into this new constellation. Lacan's theory of the four discourses (proposed in 1969, in the wake of the massive student revolts) can in this light be seen as the culmination and the formalization of this endeavor, the most developed and the most complex theory of the social tie advanced by psychoanalysis, proposing four versions of the modern functioning of authority.[20] The four discourses are at bottom conceived on the model of the three impossible professions: the discourse of the master corresponds to governance, with its obverse side in the discourse of the hysteric (and the prominent new surge of hysteria at the end of the nineteenth century was the symptom of the crisis of the master, providing the initial entry point of psychoanalysis). The university discourse corresponds to education, now largely molded by the modern institution of the university. And finally the discourse of the analyst, corresponding to the establishment of psychoanalytic experience, was designed as a "line of flight" that offers a different take on authority and proposes the possibility of a new social tie.[21] In the time that elapsed from Freud's passing remark on the three impossible professions to Lacan's grand design constructed on their basis, one can appreciate the ambition of psychoanalysis as a discourse on authority. In the tribulations of the attempts to establish psychoanalytic discourse, in the vagaries of its institutions and sectarian striving, one can appreciate the odds, the traps, and the failures. In the fifty years after the inception of this theory, in the face of the further catastrophic tribulation of authority we have witnessed in the last half century, we can appreciate the enormous odds we are confronting today.

We have seen that authority pertains to exception, a surplus, an excess, a figure standing apart, endowed with a mysterious aura. Lacan proposed to formalize this with what in his algebra is designated by S1, the master-signifier irreducible to the series of signifiers designated by S2. But this already presupposes the establishment of the symbolic order and hence the authority which upholds it—an implicit foundational authority which is supposed to vouch for the symbolic, for the discourse as a social tie, and first of all, at the simplest, the authority sustaining language itself, the process of signification, the guarantee of meaning—in one word, the status of what Lacan called the big Other. This is the authority we have to assume if we are to enter the symbolic at all, to use language, and which we have to maintain by our belief. The authority one has to presuppose as already there is paired with the authority that one eventually has to assume oneself in order to be able to speak at all—what gives me the authority of the speaker? What is my entitlement? This is what opens up the basic problem of psychoanalysis: one cannot speak without the authority of the Other, one cannot establish social ties without the Other, the Other guaranteeing the basic "social contract," the symbolic pact underlying our social relations. One presupposes the guarantee of the symbolic Other, warranting that words, signifiers, mean what they mean, that there are rules and codes, both in language and symbolic rules governing society, and one complies with them on the supposed authority that sustains them. The shorthand for this is the notion of the (big) Other.

There is a paradox at the core of psychoanalysis which is closely linked to our problem of authority. There is a Lacanian antinomy as to the nature of the Other (as the source of the supposed authority), a spectacular antinomy of two massively opposing propositions: first, "*there is the Other*," which is the essential dimension that psychoanalysis has to deal with. To put it simply, there is the Other of the symbolic order, the other of structure, the Other that one has to rely on in order to enter into language and adopt social ties. Even more, there is the Other that is essential for the advent of desire, on which desire leans as it were by identification so that we can become desiring subjects—hence the Lacanian formula "desire is the desire of the Other," which takes its support in the Hegelian master-slave dialectic, pinpointing the fundamental impasse of desire. There is the Other at the heart of all entities that psychoanalysis has to deal with, and this may be seen as a shorthand to pinpoint their common denominator, to assemble them under one heading, the heading of the Other. What they have in common is the fact that there is the

Other at their core, the Other of a qualitatively different nature in relation to the realm of One.

Yet this is but the first part of the antinomy, the part positing the Other at the core, the irremovable otherness, the alterity, which turns any intimacy extimate, in Lacan's excellent neologism. The second part of this antinomy, in stark contradiction to the first, states bluntly: "*the Other lacks*," or there is the lack in the Other, ultimately the Other doesn't exist. One can find it, for example, in this minimal and straight form in one of Lacan's last public statements: "L'Autre manque. Ça me fait drôle à moi aussi. Je tiens le coup pourtant, ce qui vous épate, mais je ne le fais pas pour cela." (The Other lacks. I don't feel happy about it myself. Yet, I endure, which fascinates you, but I am not doing it for that reason.)[22]

Now, how can the very dimension not exist on which psychoanalysis ultimately depends, on which it is premised, and which is the key to all psychoanalytic concepts? What is the status of this Other which is emphatically there, and which at the same time emphatically lacks? Can the two statements be reconciled in their glaring contradiction? If this is an alternative, is it an exhaustive one, does it cover all options? The trouble is precisely that the Other may not exist, but this doesn't mean that there simply is no Other—its nonexistence leaves traces and entails consequences that cannot be done away with. Perhaps the problem of authority should be ultimately posed precisely in the tension between the first and the second proposition, between the existence and the nonexistence of the Other. Maybe authority as such was always premised on the nonexistence of the Other and was drawing its resources from a void, as a defense against the lack in the Other; it was placed at the point of the lack of the Other, which it covered over by the gesture of authority whose alleged aura stems from the void behind it. The break in the perception of authority, brought about by modernity, implied that in premodern times it was firmly grounded in the Other, while modernity implies the downfall of the Other (the paternal law, tradition, religion, and so on). Hence the problem of authority is now presented in its pure form, without the backing of the Other. It is because of the demise of the Other that the problem of authority becomes endemic, and as already indicated above, it is through this demise that it manifests its inherent link with the dimension of the extimate that modernity properly brought about.

The birth of psychoanalysis, as I said, coincided with the modern crisis of authority and had to deal with its afterlife. Let me finish with an anecdote. This historic moment is emblematically condensed in the anecdote of Freud's one most memorable visit to Slovenia. In early April 1898 Freud spent his Easter holidays on a trip to the Adriatic coast (now the Italian part) with his brother Alexander. They visited Aquileia, Gorizia,

WHAT, IF ANYTHING, IS AUTHORITY?

Grado, and, on the way back, some subterranean caves in Karst, in Slovenia, close to the township of Divača. Freud reports about the trip in a letter to Fliess dated April 14, 1898. Let us leave aside Freud's remarkable encounter with the Slovene guide, Gregor Žiberna, and focus on his visit to the spectacular Škocjan caves, a tourist attraction already then and much bigger nowadays (it has been on the list of UNESCO world heritage sites since 1986). "The caves of St. Cangian [Škocjan] which we saw in the afternoon, are a horrifying freak of nature—a subterranean river running through magnificent vaults, with waterfalls and stalactites and pitch darkness, and a slippery path guarded by iron railings. It was Tartarus itself. If Dante saw anything like this, he needed no great effort of the imagination for his Inferno."[23] The tourist trip suddenly turns into something like a metaphysical journey, a descent into the abyss, a visit to Tartarus, the Acheron, the Dantean Inferno. The time of this visit is very important; this is the period of gestation for Freud, a year and a half before the publication of *The Interpretation of Dreams* (published in November 1899). The motto for this inaugural book of psychoanalysis was taken from Virgil: "Flectere si nequeo superos, Acheronta movebo" (*Aeneid* 7.312; "If I cannot bend the Higher powers, I will move the Infernal Regions"). There is a literal descent into Inferno, in Slovenia, prefiguring the motto of *Die Traumdeutung*—there is an appealing idea that Freud got the inspiration for this motto on this occasion.[24]

So what did Freud find in this Slovenian Inferno? The account to Fliess continues like this: "The ruler of Vienna, Herr Dr. Carl Lueger, was with us in the cave, which after three-and-a-half hours spewed us all out into the light again."[25] This inconspicuous line contains a big drama. At the bottom of the abyss, Freud met the *Herr von Wien*, as he says, namely the mayor of Vienna, one of the best known and most influential political figures of that time in that part of the world. Their common descent into the Slovene hell was their only meeting; they would never come face to face in Vienna. They had to come to this *anderer Schauplatz*, this Slovene other scene, they had to take a vacation from the center of the *Zeitgeist* to meet in the outskirts of the empire, in the Slovene underground.

Dr. Karl Lueger (1844–1910) was the head of the Christian Social Party and the mayor of Vienna from 1897 until his death; a very popular and populist leader, he was also notorious for his blaring antisemitism.[26] The best clue to his significance is to be found in Hitler's *Mein Kampf*— Hitler spent his youthful years roaming the streets of Vienna (1907–13), the same Vienna that produced all those great spiritual and artistic figures—the notorious cunning of reason must have been playing some tricks there. We find out in *Mein Kampf* that Hitler had one great model at the time, his ego-ideal: he found a great source of inspiration in Lueger, that "greatest German burgomaster of all times," "the real genius of a burgomaster," "the great and genial reformer," and particularly the great promoter of antisemitism. Lueger was the one who, for Hitler, opened his eyes as to the true nature of Jewry. Hitler particularly praised Lueger's ability to stir the feelings of the masses, to have a direct influence on the masses beyond the untrustworthy and treacherous parliamentary politicians. It was from Lueger that Hitler learned everything he needed to know about antisemitic propaganda.

Quite apart from this very drastic sequel in fascism, Lueger's antisemitism was already so notorious by then that the first time he was elected mayor in 1895, the Emperor Franz Joseph himself refused to confirm his election—and Freud says somewhere that he celebrated this occasion with an extra cigar. The emperor actually refused to confirm Lueger three more times, but he had to eventually give in to the "democratic will of the people" (and after the intercession of Pope Leo XIII). Why did the emperor so adamantly refuse to confirm Lueger's election? No doubt he was led by conservative reasons; he wanted Vienna to be ruled by a decent aristocrat, not an upstart, a troublemaker and hate-monger who catered to divisions and zealots. The emperor instinctively opposed the kind of politics that abandoned all decency, manners, decorum—everything that Hegel (among other things) brought together under the heading of *Sittlichkeit*, or "ethical life based in customs and tradition." Lueger's politics was of a type that contravened many unwritten laws and built its success on these contraventions—and the emperor instinctively understood that the unwritten laws form the fabric of society. Every populism starts by breaking unwritten rules. There is something highly emblematic in this constellation: Franz Joseph was arguably the last emperor, the last figure of a ruler as the father, the father of the nation, and being the father epitomized his *habitus*. He ruled for sixty-seven years (surpassed in length only by Louis XIV and Elizabeth II), and Freud spent three-quarters of his life under this rule. In this dispute about investiture, so to speak, the last model of the old authority confronted virtually the first model of the new type of authority, quite literally the figure who would serve as a direct model for the catastrophic rise of the new authority. The emperor, the embodiment of the old authority and its stability, did what he could to stop this ascent—a moment that one can see as the swan's song of old authority. Furthermore, it is significant that Lueger was already qualified as a populist by that time. It seems that the term "populism" first entered the general vocabulary with the rise of the People's Party in the United States at the end of the nineteenth century, in many ways with positive connotations, but the dark underside was very quick to follow. It's as if the advent of populism as a political concept and a political logic reaches directly from those times into ours, and frames the fate of psychoanalysis.

Freud's encounter with Lueger in the Slovene underground has the value of a parable. The new antisemitic master and the Jew, coming eye-to-eye in the Inferno, presents an iconic image inaugurating the century, with so many forebodings of what the century will bring. Freud met this *Herr*, who would, by a devious and mediate way, influence a good deal of subsequent European history. In a dramatic echo of this encounter, Freud will have to flee Vienna and finish his days in exile once Lueger's pupil has recaptured Vienna, almost exactly forty years after Freud met his master in the cave. And this can serve as an inaugural image of psychoanalysis and its political mission—confronting the authority after the downfall of old authorities, in the historical moment of the rise of new authorities—a mission which directly translates into our present turmoil.

Notes

1. Hannah Arendt, *Between Past and Future: Six Exercises in Political Thought* (New York: Viking, 1961), 91.

2. Plato, *Laws* III, 701b–c, trans. Trevor J. Saunders, in Plato, *Complete Works*, ed. John M. Cooper (Indianapolis, IN: Hackett, 1997), 1390.

3. If this move seems innocuous, one should be reminded that none other than Jair Bolsonaro spelled it out plainly in his presidential campaign as his goal: "authority without authoritarianism."

4. This is in parallel with a number of other heroic narratives: once there was *Gemeinschaft*, once there was metaphysics, once there was mimesis, once there was aura—perhaps all of these are mythical entities that modernity badly needed as springboards so that it could define itself; they are all endowed with a part of retroactive construction, they never existed in their full presence. But what they all have in common is that, notwithstanding, they wouldn't go away once we moderns have allegedly been rid of them—but this is a larger argument for another paper.

5. Eric Santner, *The Royal Remains* (Chicago: University of Chicago Press, 2011), 28, 61, 82, and 135.

6. I tried to argue for this line at greater length in an old paper, "'I Shall Be with You on Your Wedding-Night': Lacan and the Uncanny," *October* 58 (1991): 5–24.

7. Arendt, *Between Past and Future*, 93

8. "But all mythic, lawmaking violence, which we may call 'executive' [*schaltende*], is pernicious. Pernicious, too, is the law-preserving, 'administrative' [*verwaltete*] violence that serves it. Divine violence, which is the sign and seal but never the means of sacred dispatch, may be called 'sovereign' [*waltende*]

violence." Walter Benjamin, "Critique of Violence," trans. Edmund Jephcott, in *Selected Writings*, vol. 1, ed. Marcus Bullock and Michael W. Jennings (Cambridge, MA: Belknap Press of Harvard University Press, 1996), 252.

9. "What is a gesture? A threatening gesture, for example? It is not a blow that is interrupted. It is rather something that is done in order to be arrested and suspended. . . . It is this very special temporality, which I have defined by the term arrest, and which creates its signification behind itself, that makes the distinction between the gesture and an act." Jacques Lacan, *The Four Fundamental Concepts of Psychoanalysis*, ed. Jacques-Alain Miller, trans. Alan Sheridan, vol. 11 of The Seminar of Jacques Lacan (London: Penguin, 1986), 116. Gesture is not an act, but it acts nevertheless in the absence of the act.

10. Aristotle deals in passing in the *Nicomachean Ethics* (1114a) with the gesture of wielding a stone, brandishing it, but not throwing it, yet everybody runs for cover. The stone hits the target without ever leaving the hand.

11. The problem of structural delay intersects with Lévi-Strauss's central argument that delay stands at the core of the symbolic, and hence of the human—the prohibition of incest implies and demands a delay of immediate satisfaction, hence exogamy and the beginning of culture; and so does preparing food based on the delayed immediacy of the satisfaction of hunger, and so on. In elementary material needs such as hunger and sex, the symbolic coincides with the temporal deferral of immediacy. At bottom, there has to be a temporal economy that exchanges "now" for "later." See, from a very different perspective, Hans Blumenberg's 1980 essay on pensiveness, *Nachdenklichkeit*, in which he insists on the essential part played by hesitation and delay as the very condition of thought. Hans Blumenberg, *History, Metaphors, Fables*, ed. Hannes Bajohr, Florian Fuchs, and Joe Paul Kroll (Ithaca, NY: Cornell University Press, 2020).

12. See Lacan, *Four Fundamental Concepts*, 99–100.

13. Arendt, *Between Past and Future*, 123.

14. Jacques Lacan, *On Feminine Sexuality, the Limits of Love and Knowledge*, ed. Jacques-Alain Miller, trans. Bruce Fink, vol. 20 of The Seminar of Jacques Lacan (New York: Norton, 1999), 31–32.

15. Louis Althusser, *On the Reproduction of Capitalism: Ideology and Ideological State Apparatuses* (London: Verso, 2014).

16. See, conspicuously, Max Weber, *On Charisma and Institution Building*, ed. S. N. Eisenstadt (Chicago: University of Chicago Press, 1968).

17. Blaise Pascal, *Pensées*, ed. Philippe Sellier (Paris: Librairie Générale Française, 2000), 83.

18. "The most significant symptom of the crisis, indicating its depth and seriousness, is that it has spread to such pre-political areas as child-rearing and education, where authority in the widest sense has always been accepted *as a natural necessity*, obviously required as much by *natural needs*, the helplessness of the child, as by political necessity, the continuity of an established civilization which can be assured only if those who are newcomers by birth are guided through a pre-established world into which they are born as strangers." Arendt, *Between Past and Future*, 92, italics added to highlight the particularly problematic assumptions of naturalizing authority which served as the basis of patriarchy.

19. Sigmund Freud, "Analysis Terminable and Interminable" (1937), in *Moses and Monotheism, An Outline of Psycho-Analysis, and Other Works (1937–1939)*, trans. and ed. James Strachey, vol. 23 of *The Standard Edition of the Complete Psychological Works of Sigmund Freud* (London: Hogarth, 1964), 248. The idea was first used by Freud in the "Preface to Aichhorn's Wayward Youth" in 1925. Freud presents this as a common idea, but it's actually difficult to find any precedents.

20. See Aaron Schuster, "Impossible Professions, and How to Defend Them," in *Homestead of Dilution*, ed. Domenico Mangano, Marieke van Rooy, and Niekolaas Johannes Lekkerkerk (Eindhoven: Onomatopopee, 2017), 95.

21. The broader ambition of the present project on authority is to provide an assessment of the theory of the four discourses fifty years later. The current paper is one of the steps in this direction.

22. Jacques Lacan, "Dissolution," *Ornicar?* 20–21 (1980): 12. One can mark in passing that there is something like a draft of an ethics of psychoanalysis there: to endure in the face of the lack of the Other.

23. Sigmund Freud, *The Origins of Psychoanalysis: Letters to Wilhelm Fliess; Drafts and Notes, 1887–1902* (New York: Basic Books, 1977), 253; translation of Sigmund Freud, *Briefe 1873–1939* (Frankfurt am Main: Fischer, 1977), 249.

24. One should be reminded that the originally intended motto was to be taken from *Milton's Paradise Lost*: Let us consult "what reinforcement we may gain from hope, if not, what resolution from despair" (I, 189–91). This is appropriately put in the mouth of the devil.

25. Freud, *Origins of Psychoanalysis*, 253.

26. Probably the best historical account of Lueger and his significance is to be found in Carl E. Schorske, *Fin-de-Siècle Vienna: Politics and Culture* (New York: Vintage Books, 1980), 119–39.

Asexual Violence and Systemic Enjoyment

Alenka Zupančič

There is a proverb, attributed to Oscar Wilde, which is becoming more and more relevant: "Everything is about sex except sex. Sex is about power."[1] Perhaps this shouldn't be taken as an eternal wisdom but more as a very poignant description of the present historical—and *political*—moment. I propose to take this cue to discuss the question of extimacy from the angle of enjoyment and its social articulations. The phenomenon of enjoyment, as conceptualized by psychoanalysis, is of course one of the prime examples of the logic of extimacy: something most intimate that often strikes us as utterly foreign, other. Enjoyment in the strict sense of the term thus seems to originate not in the subject and not in the Other, but to emerge from their interaction and their "impossible" intersection. This positioning of enjoyment also provides the grounds for the central argument of this essay, which takes the concept of extimacy as opening an interesting and productive way for the conceptualization of the relationship between the subjective (psychic) and social (political) economy.

The claim that sex is about power can of course mean several different things. It can mean, and this is a more traditional understanding, that sex and sexuality are all about power games, for example women seducing men and making them do whatever they want or vice versa. We can change "men" and "women" to different sexual partners, but the point remains that sexuality, as also implied in desire, enjoyment, and love, gives you a certain power over the other person, and that this is actually what it is all about. In other words, in this understanding sex is used *for*, and *as*, power by means of using and turning *something in the other* (say their desire) against them. In this constellation, power (position of power) is not so much the starting point as it is a result, and even an "honestly earned" outcome. It is "honestly earned" in the sense that the game—which is basically the game of seduction—obeys certain rules, the fundamental one being that one can obtain this power only by inciting the other to hand it to us. One only uses against the other what one has succeeded in provoking in them. It is by responding to my seduction that the other hands me the weapon, the power.

In classical literature, one of the most prominent and interesting examples of the exploration of sexuality and desire as power-relation is Choderlos de Laclos's *Dangerous Liaisons*.[2] People's lives can be ruined by their desire, particularly women's lives, since the social setting of the times (the eighteenth century) doesn't allow for a woman's desire not to be fully covered by wedlock. But in the novel these two levels of power are distinguished: as a result of Valmont's manipulating seduction and subsequent abandonment, Tourvel dies not of social shame and exclusion but of the injury inflicted, via her love, to her being. We can say, of course, that this casting of women as beings who can "die from love" is itself deeply ideological, and it could be read this way, but this is not what is primarily at stake in the novel. What is at stake is, first, a more general proposition that lies at the origin of Valmont and the Marquise de Merteuil's pact, and also constitutes an important theme of eighteenth-century literature—namely, that even the most authentic feelings, such as love, can be "mechanically produced" by appropriate machinations.[3] Valmont decides to make Madame de Tourvel fall in love with him, so he forms a strategy and systematically carries it out step by step, leaving nothing to chance. And Madame de Tourvel does in fact fall in love with him. We'll return to this mechanical aspect later. Second, the crucial aspect of Valmont's seduction is the emphasis on Tourvel's surrendering willingly—not only willingly, but in full and sober awareness of the drastic consequences of her actions (he does not want her to give in to his seduction in a moment of passion and confusion).

Valmont thus makes his project doubly complicated, first because of Tourvel's state of mind when he meets her. She is not only known for her genuine (rather than moralizing) virtue but also for being genuinely happy in her marriage. And second because, as he keeps repeating, her surrender must be the result of reflection and sober decision and not based on her giving in to his seductive efforts in a moment of confused passion. He emphasizes this again and again, and this also constitutes the reason why he twice refuses to take advantage of opportunities to score a quick "victory" offered to him. Each time he gives the explanation that this would be too easy and not worthy of the true and capable hunter that he is. "Leave the humble poacher to kill the stag where he has surprised it in its hiding place; the true hunter will bring it to bay."[4] He also explains: "My plan is . . . to make her perfectly aware of the value and extent of each one of the sacrifices she makes me; not to proceed so fast with her that the remorse is unable to catch up; it is to show her virtue breathing its last breath in long-protracted agonies; to keep that somber spectacle ceaselessly before her eyes."[5] At stake here is clearly his own fantasy and the way in which the latter frames his enjoyment for him—it is a classic example of what Lacanian psychoanalysis puts under the clinical heading of perversion: forcing the other to subjectivize herself. Perversion, and particularly its sadistic version, is not about treating the other as object, but about treating her in such a way that would trigger, demand, "extract" a subjectivation; it is about forcing the other to become fully subject (to "decide," consciously accept, etc.).[6] A sadistic pervert wants the other to subjectivize (split) herself in response to the surplus object he makes appear for her, and to supplement her lack (division) by that same object. The pervert wants the Other to become a complete Other, a "complet(ed)" subject. Ultimately, he posits himself as the *instrument* of the impossible enjoyment of the Other.

In the case of Valmont, it is very clear that none of his seductive machinations with Tourvel are simply about sex—the whole thing is indeed about power (making her do what he wants, and proving his point). But, of course, power itself gets sexualized in this process of its "purification": the very proving of his point is for Valmont the ultimate source of enjoyment. (There is also a suggestion in the novel that at some point he has genuinely fallen in love with Tourvel, but this is another matter, and another layer of the story, which we will not pursue here.) But independently of this specific setting (of perversion), and looked at from Madame de Tourvel's perspective, it is clear that a certain subjectivation and exposure—via desire—can *always* be at stake in "sexual relations"; there is a possible dimension of power (and its abuse) that always surrounds the very event of our desire. The fact is that we risk being, and sometimes are, hanged by the ropes of *our own desire*. It seems that this dimension has been strongly repressed or erased in recent predominant debates concerning power and sexual violence, because any hint at a possible subjective participation by the victim in the configuration of abuse is perceived as an outrageous insult. This is because it appears to lend itself directly to claims such as: she was raped because she more or less secretly desired it. But this outraged dismissal of the question of desire misses the point, and it does little service to the victims.

Desire is in itself a complex, dialectical thing; it is not one-dimensional and it cannot be reduced to its supposed last instance. Nor are we as subjects simply reducible to our desire (or enjoyment) but are split by them. This is to say that if I don't want something, and I say so, this "no" cannot be dismissed by pointing to the desire that perhaps nevertheless exists. And this holds even more true in the case of enjoyment: I can be forced to enjoy what I don't want to enjoy. As Slavoj Žižek emphasized some time ago, this configuration doesn't constitute any kind of vector or revealer of truth (of what I *really* want); on the contrary, it makes the forcing even worse, it makes it *more* and not less inexcusable.[7] Also, women (and men as well) have rape fantasies, but this doesn't mean that deep down they secretly want to be raped, violated. This is not how fantasy works. Fantasy, in the strong psychoanalytic meaning of the word, is not some subjective scenario waiting and wanting to get realized. It participates in reality exactly *as fantasy*. In terms of psychoanalysis, fantasies are not the opposite of reality, but its support. What prevents fantasy from being fulfilled is not simply our fear ("lack of nerve" or other considerations), but above all the fact that fantasy fully fulfils its role *such as it is*, as fantasy. It is as fantasy that it provides the framework which guarantees (for us) the consistency of a certain segment of our reality. This is precisely why, as Žižek also insists, a "realization of fantasy" can be, and usually is, utterly devastating for the subject. Because in being "realized" as empirical content, it disappears, disintegrates as the frame that has so far held our reality together. (This is also why psychoanalytic work with fantasies does not consist in making subjects finally "realize" them, carry them out, but in gradually making them useless in their role of framing some reality for us and providing its consistency. We can henceforth relate to, or be part of, this reality in a different way.)

To take another example: if I fantasize about suddenly dying and my unfaithful lover being devastated by it, this doesn't mean that deep down I want to die or kill myself. What I want is to see (through the "window" of this fantasy, that is to say through the otherwise impossible *perspective* that this fantasy opens on my reality) the other suffer because of losing me, I want to see him realize via this loss how important I have actually been to him. It is a fantasy that helps me sustain the reality of my actual love life and not something that would constitute its future accomplishment (if fulfilled). The difference between the two is crucial, and not addressing it de facto leads to what this avoidance of addressing it wants to prevent: it makes those who fantasize indeed (feel) guilty/responsible for what happens to them in an utterly independent and brutal way. You can repeat to the victim as much as you want that it was not her fault, but if you don't provide her with the means of coping with and tackling the issues of desire and enjoyment, you've done her very little service.

In any case, this is slippery ground, and it seems to be all the more intolerable because it is slippery. And it is here that another aspect of the theme of "sexuality and power" enters, or another way of understanding the saying that "sex is all about power." It presents us not so much with the power of sexuality (power of desire, of seduction), as with the power that comes from being in the *position* to seduce, or in a position to more or less subtly blackmail the other into gratifying our sexual desires. The key word here is of course *position*—power is all about position (of power), and sex enters the game on a secondary level. This second configuration (conception) itself comprises two relatively different structures. As indicated, one emphasizes that there are certain (power-) positions which facilitate seduction and even automatically engender it, and the other exposes the abuse of power in forcing, blackmailing people to cooperate with our sexual desires. Both are real, but they are not exactly the same. The first brings us back to the other briefly mentioned theme of *Dangerous Liaisons*, the theme of the "mechanical" and inexorable causality by which even such a subjective sentiment as love can be produced.[8] There are situations, configurations, and "positions" that seem to engender something like love almost automatically. This phenomenon is also not foreign to psychoanalysis and its practical setting, with the transference (also called transference love) almost inevitably appearing during the treatment. To reciprocate this love is of course not what is expected from the analyst, and it would inevitably end the analysis and transform the nature of the relationship. But if, as Freud humorously describes this possible alternative path of transference, the analyst decides to stop the analysis and marry the patient, this is not necessarily the same as abuse. The other structure is much more perfidious; it is a matter of—often systemic and structural—blackmail. (For example: you risk your job, or miss a promotion, or have other kinds of trouble if you don't comply with the sexual desires of those in a position of power.) In this case, "sex is all about power" refers to something other than the power-games involved in seduction: you are in the *position of power*, and you use this position to solicit sexual favors, or simply exercise, impose your sexuality on persons who are in no position to say no (or who, if they say no, can face severe consequences). In this conceptual configuration, power exists outside of sexuality and is used to get sex.

In other words, in the first configuration it is sex (desire) that is used for power, it gives you power over the other person, whereas in the second configuration it is power that is used for sex. A large majority of the public discussions about sex and violence that we see today in the West belong to the second category. One could even say that the interrogation of the first (of the dialectics of desire and love) has all but completely ceded its place to the interrogation of power positions and power relations, and of sexuality as their *hostage*. I would like to suggest that there exists a very tricky side to this move in which one first entirely separates sex and power, and then reunites them in a new "sex-power" compound, defined by *abuse*. This rather overwhelmingly present link between sex and power, where sexual violence appears as a result of the abuse of power, has important consequences for both how we think about power and how we think about sex. And the particularly problematic side of this link concerns the way in which it affects our thinking about power, that is, how it efficiently narrows our critical scope when it comes to thinking about power.

The predominant talk about sexual violence as abuse of power (supported and exploited by the media) has this other side: it implicitly suggests that power is problematic *only* when it involves sexuality. Or more precisely: it suggests that it is problematic because someone *enjoys* it—with enjoyment constituting the link to sexuality. As Jean-Claude Milner succinctly describes the consequences of this kind of stance: the brutality of power is not contested per se, if nobody enjoys it. What is impermissible is for any individual to use their professional position to satisfy their own personal fantasies.[9] This is a very important observation. Of course, we can immediately cry out: Well, it should be impermissible!—Yes, but we should nevertheless not move too quickly when reading and discussing this, and rather try to see what exactly is being said.

Power, or its abuse, can be used to "get" many things, which we like to talk about, and *do* talk about a lot—particularly in the West—like sex or personal gain . . . But let us not forget, it can also be used to influence and decide major systemic, fundamental social issues such as, for example, the distribution of social wealth, general health care, military interventions, and the prosecution (and character assassination) of people who expose serious systemic malpractices and crimes. Moreover, sexual abuse cannot be separated from systemic inequalities and their "ordinary" reproduction, as feminists have always insisted. If the only thing that can be wrong about power is its unprofessional abuse, then we have no means to even begin to address these issues. The point would be the following: the systematic presentation of the link between power and sex (or personal gain/enjoyment in general) conveniently whitewashes situations where power is exercised in ways that affect our lives, all our lives, in most fundamental and often extremely brutal ways. The example of Julian Assange is paramount here: the (mere) allegations of sexual abuse (the prosecution of which was later dropped altogether) were, and still are, enough to block out in public eyes the enormous systemic and systematic crimes revealed by Assange and WikiLeaks.

Or consider this supposedly "natural" situation ("natural" particularly in the United States): a professor having sex with a student is a serious and utterly inadmissible abuse of power, whereas the fact that this same student had to pay hundreds of thousands of dollars to get a decent education is simply business as usual. This example is emphatically not meant to be about comparing the two, because they cannot be compared, nor about one evil being possibly excused on the grounds that the other is even bigger; it is about what we consider "evil" (or not at all) in the first place. The point is not that sexual abuse is not seriously evil, but that it *itself* often functions today in a much broader power game as a welcome decoy: it functions as the stain, the elimination of which whitewashes other ways in which power operates, making these look simply normal ("professional"). Here we are talking not so much about sexual abuse as about the abuse of sexuality. In other words, I'd like to suggest that the mainstream focus on sexuality and sexual scandals can *also* be an abusive stratagem, and not only a welcome indicator that sexuality and sexual abuse are finally being taken seriously (which is unambiguously a good thing). There are some extremely significant dimensions of power that we simply don't talk about, and don't have the means to talk about. But we are given the opportunity to talk about sex as much as we want.

Again, to make this absolutely clear: the point is not that we talk too much about sexual abuse and neglect other forms of violence; no, the point is that we talk about it mostly in a wrong way—that is, in a way that allows for the concealment of systemic causes of violence in general, *including the systemic causes of sexual violence*. Paradoxically, for all the talk about sex and sexuality, nobody really cares about or talks about *it*. The talk is indeed all about power, and—as the obverse side of this—about the whitewashing of power by way of eliminating the allegedly "subjective stain" of sexuality. In this situation, the issue of sex is not overemphasized but rather overexploited, yet not taken seriously in itself. An important issue at stake here, of course, is also the old issue of the difference between subjective and objective, or between subjective and systemic, violence. To quote Žižek on this question:

> The catch is that subjective and objective violence cannot be perceived from the same standpoint: subjective violence is experienced as such against the background of a non-violent zero level. It is seen as perturbation of the "normal," peaceful state of things. However, objective violence is precisely the violence inherent to this "normal" state of things. Objective violence is invisible since it sustains the very zero-level standard against which we perceive something subjectively violent. . . . It may be invisible, but it has to be taken into account if one is to make sense of what otherwise seem to be "irrational" explosions of subjective violence.[10]

The implicit context of this quote is political, referring to the difference between the "smooth" everyday functioning of power (with the amount of invisible repression/violence necessary for this smooth operation), and the visible outbursts of violence with people protesting on the streets, setting fire to cars and shops, attacking the police, and so on.

In relation to this, one could see the ideological operation/configuration that I'm trying to describe in this essay as something that casts or deploys this difference between subjective and objective violence entirely on the side of the systemic forces of power themselves, establishing this divide there. Systemic violence is perceived, habitually, as business as usual. However, the moment a serious and growing dissatisfaction and revolt appears on the side of the people, a revolt that threatens the stability of power and cannot be easily ignored, the "issue" is recognized by those in power and its causes are quickly attributed to the subjectively corrupt usurpation of power—that is, to its *abuse*. Someone abused their power, which makes the problem appear as a result of purely subjective violence. What follows therein is this axiom: power can only be wrong when it is abused. Or perhaps even more precisely; power can never be wrong, it can only be abused.

So, if objective violence is invisible, subjective violence is visible, often very visible—particularly when figures and representatives of power engage in it. And I'd like to suggest that sexuality functions today not only as one of the prominent cases of visible, subjective violence but also as an embodiment of the very *visibility/subjectivity of violence*. It seems that nowhere more than in sexual violence is the subjective factor in the foreground, and "sexual violence" has the capacity, or characteristic, of absorbing or subjectivizing all layers of violence. If it is sexual, it cannot but be personal; not in the sense of necessarily involving deep feelings, emotions, or passions, but in the sense of someone *enjoying* it and hence being personally/subjectively corrupt.

And here we come back to the already briefly mentioned notion of *professionalism*. You can do all kinds of violent things to people if you do it professionally—that is, without (visible) personal satisfaction or gain. It seems obvious that the notion of "professionalism" also underwent an important change in this contemporary ideological operation. The more classical, and in some ways laudable, notion of professionalism has been hijacked and taken in the direction of perversion, as I briefly described it earlier. The classical notion was mostly about not letting your personal preoccupations and views interfere with your job, *while taking full subjective responsibility* for the objective outcome of your actions, which is what the notion of "objective responsibility" is about in this case. The new notion and ideal of professionalism simply pretends to cut off any subjective dimension, and casts the professional as a *mere executor* of higher forces and orders; the subjective dimension is reduced entirely to just a possible source of troubles. If the execution of those orders has devastating results, it has to be because a subjective factor got in the way of their pure execution. And this is very different from taking subjective responsibility for the objective state of things that you helped to bring about. It is, more often than not, about offering a subjective *explanation* or excuse for what is in fact objectively wrong.

But the problem is that this professionalization of power (via the elimination of enjoyment) doesn't really work—as psychoanalysis keeps pointing out, you don't get rid of enjoyment so easily. Moreover, there is such a thing as *impersonal enjoyment,* and perversion is the key figure of it. Contrary to how it is often depicted in movies, the true image of perversion is not that of a horny old man observing a young girl with saliva dripping from his mouth; on the contrary, its true image is that of a cold and composed "professional" making *others* ashamed of themselves and their enjoyment. It is important to emphasize here that I am not denouncing the perverse position on the grounds that behind its "professional" posture its practitioners nevertheless enjoy and are hence bad. This would be repeating the same argument that I am trying to dismantle here. The figure of perversion is important because it challenges the idea that all enjoyment is simply and directly subjective, personal. It testifies to the existence and dimension of *impersonal enjoyment.* It testifies to the existence of what we could call "systemic enjoyment." Perverts know that it exists, and they certainly know how to put it to personal use, but that doesn't make the enjoyment simply subjective in its origin. Why is this important? Because today the key question seems to be the following: Is it even possible to conceive of power without some enjoyment sticking to it? Can there be power without this libidinal stain blemishing its purity? If we accept the question in this form and let it orient us, we end up with two possible attitudes: (1) one that claims that this should at least be our ideal (even if unattainable) and that progress lies in the potentially infinite purification of power and the invention of more and more complicated rules and prescriptions that regulate it and prevent its abuse; and (2) one that cynically gives up on these attempts, embraces enjoyment, invites us to realistically accept that there is no power without the libidinal compound, and suggests that we better get used to it and even use it fully. But, as we can see almost every day now, this is a deadlock that confronts us with a wrong and politically disastrous alternative. For isn't this precisely how our political space is structured today between "left progressive liberals" and the rise of the alt-right?

As Angela Nagle has pointed out,[11] we've been witnessing lately a curious turn in which the new populist Right is taking the side of transgression and rebellion, traditionally associated with the Left: they talk about breaking taboos (of speech, but also of conduct), they dare to speak up, say and do forbidden things, challenge established structures (including the media), and denounce the "elites." Even when in power, they continue with this "dissident" rhetoric of opposition and of courageous transgression (for example, against European institutions and their bureaucracy or else against the "deep state"). Transgression seems to be "sexy," even if it simply means no longer greeting your neighbor, because, "Who invented these stupid rules and why should I obey them?" In this constellation—after giving up on the more radical ideas of social and economic justice, and on exposing the systemic causes of injustice—the Left has paradoxically ended up on the conservative side of defending the rule of law, conserving what we have, and responding to contradictions, excesses, and plain catastrophes generated by the present socioeconomic system by means of introducing more and more new rules, regulations, and adjustments that are supposed to keep the "anomalies" at bay and prevent and punish any abuse. This growing and often impenetrable corpus of rules and sub-rules, which are usually easily disregarded by the big players but tend to drastically complicate the lives of smaller players and individuals, includes "cultural" rules and injunctions that have become, in the past decades, the main battlefield between the "Left" and the "Right," particularly in the United States.

So, on the one side we have people who want "power without enjoyment," and on the other side people who openly and boastingly enjoy it, who make it a matter of enjoyment. And the problem is that both sides are part of the same fundamental logic, which is why they mostly keep responding to each other, rather than to any social real. To at least conceptually break out of this alternative between asubjective power without enjoyment and subjectively affirmed enjoyment as power, we have to first recognize that this is a false alternative, and why that is so. The true question is *not* simply whether it is possible to have power without the subjective libidinal compound. Instead, the conceptual shift to accomplish would be to conceive of the very libidinal compound of power (which we usually associate with some subjective gain) as something that is never simply or immediately subjective but is rather generated out of the structure itself and is *symptomatic of its contradictions.*

As I have tried to develop more extensively in *What Is Sex?* the libidinal compound of power ("enjoyment"), or of any symbolic/social structure, is not simply some unavoidable human factor that comes to stain its purity, but the symptom of an inner contradiction of this structure, of a gap in it. It is this contradiction that we need to deal with, and just cutting off the enjoyment does little to help with that. The fact that there is enjoyment always points to a "leak" or contradiction, an inconsistency in the structure. If the structure were a fully consistent entity, it wouldn't produce, in its functioning, these layers and shoots of (surplus) enjoyment. The latter always occur in places of structural difficulty, interruption, discontinuity, passages from one level to the other, from the outside to the inside, and so on. We usually respond to these contradictions and shoots of enjoyment (which we can experience directly or indirectly) by subjectivizing them in different ways. The subject is not the cause of this enjoyment but a response to it. So the strong claim here would be that *no* enjoyment is simply personal and subjective at its outset; it is not subjective but *subjectivating* (inducing subjectivation), which is a different thing. It can be "subjectivized" in different ways, and the figure of the boasting, self-affirming, often authoritarian "enjoyer" doubtless gets a lot of thrust from the growing discontent that people experience in the face of the also growing amount of systemic enjoyment and its pressure, which is being methodically disclaimed by the purely "professional" executors of politics.

What is "systemic enjoyment"? It is the term with which one could perhaps address more specifically what Freud has called *das Unbehagen in der Kultur*, the discontent that grows out of different layers of our social edifice and its contradictions.[12] Freud's term points to an affect (discontent or discomfort), but to what exactly does this affect respond? It responds to the growing complexity of cultural, civilizational configurations and demands, which cannot be reduced to symbolic regulations, prohibitions, and restrictions, and which also imply and generate new forms and even injunctions of enjoyment. (The "injunction" part was added by Lacan.) For Freud, this basically meant that in dealing with and regulating drives, *Kultur* itself takes on a kind of drive-life and logic, so that the two can no longer simply be opposed but work in a singular and sometimes devastating complicity. The logical form implied in this configuration of complicity can be easily extended to political economy or, perhaps more accurately, it can even be argued that it *comes from* political economy; psychic economy is its "extimate" prolongation.

Lacan famously claimed that "Marx invented the symptom"—that is to say, the very logic and structure of what is called a "symptom"—and he coined the term "surplus enjoyment" from the Marxian concept of "surplus value." This is more than just an analogy. The Marxian concept has provided Lacan with a way to think of enjoyment as systemic, or more precisely as being generated out of a certain glitch in the "system" or social/symbolic order. And I would suggest that Lacan's theory of the four discourses is a response to this idea, a further and systematic elaboration of the fact that enjoyment is not simply a subjective category. For this theory also allows Lacan to redefine what is implied for him in the term "discourse." Discourse is not simply synonymous with language and speech, or with the symbolic order in general; it now gets to be defined as a "social bond," *le lien social*. And while Lacan held that all symbolic structures and discourses involve a contradiction or non-relation, a gap at the point of which systemic enjoyment emerges, he also suggested that they do not exactly base their entire economy on it, as is the case with the capitalist economy, which "discovered" the productivity/exploitability of this gap or non-relation. In other words, whereas the gap and the systemic enjoyment emerging at its point can function as an obstructive element of a social bond and call for repression (or some other forms of "domestification" and control), the capitalist economy discovered its positive use as a possible source of profit. Is capitalism one of the four Lacanian discourses or social bonds? I'm more and more inclined to say that capitalism, in the sense of capitalist economy, is not a social bond, yet it affects, it can affect, all social bonds. Perhaps some more than the others. It affects them with its two fundamental inventions, which involve the *countability* (as surplus value) of the surplus generated out of inherent discursive contradiction, and the systemic exploitation of this contradiction (non-relation) as the very *source* of profitable productivity (the source of "growth").[13] As Lacan put it: "the important point is that on a certain day surplus *jouissance* became calculable, could be counted, totalized. This is where what is called the accumulation of capital begins."[14] To develop this further and in more detail would largely exceed the scope of this essay, so let me return to the starting point.

What Freud has detected and called "discomfort in civilization" could be seen as his recognizing the effects of a newly established link, a complicity between symbolic structures and the (libidinal) economy of the drives, their becoming strangely *homologized* in their very heterogeneity and incompatibility (the concept of the superego clearly belongs to this register). His concept of the unconscious was born not simply out of the configuration in which symbolic prohibitions and restrictions demanded the repression of certain drives (and their representations), but out of a more dialectical configuration which revealed an unexpected complicity between drives and repression, between the (purely) symbolic and the libidinal.[15] This complicity or short-circuit could be seen as historical occurrence, yet one needs to be very precise here: the coexistence, in their very heterogeneity, of the symbolic structure and enjoyment is not historical but belongs to the very "leaking" ontology of symbolic order (and enjoyment is generated at the points of these contradictions). On the other hand, their "homologization" (in the form of a new way of counting), and the consequent massive complicity between the libidinal and symbolic, is a historic occurrence or "invention."

As Freud already pointed out: there can be huge amounts of repression that we simply know nothing about, because they are "successful" in the sense of not inducing any neurotic behavior, or simply not producing any symptoms, not leaving any further traces. Symptom has two sides or levels. On the one hand it points to a contradiction, a problem. But it points to it by means of providing a solution to it—an often strange or cumbersome solution, yet a solution nevertheless. The symptom is this solution. The symptom alerts us to the fact that repression has been engaged in a further economy and has a consequential afterlife. Neurotic behavior always involves an *economy*, it involves an economy that feeds on its own negativity, and this has far-reaching consequences and implications. If this kind of *economy* of surplus (enjoyment), which has until then remained mostly uncounted, is the invention of capitalism, does this mean that the symptoms that led to the birth of psychoanalysis were also related, connected to this historical occurrence, dependent on it? Even more brutally formulated: Does this mean that people in precapitalist times were never neurotic, or were so to a significantly lesser degree? In a way, yes, this would be the radical implication, which of course does not amount to saying that they were "happier." And it is even less to say that no repression had been at work there. On the contrary, surplus enjoyment means that its repressive use had by far exceeded its economic use, its exploitation as possible source of profit or gain, on the individual as well as social scale.

A considerable amount of Foucault's work revolves around describing and thinking this shift, which could be formulated as the shift from repression to the economy of repression (for example, from brutal punishment and torture to imprisonment and surveillance). And the economy of repression does not only mean "cashing in" on repression; it also involves what Freud discovered as the vicious spiral of repression and its "gain" or profit, a spiral in which they mutually reinforce and amplify each other. Yet even from the purely economic point of view, this complicity is not a fairy tale, as Foucault tends to suggest. For Foucault, and to put it very simply, this economy is so vicious because it is utterly unassailable; it turns everything into its profit, it capitalizes on its own contradictions rather than being threatened and endangered by them. And of course, Foucault's criticism of Freud and psychoanalysis in general is related to this point: psychoanalysis participates fully in this economy and encourages it with its own means. This is what its supposed "invention of sexuality," as Foucault phrases it, means: with sexuality and its repression, psychoanalysis discovered something that could be infinitely exploited and put to use in this modern economy.[16]

But there is another possible, and far more critical perspective on this: Freud discovered sexuality as the privileged territory of symptoms, of precisely everything which, in this allegedly "perfect" economy, *does not work*. More precisely, he discovered it as the symptom of everything which, in this perfect economy, produces an *additional*, further, second-degree "surplus" which cannot be put back to profitable use, but constitutes disruption, a breakdown, a serious crisis. In other words, what Freud saw so well in relation to the "libidinal economy," and what he called *das Unbehagen in der Kultur*, was not only how this economy feeds on the profits of repression but also the fact that it comes with accumulating costs, and that the latter were about to burst. They did burst eventually, although in a rather unexpected, spectacular global "political" way—in nothing less than a world war. The latter was the catastrophe that had, among other things, the effect of stabilizing the economy for a while.

Everything can be put to use or made to count. Yes. The problem— a possible crisis of the capitalist order—does not come from the fact that some things, however, cannot be put to use, and resist this use. The threatening, critical point is not resistance but the fact that another kind of useless surplus gets produced/constituted *while* everything is put to use; it is produced as the other side of this expanding inclusion. The more inclusive a capitalist economy becomes, the more exclusion it generates. This is paradoxical only if we don't recognize the difference between the two levels on which this operates. Absolute uselessness is not something that resists being put to use; it is what remains or is generated out of things being put to use. This accumulating, unbound, useless surplus—what I refer to as the contemporary form of "systemic enjoyment"—is not what offers resistance to the capitalist economy; rather, it is something that threatens to make it explode.[17] But it can be put to use on another level, at least temporarily—more precisely, it can be *bound* by means of politics and ideas rather than directly by economy (although some economic use or benefit can also result from this bounding). This, for example, is what we today call populism. What is wrong with populism is not that it engages the masses, not even that it advances by gross simplifications, but that while leaving the economy of repression intact (and growing), it bounds the real and growing dissatisfaction of people in all kinds of imaginary ways, which nevertheless can have very palpable material consequences. The rise of populism, which we talk about a lot these days, is emphatically not simply about the personal style of populist leaders. Their bet on enjoyment as a political factor may be a good match for their personal affinities, but the libidinal compound they so aptly and amply use is not generated there—that is, by them and their personalities. It is generated by the contradictions and impasses of the social space in which these leaders manage to prevail and thrill.

Let me conclude with a brief remark, very much related to this, concerning the terminological shift that has taken place in the last decades in academic debates, the shift from the possibly controversial notion of *politics* to the (also academically) more glamorous notion of *power*. This terminological shift is quite significant, because the two notions allow for very different sets of distinctions, implying very different levels of reflection, critique, and action. "Politics" can be judged as good or bad, right or wrong, and it can be judged as bad or wrong even if there is no direct personal gain or abuse involved. A morally good person can have very bad politics (and vice versa). Politics allows for discussion, controversy, rebellion, militancy, (counter-)organization, and so on. "Power," as the term is mostly used today, is something else. As suggested earlier, power can never be wrong, it can only be abused. Of course, we can say that it is *always* bad (or wrong), but then we haven't said much. Yet the moment we introduce some distinctions and criticism, we usually end up somewhere along the following two divides: professionalism/abuse (corruption) or else benevolence/wickedness. And these are all subjective, not social, categories. People can organize and protest against wicked leaders publicly, but the structuring of this protest is very different. Abuse/corruption (if manifest or proved) is directly accused (and subjected to outrage) and demands elimination. And this is fine. But we should not forget that this has a clear limit—the bottom line is that if we eliminate the abuser, or cut out the corruption, everything will be well and sound (again). This is why, in a strange sort of mirroring, many of Trump's liberal critics all too eagerly succumbed to one of *his* favorite slogans. They seemed to believe that if Trump was eliminated as president, America would become great again.

Notes

1. This article is a result of the research programme P6–0014 "Conditions and Problems of Contemporary Philosophy" and two research projects: N6-0286 "Reality, Illusion, Fiction, Truth: A Preliminary Study" and J6-4623 "Conceptualizing the End: Its Temporality, Dialectics, and Affective Dimension," which are funded by the Slovenian Research and Innovation Agency.
2. This famous eighteenth-century epistolary novel has also seen many screen adaptations, the best known of which is probably Stephen Frears's 1988 film, *Dangerous Liaisons*, with Glenn Close, John Malkovich, and Michelle Pfeiffer in the leading roles. The novel is constructed as an exchange of letters from which we can reconstruct the story. The two main characters, Marquise de Merteuil and Vicomte de Valmont, have broken up their carnal relationship in order to stay more true to the pact which binds them at the level of their principles and ideas. This pact and the "duty" following from it basically consists in seducing

and manipulating other people (as many as possible) into doing whatever they want them to do. The main storyline involves Valmont's seduction of a particularly difficult target, Madame de Tourvel. I discuss Laclos's novel in much more detail in *Ethics of the Real* (London: Verso, 2000).

3. La Mettrie's famous work *L'Homme machine* constitutes the obvious background of this plot. See Julien Offray de La Mettrie, *Machine Man and Other Writings*, trans. and ed. Ann Thomson (Cambridge: Cambridge University Press, 1996).

4. Choderlos de Laclos, *Les Liaisons dangereuses*, trans. P. W. K. Stone (Harmondsworth, UK: Penguin Books, 1961), 63.

5. Laclos, *Les Liaisons dangereuses*, 150.

6. Another example would be the novel *Sophie's Choice*, and the also quite famous film by Alan Pakula (starring Meryl Streep) based on it. I'm referring, of course, to the traumatic kernel of the story: Meryl Streep arriving at Auschwitz with her two children, a boy and a girl, and the sadistic German officer forcing her to choose one that will survive (or else both would be killed).

7. Slavoj Žižek, *How to Read Lacan* (New York: Norton, 2007), 55.

8. For more on this, see Mladen Dolar, "La Femme-machine," *New Formations* 23 (November 1994): 43–54.

9. Jean-Claude Milner, "Reflections on the Me Too Movement and Its Philosophy," *Problemi International* 3 (2019): 85.

10. Slavoj Žižek, *Violence* (London: Picador, 2008), 2.

11. See Angela Nagle, *Kill All Normies* (Zero Books, 2017).

12. I'm not the only Lacanian using this term. Samo Tomšič uses it in a similar way in his excellent recent book *The Labour of Enjoyment* (Berlin: August Verlag, 2019).

13. I develop this point concerning the discovery and exploitation of the contradiction (non-relation) as a source of profit more extensively in *What Is Sex?* (Cambridge, MA: MIT Press, 2017).

14. Jacques Lacan, *The Other Side of Psychoanalysis*, ed. Jacques-Alain Miller, trans. Russell Grigg, vol. 17 of The Seminar of Jacques Lacan (New York: Norton, 2007), 177.

15. Sigmund Freud, *Civilization and Its Discontents*, trans. and ed. James Strachey, vol. 21 of *The Standard Edition of the Complete Psychological Works of Sigmund Freud* (London: Vintage, 2001).

16. See Michel Foucault, *The History of Sexuality*, vol. 1, *An Introduction*, trans. Robert Hurley (Harmondsworth, UK: Penguin Books, 1978).

17. We can recognize the same logic in the case of the climate crisis, global warming, and its core cause, carbon emissions. The latter are essentially *by-products* of the capitalist economy and its use of resources. The climate has not been changed simply by our direct efforts, by what we created and built, but mostly because of what has accumulated in this process: pure waste. The ecological crisis is not simply a problem of the word's finitude, a problem regarding the fact that natural resources will run out. This obviously can (and will) cause shortages, wars, and so on. The problem of climate change strictly speaking comes from elsewhere—namely, from what *comes into existence* when we burn these resources.

If we were able to just use up these resources with no remains or surplus, we wouldn't be talking today about climate change. We talk about it because of the emissions, which are a kind of useless "surplus" of the industrial exploitation of natural resources. In other words, the problem is not only that natural resources are running out (which obviously *is* a problem), but that while running out they seem to be returning, reentering our space from another side, from a "beyond," from the real—in the form of another kind of surplus, a menacing disaster.

"For Thought to Dwell Where Evils Have No Entry"

On Oedipus and the Extimacy of Anger

Amanda Holmes

There is a striking moment at the end of Sophocles's *Oedipus Rex* just after Oedipus has blinded himself in his infamous outburst of rage; it is a moment when he wishes he could go even further in his self-mutilation. After destroying his ability to see by gouging out his own eyes, Oedipus laments that he is unable to close up his ears and thereby do away with his power of hearing as well:

> Once I brought to light such a stain as mine,
> could I look with steady eyes on all of this?
> No! And if there were a way to plug up my ears
> and clog the springs of hearing, I'd not refrain
> from sealing up this wretched corpse of mine,
> blind and deaf to everything. It would be sweet
> for thought to dwell where evils have no entry.[1]

The fantasy articulated here is one of recoiling from the world in the pursuit of an absolute separation from it. The wish of sealing up one's corpse exposes the desire for a certain impossibility: the desire for an existence which refuses to be marked by an outside. Oedipus wants to become a place where thought might dwell without corruption from the external world; he wishes to be a purely thinking thing. A strange bedfellow to the "thinking thing" of Descartes's *Meditations*, Oedipus's fantasy is to become a thinking thing closed off from any relation to the outside, to seal up all points of entry, and to shutter whatever is internal from everything that is external. It is not enough that he has blinded himself; Oedipus desires to shut himself up entirely from the world by stuffing up his ears and becoming deaf as well. It is with this bizarre image given in

Oedipus's "sweet" fantasy of the sealed-off, living, thinking corpse that we begin to see the stakes and the affects of *extimacy*.

The concept of *extimacy* (*extimité*) names the condition of subjectivity whereby the subject's most intimate interiority is located in its exterior. As a sort of pun that combines *intime* (intimate) and *extériorité* (exteriority),[2] the Lacanian formulation of extimacy describes the condition of subjectivity as one in which the subject is always locating itself outside itself. The subject finds itself "internally excluded from its object" and is itself "excluded in the interior."[3] That is to say, there is an inside-out structure of subjectivity whereby the core of the subject is internally excluded. Lacan claims that the only index for this strange concept is to be found in topology; it is "the generating sign of the Möbius strip" that Lacan designates as the "inner eight."[4] This warped structure contorts the distinction between internal and external, subjective and objective; it marks a strange, twisted surface whereby one side cannot be neatly distinguished from the other.

The extimate structure of the Lacanian subject poses a challenge to the traditional binary oppositions between inner and outer, subjective and objective. It is by blurring the line between the internal and the external that extimacy encapsulates the central provocation posed to philosophy by psychoanalysis. This challenge is one of thinking the specific negativity at the heart of the psychoanalytic subject. The negativity of the extimate subject is most readily cast as a structural concept, one that allows us to think the structure of the subject as built around this internal exclusion. But the concept of extimacy also implicates the question of affect. To conceive of the extimate structure of subjectivity is to name the very condition of a being who can be intimately affected by its outside. That is to say, there is an implicit theory of affect within the concept of extimacy.

The extimate condition of the subject has usually been discussed in relation to the affects of the uncanny, horror, and most of all anxiety. Indeed, in his touchstone essay on Lacan and the uncanny, Mladen Dolar argues that the invention of *extimité* was Lacan's attempt to translate the German word *Unheimliche* (uncanny) into French.[5] Dolar shows that there was not an adequate way to translate the strange word *Unheimlich* into French, and so Lacan had to invent the term *extimité* to convey the combination of the familiar and intimate with the strange and threatening as this combination was thematized by Freud in his essay on the *Unheimliche*. In an important sense, then, the extimate is something uncanny and is linked to the affects of anxiety and horror, as Dolar has so critically shown. What the invention of *extimité* adds to the notion of the uncanny or the *Unheimlich* is an emphasis on the structural determinations of the uncanny as an affect. The invention of extimacy emphasizes that the kind of being who is capable of experiencing the uncanny is one whose fundamental structure is organized around an internal exclusion. What I will pursue in this essay is a different dimension of extimacy, one which exposes another element of the affective density of the subject's extimate structure—namely, anger. I propose to extend the domain of the affects associated with extimacy to include anger because like the uncanny, horror, and anxiety, eruptions of anger mark a certain encounter with the real. Anger discloses the odd fit between the internal and the external; it exposes the subject's condition of extimacy.

The turn to anger proposed here is not an arbitrary choice of one affect among others. Rather, an investigation into anger will reveal its proximity to anxiety, which has already been identified as one of the privileged affects of the uncanny, extimate structure of subjectivity.[6] We begin by addressing the etymological proximity between anger and anxiety. In English, one can clearly identify the relation between the English word "anger" and the German *Angst* (anxiety). The root word that both anger and *Angst* share is *angh-*, a proto Germanic word that means "tight" or "painfully constricted."[7] The idea that anxiety entails a painful constriction resonates with the definition of anxiety from Lacan's tenth seminar, where he establishes that anxiety is when lack lacks.[8] Anxiety involves a relation to the Other that is *too* much; when there is a suffocating proximity of the Other, anxiety is the response or the signal. And it is precisely this sense of constriction or binding (*angh-*) that anxiety, or *Angst*, has in common with anger.

Of course, for Lacan, working between German and French in his readings of Freud, this etymological proximity between anger and *Angst* was not the case. The French word *colère* does not expose its relation to anxiety, *l'angoisse*, as readily as it does for us working in the English translations, somewhere between Freud's German and Lacan's French. However, Lacan consistently returned to the affect of anger any time he approached the discourse on affects during the first ten years of his seminar. Although Lacan was usually dismissive of the discourse on affects, whenever he mentioned affects he claimed that he had already said enough about affects in what he said about anger. For example, in the tenth seminar, just after he says that anxiety is an affect, Lacan addresses the claim that he has nothing to say about affects: "I've tried, on occasion, to say what an affect is not. It is not Being given in its immediacy, nor is it the subject in a raw form either. . . . The relationship between affect and the signifier would necessitate a whole year on the theory of affects. I've already hinted at how I understand it. I did so with regard to anger."[9] Lacan's definition of anger is somewhat enigmatic, but it is always the same: "Anger is what happens in the subject when the little pegs won't fit into the little holes."[10] This definition highlights the structuralist approach to the question of affect upon which Lacan insists. That is, the question of affect for Lacan is a question about the structure of the subject. And anger highlights this structure because anger is set off when there is something within it that does not quite fit. Anger is the failure of the structure to fit with itself.

This strange image that Lacan conjures up—namely, of a moment when the little pegs do not fit into the little holes—is borrowed from Charles Péguy. As Lacan explains it in the third year of his seminar, this formulation refers to "people who, when the great catastrophe declares itself, want to retain the same relationship with things as beforehand."[11] So early on, this formulation is used to describe something like a response to catastrophe, but it is not necessarily a definition of anger when Lacan first introduces it. It is only in later years of the seminar that Lacan returns to this expression to define anger. As he elaborates in his tenth seminar, "anger is what happens in the subject when the little pegs won't fit into the little holes. What does that mean? When, at the level of the Other, of the signifier, that is to say, always more or less, at the level of faith, of *bona fides*, the game isn't being played. Well, that's what sparks off anger."[12] So, here we have the Lacanian definition of anger: it is what happens when the little pegs won't fit into the little holes, when the game isn't being played.[13] Anger then has something to do with the dimension of expectation, with the response to some great catastrophe that abruptly changes the order of things.

Anger occurs when we assume that we know what is coming, that we have a sense of how to play the game and things seem to be going well, and all of a sudden someone or something else breaks the rules, disrupts the order, and foils our plans. There is a sudden constriction, which is not anxiety but anger. Lacan elaborates this in the sixth year of the seminar where he gives the following complementary definition:

> It is hard not to see that a fundamental affect like anger is nothing but the following: the real that intervenes at the very moment at which we have woven a fine symbolic web, where everything is going well, order, law, our merit, and our pleasure. We realize suddenly that the square pegs do not fit into the round holes. That is the origin of anger as an affect. All is well on the bridge formed by the ships on the Bosphorus, but a tempest blows in that whips up the sea. All anger involves whipping up the waters.[14]

There are a couple of things to emphasize about the definition of anger that Lacan provides in this passage. First, anger is what happens when the Real intervenes at the very moment when things seem to be going well, when everything is precisely in order at the level of the Symbolic. It does seem to be the case especially for those who keep things in order, or for those whose enjoyment in life seems very tightly bound to the tidy arrangement of ideas and of things, that anger is quite often at the ready. The crucial problem is that most orders, however firmly enforced, are actually as delicate as the order of the ships on the Bosphorus; they are formed only by a contingent and tenuous state of affairs and can be split apart, torn asunder by even slight disturbances. The image of anger as the moment when all of a sudden the square pegs do not fit into the round holes supplements the other image we get from Lacan: anger involves a whipping up of the waters. In both cases we have an image of a sudden intrusion, the moment when things no longer seem to fit or go together as they should, the abrupt collapse of an expected order in the rise of a tumult.

We find another elaboration of this definition of anger in the seventh year of the seminar. Lacan clarifies this image of anger as a whipping up of the waters and as a moment when the pegs won't fit into the holes. In this passage, he even describes anger as a feeling and as a passion. He says: "anger is no doubt a passion which is manifested by means of an organic or physiological correlative, by a given more or less hypertonic or even elated feeling, but that it requires perhaps something like the reaction of a subject to a disappointment, to the failure of an expected correlation between a symbolic order and the response of the real, in other words, . . . it's when the little pegs refuse to go into the little holes."[15] In this passage, we are given a more physiological explanation of the structural definition of anger as when the square pegs won't fit in the round holes. In an uncharacteristic moment, Lacan offers an almost phenomenological description of the feeling of anger; it is hypertonic and almost elated. What is repeated here is that anger is about a failed expectation; but what is added is that this situation generates a certain pressure in the organism's relation to its outside. There is an element of surprise: something happens that was not anticipated within the symbolic order; something does not fit into the schema with which we were at a certain point conceiving of the world and of our place in it, situating ourselves as subjects within the symbolic order. In short, anger is when the real breaks in and overwhelms the symbolic structure, and such an instance results in the sense of a split between the subject and its environment. What it is that does not fit is not only the little pegs in the little holes, but the internal torsion of the subject as it does not conform to its outside.

Anger here begins to reveal the extimate structure of the subject. The experience of anger exposes a moment of ill fit between the internal and the external; it is a by-product of extimacy.

What these passages from Lacan's various descriptions of anger all have in common is that they describe anger as a moment when something doesn't quite fit between the internal, or the symbolic order through which the subject orients itself, and the external, or the elements of reality that interfere with this order. Among all the affects, anger bears a relation to the situations that cause a disturbance in the delicate order of the internally excluded relation of the subject to its outside. In short, anger is precisely about the strange extimate relation of the subject to its situation. It seems that when the little pegs do not fit in the little holes, we have the structure of anger insofar as it is about a sudden dissonance in the way the symbolic regulates reality. As Colette Soler puts it, anger "is the affect that arises when something in reality (*du réel*) poses an obstacle to desire's enterprises, the latter always being organized by the symbolic."[16] Anger arises when the structure that one uses to make sense of the world does not map on to something confronted, when some aspect of reality that hadn't been accounted for throws a wrench in the order of desire as it has been set up within the symbolic. Anger does not mark a complete collapse of this order, but rather marks the way in which the subject and reality come to a point of not quite fitting together as expected.

We might return to the image of Oedipus blinding himself and longing to plug up the springs of his hearing, in order to elaborate and connect the definition of anger that we find in Lacan's thought with the structure of extimacy. In general, Oedipus is an angry character; he has good reasons to be angry. What is strange about the anger of Oedipus is that he seems to be angry before he even knows that he has these reasons. There are at least three notable moments in Sophocles's depictions of Oedipus that foreground his anger. First, there is the anger that was at work in the prehistory of *Oedipus Rex*: the anger, or more properly the road rage that caused Oedipus to unwittingly kill his own father at the crossroads where three roads meet. Second, there is the anger that drives Oedipus's investigation into the murder of Laius. This is an anger directed in large part against Tiresias, who refuses to tell Oedipus exactly what has happened. As soon as Oedipus perceives his authority to be threatened in even the slightest way by Tiresias, Oedipus lashes out at him angrily.[17] Tiresias's suggestion that he should not investigate the death of Laius leads to an angry episode in which Oedipus accuses him of conspiring with Creon to take over Thebes and to unseat Oedipus as king. Finally, there is the anger that explodes when Oedipus has discovered the truth of his deeds and realizes his own condition of unthinkable sin. This is a moment that entails not only anger but also despair, sadness, and anguish. But it is only anger that has accompanied Oedipus all along.

Anger is important for thinking about the character of Oedipus because it seems to be precisely what gets him into so much trouble. Anger serves as the motor of the tragedy's narrative insofar as every major development in the story (killing the father, investigating the truth about who killed Laius, and finally blinding himself) starts from some angry outburst. Often, the anger of Oedipus reveals precisely this structure of little pegs not fitting into little holes. In particular, the investigation into the murder of Laius proceeds with various moments of encounter with some set of facts or accounts of the murder that do not quite fit with what Oedipus had expected. For example, there is some confusion about how many murderers there were at the scene of Laius's killing. The number of people involved never quite matches up in the various accounts that are given. Oedipus had been told that Laius was killed by several men and insists on this point: "it was a band of robbers that attacked and killed him, not one but many hands."[18] This important difference between the one and the many is important for Oedipus's own innocence because he knows he himself had been involved in a violent altercation on his way to Thebes. But because he is not himself many, he surmises, "I could not have done it, because one is not the same as many."[19] These accounts of the murder do not fit with the schema upon which Oedipus had relied up until the beginning of the play. So when the accounts begin to show their dissonance, Oedipus's anger provokes further inquiry. This ill fit intensifies Oedipus's angry and frenzied investigation into the truth of Laius's death. The truth here is not pursued because of curiosity but because of anger.

When Oedipus finally learns the truth of his various familial relations, he gives us the supreme example of a case in which things do not quite fit together in the symbolic: his mother is his wife, his daughters are his sisters, his sons are his brothers. The pegs do not fit into the little holes, and what this causes is a catastrophic anger. All of a sudden the symbolic positions of each relation are contorted into an odd shape. The definition of anger, as a not fitting together of little pegs and little holes, is a precise characterization of Oedipus's situation. His anger precipitates a violent self-destruction, and the cause of Oedipus's anger is nothing other than the breakdown of the Symbolic structures on which his life was ordered.

If extimacy marks that uncanny moment "where the most intimate interiority coincides with the exterior and becomes threatening, provoking horror and anxiety,"[20] then Oedipus's blinding and his wish to seal up his ears and become a thinking thing can be understood as a violent and angry reaction to the anguish of extimacy. Oedipus's blinding and his wish to plug up his ears reveals a radical reaction to the human condition of extimacy because it marks his impossible desire to set up a strong border between the internal and the external. What Oedipus refuses, or rather what he *wants* to refuse, is precisely the condition of desire as that which warps the boundary between inner and outer. What Oedipus can no longer bear is the condition of his own extimacy.

Read in this way, Oedipus's anger is not sparked by the simple fact (horrible as it indeed is) that he unwittingly killed his own father and married his mother; it is rather that his desire is revealed to him to have never been *his* at all. For most of his life, Oedipus had conceived of himself as a rather clever fellow. He enjoyed the autonomy of reason: having fled the terrible prophecy, he solved the riddle of the Sphinx and obtained his place as king of Thebes. When Oedipus realizes all of a sudden that the course of his life has led to nothing other than the fulfillment of his terrible fate, he is confronted with the extimacy of his desire. That is, while acting in accordance with what he thought was his own desire, he realizes it had been determined by something other than him, something outside of him, all along. In confronting the truth of what he has done, he is shown the extimate nature of his desire. Everything he believed himself to be up until this point, including his most intimate sense of who he was, is revealed to have been wholly determined by something other than and external to him. He did not in fact escape the fate he was fleeing. And his despairing response marks an attempt to shut himself off from his externality entirely. This realization provokes a tremendous anger that brings Oedipus to blind himself, and it sparks his fantasy of a total recoil. Oedipus's blinding and his longing to go even further in separating himself from the world by stuffing up his ears marks a moment of ultimate cringe.

This reading of Oedipus's blinding as an attempt to seal up his corpse and to reject the extimate nature of his desire illuminates something about what is at stake in the Oedipus myth beyond the narrative of unconsciously desiring the mother and being in competition with the father. It reveals something else about the structure of desire as such. It is a reading that casts new light on Oedipus's act of self-blinding. As Alenka Zupančič has argued, Oedipus's act of blinding himself is not so much an act of self-punishment, as is often suggested; rather, it is an act of identifying with his symptom. That is, Zupančič shows that the act of blinding himself does not mark a self-punishment as much as it marks a return to not seeing for Oedipus. Zupančič writes: "In sum, Oedipus has always been blind, he has been blind his entire life—but then, when he finally gained the power of sight, when he saw what he had done, he 'tore away' his eyes, saying: I prefer to continue being blind!'"[21] Oedipus's fantasy of plugging up his ears extends this point even further. It shows that he not only wants to return to a condition of blindness, but he desires to radically cut himself off from the reality he is confronting altogether. Oedipus's act of blinding himself is motivated by the desire to destroy his every capacity for perception, both visual and auditory, and thereby to cut himself off completely from the external world.[22] Oedipus's desire for blindness and deafness illustrates the pain of encountering the origin of one's desire outside of oneself. In other words, Oedipus shows that anguish, anger, and anxiety are three related responses to the condition of extimacy.

At the height of his anger, Oedipus's most ardent desire is precisely to refuse the extimate structure of his being and to close himself off from the world entirely by sealing up all possibilities of perception. His attempt to refuse any relation to the outside expresses this fantasy of being completely cut off. Through this fantasy we catch a glimpse of the root of anger. Oedipus is himself an image of anger. If *Antigone* offers an image of desire, as Lacan argues in his seventh seminar, then Oedipus, we might suggest, gives us an image of anger. According to Lacan, Antigone is "desire made visible."[23] Lacan claims that "Antigone reveals to us the line of sight that defines desire";[24] her "unbearable splendor" gives us an image of desire itself. Similarly then, Oedipus give us an image of anger.[25]

If we turn to Sophocles's *Oedipus at Colonus*, there is even more evidence that Oedipus is an image of anger itself. We see Oedipus in this tragedy as an angry and embittered old man who seeks a certain vengeance on the city of Thebes. When Ismene comes to tell wandering Oedipus of the new foretelling from the Oracle at Delphi, she says that he is wanted in Thebes again because it has been predicted that if he does not return, the Cadmeans will feel "the force of Oedipus's anger."[26] The Greek word used here carries an interesting resonance for our purposes of exploring the relation between anger, extimacy, and desire. The word is *orgē*, which means "anger" and is consistently translated as such in most English translations of *Oedipus at Colonus*.[27] The Greek word *orgē* also, however, has an etymological connection to sexual desire and is the root word of the English "orgasm."[28] As Christopher Faraone points out, "although the noun *orgē* primarily means 'anger,' in its original meaning it apparently indicated 'natural impulse' or 'propensity' and was closely related with the verb *organ*, which describes the state of a man 'swelling with lust.'"[29] So, the legacy of Oedipus is his anger. The Cadmeans are destined to deal with the force of his anger, which indicates not only his rage as it was manifest throughout *Oedipus Rex*, but more broadly connotes the effects of his sexual desire—namely, the war that will rage between his sons. The legacy of Oedipus's desire and his anger is precisely the havoc that will be wrought on Thebes in the context of the tragedy of *Antigone*. The force of Oedipus's anger sets the stage for Antigone's desire.

This constellation of anger, extimacy, and sexual desire at work in the figure of Oedipus elucidates the psychoanalytic uses of the Oedipus myth. In particular, in emphasizing the anger of Oedipus we can locate the operation of extimacy within the Oedipal structure itself. That is, Lacan's structural reformulation of the Oedipus complex can be more clearly delineated in the reading of Oedipus that emphasizes this moment of rage against his own most extimate condition. When Oedipus wishes to become a sealed-off, living, thinking corpse, a place to dwell where evils can have no entry, his desire gives voice to one point of suffering for a being whose condition is fundamentally extimate. Oedipus's anger entails a moment of rage against this very extimacy. And this is what is at the core of the Oedipus myth: that one must confront the fact that desire is in an important sense never properly one's own.

As Lacan develops the import of the Oedipus myth for psychoanalysis, it is not just the old family romance of loving the mother and being in jealous competition with the father that makes Oedipus resonate as a myth about the origin of desire. Instead, the Oedipus complex names the coming into being of the subject in relation to the symbolic order. It describes the process of a subject developing as a being whose most intimate core is located outside of itself, whose desire grows around an internally excluded lack of object, and whose structure can only be described as extimate. The experience of the Oedipal stage is a grappling with this internal exclusion. As Lacan explains, "we should be arranging the entirety of the [Oedipal] experience around the notion of the lack of object."[30] This is not a simple lack of object that might be opposed to the presence of object; rather, this is exactly the lack that later develops into the notion of the intimate externality at the core of the subject. It is in these passages on Lacan's structuralist revision of the Oedipus complex that we find the origins and the necessity of thinking the notion of extimacy. As Lacan writes: "What is ultimately at stake in the Oedipus complex? Well, it's about the subject himself having to be caught in this lure in such a way that he finds himself committed to an existent order, an order that is different from the psychological lure through which he came into it."[31] In short, the Oedipus complex is about situating oneself in relation to the structure of extimacy, it is about finding oneself in a symbolic order that is always already there and coming to find a strange kind of fit for oneself within it. The symbolic order preexists the subject in this sense; or rather, the subject is a by-product of it. What Oedipus's anger shows us is a violent example of how one learns to grapple with this fact; it is a process often characterized by anger.

I have suggested here that *Oedipus Rex* dramatizes the primacy of anger in relation to desire's *extimate* structure. In reading the moment of Oedipus's angry outburst as a key to the structural reading of the Oedipus complex in Lacan's formulation, I have argued that anger, along with anxiety, horror, and the uncanny, is an affect that can best be thought through extimacy. By way of a conclusion, it is helpful to note that Freud's very first formulation of the Oedipus complex is found in a discussion about death wishes. In a section titled "Dreams of the Death of Persons of Whom the Dreamer Is Fond" in the *Interpretation of Dreams*, Freud analyzes the death wishes that children often direct against loved ones. In particular, he discusses the fact that children often wish for the death of their siblings. These wishes, Freud explains, are merely the result of a childish egoism. They are merely a wish to have no rivals. Things get more complicated in relation to the death wishes that are directed towards parents. These death wishes are very strange and raise an important question: How are we to explain these death wishes against those very people "who surround [the child] with love and fulfill his needs and whose preservation that same egoism should lead him to desire?"[32] In other words, if the anger one experiences towards siblings can be explained by a selfish egoism, how is the anger towards parents to be thought when parents are in the service of this very egoism? The anger of Oedipus offers elements for developing a response. These elements are not, however, to be found only in the narrative of the story as it is so often described in the Oedipal love triangle. Oedipus gives an image of anger and explains the strange death wishes against parents in his violent reaction to the extimate nature of his desire; the clue we find in Oedipus is contained in the angry wish to become the place where thought might dwell where evils have no entry.

As Freud reminds us, "There must be something which makes a voice within us recognize the compelling force of destiny in the *Oedipus*.... His destiny moves us because it might have been ours—because the oracle laid the same curse upon us before our birth as upon him."[33] Perhaps there is a revealing ambiguity here because the oracle laid down a curse on Oedipus more than once. The curse of Oedipus is not only that he was destined to marry his mother and to kill his father; it is at least also to be found in what the oracle foretold just before Oedipus's death. The curse is what the Cadmeans are destined to feel when they stand at the tomb of Oedipus—namely, the force of his anger.

Notes

1. Sophocles, *Oedipus Rex*, in *The Greek Plays: Sixteen Plays by Aeschylus, Sophocles, and Euripides*, trans. and ed. Mary R. Lefkowitz and James S. Romm (New York: Modern Library, 2017), lines 1384–90.
2. Jacques Lacan, *The Ethics of Psychoanalysis*, ed. Jacques-Alain Miller, trans. Dennis Porte, vol. 7 of The Seminar of Jacques Lacan (New York: Norton, 1992), 139.
3. Jacques Lacan, *Écrits: The First Complete Edition in English*, trans. Bruce Fink (New York: Norton, 2006), 731; Lacan, *Ethics of Psychoanalysis*, 101.
4. Lacan, *Écrits*, 731.
5. Mladen Dolar, "'I Shall Be with You on Your Wedding Night': Lacan and the Uncanny," in "Rendering the Real," ed. Parveen Adams, special issue, *October* 58 (Autumn 1991): 5–23.
6. See, for example, Joan Copjec, "Vampires, Breast Feeding, and Anxiety" in "Rendering the Real," ed. Parveen Adams, special issue, *October* 58 (Autumn 1991): 25–43.
7. *Oxford English Dictionary*, s.v. "ange," www.oed.com/view/Entry/7456.
8. Jacques Lacan, *Anxiety*, ed. Jacques-Alain Miller, trans. A. R. Price, vol. 10 of The Seminar of Jacques Lacan (Cambridge: Polity, 2014), 42.
9. Lacan, *Anxiety*, 14.
10. Lacan, *Anxiety*, 14.
11. Jacques Lacan, *The Psychoses*, ed. Jacques-Alain Miller, trans. Russell Grigg, vol. 3 of The Seminar of Jacques Lacan (New York: Norton, 1981), 120–21.
12. Lacan, *Anxiety*, 14.
13. As Lacan says in the seventh seminar, "anger is essentially linked to something expressed in a formulation of Charles Péguy's, who was speaking in a humorous context—it's when the little pegs refuse to go into the little holes." Lacan, *Ethics of Psychoanalysis*, 103.
14. Jacques Lacan, *Desire and Its Interpretation*, ed. Jacques-Alain Miller, trans. Bruce Fink, vol. 6 of The Seminar of Jacques Lacan (Cambridge: Polity, 2019), 141.
15. Lacan, *Ethics of Psychoanalysis*, 103.
16. Collette Soler, *Lacanian Affects: The Function of Affect in Lacan's Work*, trans. Bruce Fink (New York: Routledge, 2016), 88.
17. See Barbara Renger, *Oedipus and the Sphinx: The Threshold Myth from Sophocles through Freud to Cocteau*, trans. Duncan Alexander Smart and David Rice (Chicago: University of Chicago Press, 2013).
18. Sophocles, *Oedipus Rex*, line 123.
19. Sophocles, *Oedipus Rex*, lines 844–45.
20. Dolar, "'I Shall Be with You on Your Wedding Night,'" 6.
21. Alenka Zupančič, *Ethics of the Real: Kant, Lacan* (London: Verso, 2000), 177.
22. For a helpful analysis of this point, see John Steiner, "Two Types of Pathological Organization in *Oedipus the King* and *Oedipus at Colonus*," in *Psychic Retreats: Pathological Organizations in Psychotic, Neurotic, and Borderline Patients* (London: Routledge, 1993).

23. Lacan, *Ethics of Psychoanalysis*, 247.
24. Lacan, *Ethics of Psychoanalysis*, 247.
25. Lacan, *Ethics of Psychoanalysis*, 247.
26. Sophocles, *Oedipus at Colonus* in *The Greek Plays: Sixteen Plays by Aeschylus, Sophocles, and Euripides*, trans. and ed. Mary R. Lefkowitz and James S. Romm (New York: Modern Library, 2017), line 411.
27. *A Greek-English Lexicon*, ed. Liddell, Scott, Jones (Oxford: Oxford University Press, 1996).
28. *A Greek-English Lexicon*.
29. Christopher A. Faraone, *Ancient Greek Love Magic* (Cambridge, MA: Harvard University Press, 1999), 123.
30. Jacques Lacan, *The Object Relation*, ed. Jacques-Alain Miller, trans. A. R. Price, vol. 4 of The Seminar of Jacques Lacan (Cambridge: Polity, 2020), 46.
31. Lacan, *Object Relation*, 193.
32. Sigmund Freud, *The Interpretation of Dreams*, ed. James Strachey and Anna Freud, trans. James Strachey, vol. 4 of *The Standard Edition of the Complete Psychological Works of Sigmund Freud* (London: Hogarth, 1953), 255.
33. Freud, *Interpretation of Dreams*, 262.

On Ambivalence as a Key Freudian Concept

The *Vaterkomplex*'s Edifice

Alejandro Cerda-Rueda

Once upon a time Freud declared that in every psychosexual development, a concept emerges whose main role is to account for certain structuring processes for the psychical apparatus but also for our insertion into culture. This process is what Freud defined as the *kern-komplex* of neurosis, the bond with the parents governed by incestuous appetites—namely, the Oedipus complex. Perhaps such an outdated concept needs revision given the contemporary criticism that has attempted to topple psychoanalysis with a deadeye single-shot, making it witness to its own debacle.[1] No matter how the dimensions of this concept may be extended within psychoanalytical schools (object relations, ego psychology, or Lacanian), this has also led to a diverted understanding of psychoanalytical practice. If, according to Lacan, the Oedipus complex is both universal and contingent, then there is a key aspect within the concept itself that led Freud to place it amid a continuous ambivalent construction.[2]

Yes, Freud posed a certain universality to this concept. However, this contentious characteristic of the Oedipus complex, extensively disputed by feminist activism, post-'68 French philosophy, and sociocultural movements, has been grounds not only for a misreading of Freudian metapsychology, but for a misconception of such universality itself. Perhaps it is Freud's own biased account that should be fundamentally addressed, since it is precisely *this* "universality" that gets misplaced on the grounds of its partiality—only the masculine universality is considered. According to Verhaeghe, in his reconsideration of the Oedipus complex, Freud's (and Lacan's) oedipal theory only supports the masculine side, thus knocking over the phallocentric universal mythos quite duly.[3] His theory of sexual difference notwithstanding, Freud's universalization of the Oedipus complex should not be read or placed in this misleading sense; instead it should be studied beyond his own neurotic solution.

It is fair to claim that the Oedipus complex is not the caricature it has often been presented as, dwindled into bourgeois roles or cardboard figures (i.e., mummy-daddy issues alike); instead, the kernel should be situated in the function itself. The aim of this essay is not only to study the genealogy of this *kern-komplex*, allocating a particular emphasis to the *Vaterkomplex* (a concept completely abandoned by post-Freudians), but also to understand it as a genuinely extimate function—that is, to show that the universality of this complex is precisely in its own ambivalent structure.[4] If, according to Lacanian psychoanalysis, what is considered to be extimate is that which is most proximate, something "nuclear" that hasn't rejected its "exteriority"—that is, the *Nebenmensch* understood in Freudian terms as an origin that allows us to cogitate but also to converge love/hate into a single object—then our reading of Freud's notion of ambivalence illustrates its bearings as a form of extimacy. In short, our main purpose is to address the *kern-komplex* as ambivalent and therefore, to highlight a form of extimacy that otherwise would go unnoticed from a clinical and theoretical perspective.

Freud's Self-Analysis: Mourning Becomes Oedipus

The idea of the Oedipus complex first occurred to Freud during *yahrzeit* while mourning the loss of his father (Jacob), who passed away on October 23, 1896. Coming from a Galician Jewish background, Freud subversively wasn't very much attached to religious rituals. However, it is significant that similar to every mourning culture, the Jewish tradition has its own temporal modes of bereavement. The first seven days after the death of the beloved person (the *shiva*, which literally means "seven days") is followed by *shloshim*, which is held thirty days after the funeral service, and usually conveys the unveiling of the tombstone (and shaving the beard). All children from the deceased parent are expected to remain grieving until the first lunar year is over; after these eleven months, the mourning process is lifted. For Sephardic Jews, for example, this commemoration is named *nachala*, or "legacy."

During this period, Freud underwent the capstone moment of his own self-analysis, an endeavor he began around 1894 and "concluded" in 1897. Since there was no other psychoanalyst at the time to consult, his dear friend Wilhelm Fliess, through his heartfelt correspondence detailing personal anecdotes, memories, patient analyses, and dreams, functioned as Freud's big Other—that is, a sort of blank screen onto whom transference was made possible. It is well known that Freud insisted to Fliess on the enormous impact that his father's death had on him. Years after his disengagement with his Berliner colleague, in the preface to the second edition of *The Interpretation of Dreams*, written in 1908, Freud declared: "For this book has a further subjective significance for me personally—a significance which I only grasped after I had completed it. It was, I found, a portion of my own self-analysis, my reaction to my father's death—that is to say, to the most important event, the most poignant loss, of a man's life."[5]

As Peter Gay has described, during this time Freud did not only grieve his father's death, but also shifted his neurological studies into psychological pursuits, a serious theoretical and personal change in his scientific doctrine.[6] The contentiousness of Freud's self-analysis was precisely the way in which he was able to "translate feelings into theory," that is, apply his personal experience to a generality with the support of his case studies. In this regard, Gay writes: "It was exceptional, too, in the way he put it [his father's death] to scientific use, distancing himself from his loss, and at the same time gathering material for his theories."[7] Granting universal value to a singular case can be misleading and inadequate, but, as Forrester points out, "thinking in cases" is what has led psychoanalysis to comprehend a certain particularity through a systemically enriching task.[8] Freud's famous case studies depict this essentially: they illustrate a form of incorporating the singular simultaneously with the universal.

In his correspondence with Fliess, we find a few letters that can help explain this. For example, in "Draft N" (May 31, 1897), the first glimpse of the Oedipus complex is described as follows: "Hostile impulses against parents (a wish that they should die) are also an integrating constituent of neuroses. . . . It seems as though this death wish is directed in sons against their fathers and in daughters against their mothers."[9] This draft is defiantly completed by stating that incest is antisocial.

Likewise, in "Letter 69" (September 21, 1897), after completing his *yahrzeit*, Freud asserts: "I no longer believe in my *neurotica*."[10] This *neurotica*, although many people have confused "her" with one of his patients, is clearly Freud talking about his theory—more precisely, his seduction theory. He no longer believed that trauma was caused by a direct impact upon an individual in some sort of factual seduction (e.g., perverted fathers or child abuse), but by the production of fantasies that entail incestuous or parricidal desires. Thus, Freud shifts from his theory of seduction to his theory of fantasy. In his next letter, written on October 3, 1897, Freud expresses his ambivalent feelings concerning the active role his deceased father had played during his life, especially during the past year.

Finally, in "Letter 71" (October 15, 1897), barely a year after his father's death, we find the first eponymous statement concerning the Oedipus complex: "A single idea of general value dawned on me. I have found, in my own case too, [the phenomenon of] being in love with my mother and jealous of my father, and I now consider it a universal event in early childhood."[11] Hence, we are left with two impressions concerning the initial edification of this concept: first, the Oedipus complex supplants the resolution of Freud's period of mourning, thus his "legacy" (or merely his neurotic solution) is granted, and second, it is universal (but only from a masculine perspective). Indeed, these contradictions need further clarification.

During Freud's Easter holidays in 1898, something curious took place in the caves near the town of Divača, in Slovenia (Rudolfova Vilenica, as the cave was called back then).[12] In his letter of April 14, 1898, describing an encounter he had, Freud tells Fliess "it was Tartarus itself" and then makes a brief reference to Dante's *Inferno*.[13] Who did Freud engage with in the dark depths of Slovenia? Nobody other than Karl Lueger, the mayor of Vienna and the founder of the Christian Social Party, a political party with a strong antisemitic doctrine. As Mladen Dolar underlines: "The image deserves to be seen, in retrospect, as an emblematic icon inaugurating the century, laden with forebodings of so much of what was to happen."[14] In addition, this image is also suitable to contemplate on Freud's enduring mourning process and working-through (wasn't this "the most important event, the most poignant loss, of a man's life"?). We can speculate that while going into a cave resembles entering a grave, Freud proceeded into the realms of the (unconscious) underworld in search of his *dead father*, but instead he found a more ominous figure, an *Unheimlich* to his ambivalent affliction, he came across the *dark father* (Lueger).

Certainly, Freud was busy with his self-analysis—an activity he performed daily, even ceremoniously—and his shifting theory. Still, the outcome of this enterprise came to fruition, and we can acknowledge two major assets for such meritorious efforts: (1) the discovery of infantile sexuality (the emergence of the Oedipus complex), and (2) dream analyses (the emergence of the unconscious). Infantile sexuality and the unconscious intertwined to inaugurate what Freud would properly coin back in 1896 as psychoanalysis.

If, indeed, Freud's neurotic resolution of his mourning process was the Oedipus complex turned into a "universal event," then we must consider that this was, at least partially, an unfair characterization. Let us remember that in his seminal work *Three Essays on the Theory of Sexuality*, published in 1905, he never mentioned the complex by name, other than two extended footnotes that were incorporated into the text in 1920, and a brief allusion to the sphinx's riddle.[15] However, this sort of grieving outcome led Freud to understand that this *kern-komplex* brought in itself an add-on, not as a supplement or positivity, but as a remainder of the function as such, an extant model of the mind with a singularity concerning its structure—the feelings Freud expressed during this period were all too ambivalent. Freud's solution was not the "universal" construction that has been refuted correctly (i.e., masculine universals), but the fact that in its kernel the oedipal function is, essentially, ambivalent. This ambivalence presents itself as the extimate relation of the particular and the universal, whereby Oedipus as a nomination exposes Freud's own irresolution with regard to the function of the *Vaterkomplex*.

The Question of Universals on the Couch, a Particular Extimacy

Why is it crucial to undertake the question of universals (at least from a psychoanalytical perspective), given that there is a generation of contemporary thinkers and militant political activism that seems to repudiate it on decolonial grounds? In this sense, we must lay the ground of what specifically extimacy grants towards a different comprehension of universals. This is the central interest in turning to the topic of the *kern-komplex*.

In 1901, Freud modestly described his self-analysis as a sheer "self-observation." A question thus immediately arises: What is behind this pioneering attempt that allows for an individuality to emulate a universal status? As we have seen before, Freud's case studies, although erroneous in many interpretative ways, point towards the fundamental anchor for psychoanalytical praxis, its particularity demarcated from other discourses, and hence its singularity. While other scientific fields, according to Dolar, guarantee the form of the repeatable as an experiment that is "universally available" and thus assure "objectivity and verification," psychoanalysis differs considerably: "in psychoanalysis one constantly deals only with the singular, the singularity of symptoms, the singularity of a particular unconscious, i.e., one deals with the non-repeatable, and it is from the singular that the universal has to be constructed."[16] Here we run, though, into a sticky situation. Can we consider private observations of one's own neurosis (at best!) to be a repeatable experience for the generality of cases? In other words, is this form of universality just another mode of production due to Freud's epochal and woeful bereavement—that is, a self-reflection at most?

In its history as a psychoanalytical concept, the Oedipus complex has been decidedly criticized for its claim to universality. Althusser described it as a production stemming from a field of knowledge, properly speaking, an *episteme*, where the concept would be reduced to merely an ideological state apparatus. Lévi-Strauss could not endorse its universality given the "elementary" structures of kinship; for Deleuze and Guattari in *Anti-Oedipus* (already a title giving a subtle impression of coming attractions), the complex is the ultimate territoriality; Irigaray refuted it by questioning the control placed on female sexuality centered entirely around the lack and penis envy, while opening a new chapter to psychoanalytical theory and praxis. But what exactly is at stake here?

Nevertheless, despite these criticisms, allow me to mention two comments about the mishaps of psychoanalysis and explain this situation from a different angle. First, Judith Butler, while discussing the notion of hegemony, stresses the proclivity for establishing universals while not rethinking what they actually mean.[17] She writes: "The fear, of course, is that what is named as universal is the parochial property of dominant culture, and that 'universalizability' is indissociable from imperial expansion."[18] In such a case, universality is not a cultural translation of phenomena, nor should it be considered as an "empty" place which can be filled by specific contents (e.g., colonial aims). In this remark, Butler argues that "no concept of universality can ever be all-encompassing, and that were it to enclose all possible contents, it would not only close the concept of time, but ruin the political efficacy of universality itself. Universality belongs to an open-ended hegemonic struggle."[19] It is on this "open-ended struggle" that we should focus our attention, since the intention of the *kern-komplex* from a Freudian perspective (that is, metapsychology) is not meant to enclose a certain particularity; on the contrary, it is there to unfasten it. Yet this is also where I diverge from Butler's thesis, as she argues that to sustain the universal as universal is possible "only to the extent that it remains untainted by what is particular, concrete, and individual."[20] Clearly, this is at odds with what I have described regarding psychoanalytic singularity and its universal meandering.

Second, recall Paul B. Preciado's now infamous intervention on November 17, 2019, at the 49th *Journées* of the École de la Cause Freudienne. In short, Preciado argued against the binary position of the sexes in psychoanalysis, a clear jab at oedipal theory, as well as its heteropatriarchal colonialism, an impressive uppercut to psychoanalytic practice.[21] Preciado is partly correct in making these attacks when he states that psychoanalysis, since its origins, was always outdated in its repetitive imposition of ever-normalizing models of adaption onto individuals. By committing to his criticism that psychoanalysis only accommodates its subjects to heteronormative standards (or colonial patriarchy), especially when "shaping" the sexes into binary positions (a project already studied by Foucault in the 1970s), Preciado appears to point to an undiscovered dimension of psychoanalysis. In this sense, he is rightly certain that there are particular practices that have operated like this within the psychoanalytical dome. However, what Preciado seems to miss is the fact that Freud's theory of sexuality originated from a universal premise: bisexuality (i.e., non-binary). There is no a priori quality to the Oedipus complex other than its symbolic function, and thus the way contingency accommodates itself has, evidently, an outpouring on sociopolitical ideologies that manifest themselves as driving forces of subjection (not subjectivity).[22] Can we think of psychoanalysis as a queer practice, or, in such terms, having a proper *trans-* methodology? This is unlikely, not because of counter-indicative reasons, but mainly due to the fact that such mutant qualities are substantially at the core of psychoanalysis, so such delimitation seems a bit redundant. In this regard, psychoanalysis has always been queer,[23] and trans- too, or as Patricia Gherovici points out, "the human infant *becomes sexed* without fully symbolizing unconsciously a normal, finished sexual positioning."[24] Clearly, the psychoanalytical phallic dream of totality is utterly pointless, but it is not without its adverse mechanisms that require bold refutations such as Preciado's viewpoint.

Therefore, how are we to argue against these positions, when we support their political efforts that openly demand justice in the face of psychoanalytical misdemeanors? Must we discuss these positions from a different theoretical perspective? All in all, is the Oedipus complex universal, or is it simply a contingent production that has lingered in popular culture all through the Second World War up to today? In this context, our examination of Lacan's early seminars provides us with an intricate solution to Butler's and Preciado's challenges, not only at the level of extimacy but further in formulating a contradistinctive interpretation to the *kern-komplex* posed by Freud. In his second seminar, Lacan states that "the Oedipus complex is both universal and contingent, because it is uniquely and purely symbolic."[25] This statement cries out for an immediate explanation. In order to understand this provocative claim, we should first briefly consider what exactly the symbolic order is. According to Lacan, the symbolic universe functions much like a totality: "In order to conceive what happens in the domain proper to the human order, we must start with the idea that this order constitutes a totality. In the symbolic order the totality is called a universe. The symbolic order from the first takes on its universal character. It isn't constituted bit by bit. . . . Constituting the emergence of the symbolic function as such in human life, [the symbols] imply the totality of everything which is human."[26] This, evidently, is the marrow of the bone: while individual symbols are constitutive of the symbolic order, it is only through the universality of this (symbolic) function that this contingency of symbols is actually made possible, and thus the connection between the singular achieving a universal condition is only comprehensible if such a function actually exists.

Although Butler's objection may indicate that "the universal will not be founded in a linguistic or psychic condition of the subject" (as she follows Zerilli's rebuttal to Laclau's definition), it is important to point out why this feature is crucial in order to grasp the difference between the psychoanalytical subject and other definitions. This is why bestselling books on dream interpretations really only offer a quasi-universal solution by leaving the arbitrariness of the signifier out of the equation. While the founder of psychoanalysis was using his own dreams as an additional source of material (but not exclusively), he reflected intensely upon the commitment to a contingent origin and its universal function. This is, thus, what is accepted as the Oedipus complex's genuine extimacy: the non-duplicity of each patient shouldn't be taken as an obstacle for praxis; rather, it should be granted as the key to confronting the perils of a closed and sterile theory. The exterior folds onto itself as it constitutes an interiority that unfolds a singular and unique historicity. As hinted above in our introductory remarks, to be extimate is comparable to being "proximate" (*Nebenmensch*), where what is "nuclear" comprises its "exteriority" in an ambivalent nature of shifting subjectivities: extimacy is precisely the constitutive fracture of the universal.

Another note that may be useful to understanding this claim is Lacan's intervention in Baltimore in 1966. By being invited to participate in a "structuralist" symposium, Lacan returned to a concept he had previously exposed in his third seminar ten years before: *l'immixtion des sujets*. The notion of "inmixing" corresponds to the subjects (in plural) not as isolated but also not as collective. During one of his responses, Lacan ardently insisted that Goldmann's subject is "the subject of knowledge, the support (false or not) of a whole world of objects." And Lacan continued: "What seems to me to be the subject is really something which is not *intra* nor *extra* nor *inter*subjective. . . . Such then is my question, on the level of this *gap*—which does not fit into *intra* or *inter* or *extra*subjectivity— that the question of the subject must be posed."[27] This is perhaps one of the most exquisite definitions of extimacy that we can come across in all of Lacan's teaching. If the subject is neither individual nor collective, there must be an extimate function for its proper constitution, and such an operation can only be attainted precisely through the symbolic universe: ergo, the function of a limit by placing the subject on the level of this gap.

In such case, we must still contest the idea as to why we allow ourselves to take Freud's working-through and turn it into an influential theory. In this regard, Žižek commits himself to a similar approach while asking why Kieslowski is still relevant and universal. In *The Fright of Real Tears*, Žižek explains: "All great historical assertions of universal values... are firmly embedded in a concrete social constellation. However, one should avoid here the historicist trap: this unique circumstance does not account for the 'truth' and universal scope of the analyzed phenomenon. It is precisely against such hasty historicists that one should refer to Marx's famous observation apropos of Homer: it is easy to explain how Homer's poetry emerged from early Greek society; what is much more difficult to explain is its universal appeal, i.e., why it continues to exert its charm even today."[28] Why, after all these years of attacks on oedipal theory, are people (and psychoanalysts) still clinging to this "obsolete" concept? Let us look at this from a different angle—that is, from Freud's couch. An item of furniture that is more than furniture itself, its main purpose—beyond any form of nostalgic anachronism and the obvious incitement of free association—is to serve as a locus where an unprecedented production may occur. Thus, every oedipal singularity is to be considered exceptional. The experience of analysis is precisely this aperture that involves the lodgment of contingency and the effects it has on encountering universality.

On Ambivalence, or Not

In psychoanalysis, "ambivalence" arrived through Swiss psychiatry. On multiple occasions, Freud didn't hesitate to acknowledge the influence that Eugen Bleuler and his "happily chosen" (*glücklich*) term had on his theory, a concept borrowed from his article "Vortrag über Ambivalenz," published in the *Zentralblatt für Psychanalyse* in 1910. What is important to highlight is that for Bleuler, "ambivalence" held three registers for the comprehension of schizophrenia: (1) volitional (on action: to eat or not to eat), (2) intellectual (a single sentence may include an affirmation and its opposite simultaneously), and (3) affective (dissociation between love and hate). This last record, indeed, caught Freud's attention. In an excerpt that he added to the 1915 edition of *Three Essays*, Freud states that sexual organization "is further characterized by the fact that in it the opposing pairs of [drives] are developed to an approximately equal extent, a state of affairs described by Bleuler's happily chosen term 'ambivalence.' "[29] In addition, merged with the multiple footnotes that Freud added to this text throughout the years, we observe that the complete sixth part of the second essay, "The Phases of Development of the Sexual Organization," was aggregated in its entirety in 1915, including the "Pregenital Organizations" and "Diphasic Choice of Object" sections. It comes as no surprise that Freud employed the concept of ambivalence successively throughout his entire opus, from his case studies throughout his papers on technique up to his last days, inasmuch as when he announced, in 1938, in *An Outline of Psychoanalysis*: "This transference is ambivalent: it comprises positive and affectionate as well as negative and hostile attitudes towards the analyst, who, as a rule, is put in the place of one or other of the patient's parents, his father or his mother."[30] In short, both transference and sexuality are effectively traversed by ambivalence.

According to Freudian theory, the weight granted to this concept goes beyond any single source (e.g., father, religion, grief). In a strict sense, Freud's notion of ambivalence had a deeper influence on the rest of his theory, especially on the roots of subjectivity (and Lacanian extimacy), as demonstrated in the previous section. Thus, it is important to reassess the influence this concept had upon sexuality, object-choice, and transference, since it is mainly due to this term that most of his metapsychological oeuvre can be formulated, notably in the heart of drive theory. Nevertheless, psychoanalytical ambivalence, in a Freudian sense, must not be understood as a "triumph of emotions," as Tadej Troha demonstrates in his remarkable article "On Ambivalence."[31] The concept does not appear at the level of the predicate as an expression of the type "I feel ambivalent." On the contrary, it is the fundamental condition that remains situated at the level of the subject as the core of experience. To sum things up, ambivalence does not necessarily exist as the opposition of pairs, or oscillatory forces, but above all it is there to indicate a clear-cut division, a gap—a sort of neither here nor there, and/or split in subjectivity—an intrinsic constitutive "exteriority," so to speak.

For sure, many post-Freudians left the concept of ambivalence almost neglected. This inattention is perhaps mainly due to the fact that Karl Abraham was one of the first-generation Freudians to actually develop a theory about it, sadly an approach that diverged from Freud.[32] Abraham's notion of ambivalence, which later influenced Melanie Klein's theory, postulated three stages in relation to libido organization, while achieving character formation and object-love: (1) pre-ambivalent (autoerotism, without object), (2) ambivalent (narcissism, incorporation, partial love, exclusion of genitals), and (3) post-ambivalent (object-love). Abraham's theory insinuates that ambivalence is something to overcome in order to achieve object-love at a genital stage. Unfortunately, this misses the target precisely because it implies the possibility of integrating an object into a totality while leaving the contingency of the drives reduced to a sheer genital function. Weren't the drives above all invariably partial? This theoretical approach already has many rightly at the brink of indignation.

For his part, Lacan was never comfortable with this coinage. Perhaps it reminded him of the inappropriate steps taken by Lagache's rather prudish article "L'Amour et la haine" ("Love and Hate"), published in 1939. Despite his harsh criticism of Freudian "ambivalence," Lacan did not hesitate to propose an alternative that is quite debatable. In his seminar "Encore," Lacan begins his lecture on March 20, 1973: "What I willingly write for you today as *hainamoration*,[33] is the depth (*relief*) psychoanalysis was able to introduce in order to situate the zone of its experience. . . . If only it had been able to call it by some other name than the bastardized one of 'ambivalence,' perhaps it would have succeeded better in shaking up the historical setting in which it inserted itself."[34] Here, Lacan equips his neologism to illustrate precisely what is called the "zone of experience," or the couch's contingent core.

Apart from understanding ambivalence as the struggle between opposites that fluctuate from one end to the other, from love to hate and vice versa, what Troha detects in the Freudian concept of ambivalence is not only an abounding gratitude towards Bleuler but the conditions to comprehend this "oscillation." (In this regard, this is what we consider the core element of extimacy: the inner world as a folding of history, economics and culture.)[35] According to Troha, Freud discovered not simply that "ambivalence exists only in the material that appears in the form of a multitude of ambivalences": for example, pairs of opposites, positive and negative transference, *Vaterkomplex*, affects, drive theory.[36] But mainly, according to Troha, Freud recognized another signature to speak about the kernel of psychoanalysis: analytical experience. When ambivalence speaks, the experience on the couch "stops not being written."

As such, ambivalence can be examined as simply another name for analysis. Due to this peculiar characteristic, psychoanalysis is not meant to be a "cure" for civilization and its discontents, but it is mainly because of this distinctiveness that psychoanalysis posits itself *as* civilization's discontent. That is why, given their ambivalent traits, Freud considered politics, education, and psychoanalysis as impossible professions.

What Is the *Vaterkomplex*?

In *Vocabulaire de la psychanalyse*, perhaps the most popular dictionary in psychoanalytical literature nowadays, the following scanty description appears concerning the entry *Vaterkomplex*: "Term used by Freud to designate one of the chief dimensions of the Oedipus complex: the ambivalent relation to the father."[37] It is worth noting that after such a concise definition is offered, there is no thorough explanation that follows (unlike most of the entries included in the dictionary). Immediately the authors guide the reader towards the entry *Oedipus complex*, but there is not much attention given to the expression there either. It almost feels like this picture is left inconclusive intentionally, even fragmentary. The same inadequacy is present in other psychoanalytical lexicons, where the aforementioned concept is not even included in many of them. Only Pierre Fédida's work of 1974 does justice to Freud's encompassing concept: "[*Vaterkomplex*] designates the ambivalent relation with respect to the father, and at the Oedipus's center entails this complex. This ambivalence (admiration, love, fear) is conceived at the same time depending on the cross-game of identifications, taking into account the bisexual position of the subject with his parents."[38] Indeed, the *Vaterkomplex* is at the epicenter of ambivalence. As we can observe, the discarded concept (by many) is open to more signification than the centrality of a father figure; it is coalescent of deeper metapsychological implications such as identification, sexuality, and object-choice.

Freud made few direct references to the *Vaterkomplex* and never offered a concrete and ultimate definition of it, but *Totem and Taboo* is perhaps where this term is most extensively defined. Although this is not the place to inquire into each annotation, it is clear that Freud commits his theory to the existence of ambivalence in relation to the *Urvater* (or totemic animal), religion, loss, cannibalism, grief, and particularly love. For example, regarding the displacement of the father onto other figures, Freud states: "The child finds relief from the conflict arising out of this double-sided, this ambivalent emotional attitude towards his father by displacing his hostile and fearful feelings on to a *substitute* for his father. The displacement cannot . . . bring the conflict to an end, it cannot effect a clear-cut severance between the affectionate and the hostile feelings."[39] Freud here is clearly reminiscent of Little Hans. But, what about the mother?

In popular Freudianism, the function of a limit (castration) usually implied the father exclusively. In this traditional sense, it seems that Freud reduced the purpose of the mother to a mere breast-function or partial object. However, this is not the case, or at least this is not my reading of Freudian metapsychology. Nevertheless, the *Vater* involved in the *komplex* does signal towards a possible particularity, leaving the *Mutter* side completely unaddressed. André Green has pointed in this direction by stating the equal function of a *Vaterkomplex* sidelong to a *Mutterkomplex*, thus eliminating any gender-based argumentation.[40] Thus, wasn't Lacan's attribution of omnipotence to *la mère crocodile* not a clear opposition corresponding to Freud's almighty *Urvater*? So, we must emphasize that in psychoanalysis not everything is about the father or about the mother; it involves both and concurrently it doesn't. The predominance of this *kernkomplex* rests solely in their symbolic function and its ambivalence. Their extimate function is only present as that which "cannot bring the conflict to an end." To this extent, this should not be read as an apologia for the father/mother figures, since such cases don't need justification because they have proven to falter. What is in need of defense is their (symbolic) function, the remainder of what is left after such figures wobble (isn't this the whole objective of adolescent years?). The question is not whether we are to prevail in a hysterical discourse endlessly, but rather, are we condemned to cathect the world and others ambivalently forevermore?

One way to look into this problem is by going back to Lacan's discourse theory.[41] In his seminar *The Other Side of Psychoanalysis*, Lacan explains how a master position hides an inner division. The S_1 (the master-signifier) thus disguises itself in order to bury the essential $, or constitutive split. In this sense, the conclusion that Lacan attends to is that the "reverse" side of psychoanalysis is, in fact, the master's discourse. Henceforth, there is no certainty that psychoanalysis will tilt back to dire mastery other than the maneuver set forth by the ethics of desire; in other words, the analytical experience that has stumbled upon the rock of castration (a limit in itself) and what has remained of this process, consequently, ambivalence.

As of 1913, Freud's main concern was not only focused on the origins of culture. He was also trying to reassure the politics of the psychoanalytical institution (the International Psychoanalytic Association was founded in 1910) while setting the grounds for a properly "enlightened" technique: this period presented an ambivalent struggle vis-à-vis hostile feelings towards Jung and an endearment towards Ferenczi. Indeed, we can only speculate if this conflict turned the IPA into still another association for the continuation of the *Urvater* rather than confronting the ambivalence arising from the *Vaterkomplex*, a parochial endeavor dangerously transforming psychoanalysis into a deplorable possible "new religion."[42] Thus, from a political perspective, Preciado's intervention is truly outstanding for the reason that the institutionalization of psychoanalysis, while necessary for its growth and development, has also meant its enclosure and debacle, thus harboring an elitist normative discourse (heteropatriarchal colonialism) for the adjustment of the sexes at its heart. However, Preciado fails to attend to a key element that precisely contributes to what we have called "analytical experience." While every (sexual) body is marked by a medical or juridical discourse, much too violently imposed, it is important to understand that the "apex of contingency" (the singularity of each body) "stops not being written," pushing Lacan to enunciate the following: "Analysis presumes that desire is inscribed on the basis of a corporeal contingency."[43] But what does this mean regarding extimacy?

Advocating against decrepit psychoanalytical father-models and transforming them into new epistemologies of sexuality, indeed, implies the utmost necessary renovation of psychoanalysis in light of the contemporary challenges set forth by its sociopolitical reality (i.e., gender politics). However, these "new" epistemologies, which we need to rethink adamantly as psychoanalysts, seem to bring forth an ambiguous objection in the form of "choice" viewed not only as "the hallmark of modernity" but also as infinite; in short, they tend to imply that all possibilities are to be made available. In his rebuttal to Preciado's intervention, Jean-Claude Maleval is clear to point out that analytical experience (or the pass, in Lacanian terms) reminds us that a limit (and thus a split/division) is always at hand to stumble upon,[44] be it castration or *jouissance*.[45] Isn't analytical experience essentially the experience of skimming such a limit? In this fashion, the experience of analysis is nothing more than the actualization of this clear-cut limit by the contingency of the signifier through a corporeal struggle (no matter what the choice may be). It is strictly due to this peculiarity that analysis is a ceaseless exertion, coeval with its perpetual impossibility of not relinquishing the core element in its practice—specifically, ambivalence as something not to abdicate but to endure. Aren't these *trans-* qualities a constant psychic achievement we see in everyday analysis through transference?

What, then, is the intention of transference, other than to solely remain ambivalent continuously? Transference is meant to be dissolved, understood in Freudian terms as an *Untergang* (so is the Oedipus complex). But does this imply the complete evanescence of ambivalence in order to suppress the *kern-komplex* which is almost obliterated in contemporary debates? I believe not. This sort of resolution is what could be described as an intervention sprouting from a notion of psychoanalysis as a "deficit theory"; for example, if there is a lack to readjust, then the psychoanalyst holds the fortunate remedy for it. On the contrary, I believe that psychoanalytical praxis is more akin to what Althusser defined as a "conflictual science,"[46] an engagement where the resolution is not a patch on the animosity between systems, or oppositions within bickering arguments, but an "open-ended struggle." Without the necessary conflict involved from internal/external forces—extimacy par excellence—there would be no subjectivity. In this way, the Other is not there to cover or disavow lack itself but rather to reveal it. So, in agreement with Lacan, without this symbolic function (*kern-komplex*), transference would be utterly inconceivable.[47]

Finally, recalling a Kantian "joke" that Dolar once told during a seminar, one cannot help but wonder about the adequacies of Kant's lesson for today's politics. In *The Contest of Faculties*, Kant places philosophy not only on the weaker side of the faculties (in opposition to the stronger faction such as theology, law, and medicine), but also on the left side of the body.[48] It is then that he pursues his claim by declaring that Prussian infantrymen know this assertion by heart, since they are trained to step on the left foot in order to jump over a ditch and give way to the right foot ready to attack. What Dolar comically points to is that philosophy is not only considered to be on the weaker side of the faculties but also on the Left, only to allow for the Right to emerge . . . and attack! Thus, the problem arises not on which side we are to be situated, but how to endure the everlasting marching movement of the Left and Right in perpetuity. Consequently, a radical obverse side to ambivalence is what is disastrously known as polarization.

In conclusion, analytical experience can simply be viewed as another form of ethical witness where transference marches on, confronting ambivalence as it dissolves what ideology has unified and enclosed, purely a ditch or a gap to jump over repetitiously, an attempt to break through the *Vaterkomplex*.

Notes

This essay is dedicated to Joan Copjec.

1. A clear example of such contemporary criticism can be found in Lacan's statement of how "the dimension of the unconscious" had been completely forgotten by many psychoanalysts around the 1950s, something that Freud alluded to quite often at the turn of the century as well. "The unconscious had closed itself up against his message thanks to those active practitioners of orthopaedics that the analysts of the second and third generation became, busying themselves, by psychologizing analytic theory, in stitching up this gap." Jacques Lacan, *The Four Fundamental Concepts of Psychoanalysis*, ed. Jacques-Alain Miller, trans. Alan Sheridan, vol. 11 of The Seminar of Jacques Lacan (New York: Norton, 1998), 23. In this regard, it is precisely the next generation of psychoanalysts who have sealed off the gap of the unconscious by filling it with present-day contingent

substitutes like cognitive-behavioral therapies and overly demanding pharmaceutical interventions, or even by posing neuropsychology as the next phase of psychoanalysis. While many rebuttals have come from other disciplines, I will focus on the work exercised by contemporary psychoanalysts in order to give way to such disproof.

2. Jacques Lacan, *The Ego in Freud's Theory and in the Technique of Psychoanalysis*, ed. Jacques-Alain Miller, trans. Sylvana Tomaselli, vol. 2 of The Seminar of Jacques Lacan (New York: Norton, 1991).

3. Paul Verhaeghe, *New Studies of Old Villains* (New York: Other Press, 2009).

4. Although many traditions (i.e., sociology, feminism, or phenomenology) have insisted on ambiguity as a condition for subjectivity, I will focus my attention on the Freudian concept of ambivalence. While the term "ambiguous" stems from the sixteenth-century Latin root *ambiguus*, connoted as "having double meaning, doubtful," the concept of ambivalence originated much later in 1910, coined by Eugen Bleuler and referring not only to affects but also to a force: *ambi-* (both sides) + *valentia* (strength).

5. Sigmund Freud, *The Interpretation of Dreams*, trans. and ed. James Strachey, vol. 4 of *The Standard Edition of the Complete Psychological Works of Sigmund Freud* (London: Hogarth, 1955), xxvi.

6. Peter Gay, *Freud: A Life for Our Time* (New York: Norton, 2006).

7. Gay, *Freud*, 88.

8. John Forrester, *Thinking in Cases* (Cambridge: Polity, 2017).

9. Jeffrey Moussaieff Masson, trans. and ed., *The Complete Letters of Sigmund Freud to Wilhelm Fliess* (Cambridge, MA: Belknap Press of Harvard University Press, 1985), 250.

10. Masson, *Complete Letters of Sigmund Freud to Wilhelm Fliess*, 264.

11. Masson, *Complete Letters of Sigmund Freud to Wilhelm Fliess*, 272.

12. This reference comes directly from Mladen Dolar's article "Freud and the Political," to which I am greatly indebted. See Mladen Dolar, "Freud and the Political," *Unbound* 4, no. 15 (2008): 15–29.

13. Masson, *Complete Letters of Sigmund Freud to Wilhelm Fliess*, 309.

14. Dolar, "Freud and the Political," 16.

15. The Oedipus complex first appeared in psychoanalytic literature in 1910. See Sigmund Freud, "A Special Type of Choice of Object Made by Men (Contributions to the Psychology of Love I)," in *Five Lectures on Psycho-Analysis, Leonardo da Vinci, and Other Works*, trans. and ed. James Strachey, vol. 11 of *The Standard Edition of the Complete Psychological Works of Sigmund Freud* (London: Hogarth, 1955), 163–76.

16. Dolar, "Freud and the Political," 18.

17. Judith Butler, "Restaging the Universal: Hegemony and the Limits of Formalism," in *Contingency, Hegemony and Universality*, by Judith Butler, Ernesto Laclau, and Slavoj Žižek (London: Verso, 2000).

18. Butler, "Restaging the Universal," 15.

19. Butler, "Restaging the Universal," 38.

20. Butler, "Restaging the Universal," 23.

21. Paul B. Preciado, "Intervención en las Jornadas No. 49 de la École

de la Cause Freudienne" (presentation, November 17, 2019), drive.google.com/file/d/1qRc0SPPhfKkM2cu1ByLnNfpC_z50lke0/view. See Paul B. Preciado, *Can the Monster Speak? Report to an Academy of Psychoanalysts* (South Pasadena, CA: Semiotext(e), 2021).

22. For a further debate, see Lacan's formulae of sexuation. In short, the feminine and masculine positions are different ways to relate to castration, two views that seem to intersect but never actually blend.

23. Jamieson Webster, "Interview with Jamieson Webster," interview by Fiona Alison Duncan, *The White Review*, January 2020, www.thewhitereview.org/feature/interview-jamieson-webster/.

24. Patricia Gherovici, *Please Select Your Gender* (New York: Routledge, 2010), 5.

25. Lacan, *The Ego in Freud's Theory*, 33.

26. Lacan, *The Ego in Freud's Theory*, 29.

27. Jacques Lacan, "Of Structure as an Inmixing of an Otherness Prerequisite to Any Subject Whatever," in *The Structuralist Controversy*, ed. Richard Macksey and Eugenio Donato (Baltimore, MD: Johns Hopkins University Press, 1972), 121–22.

28. Slavoj Žižek, *The Fright of Real Tears* (London: Palgrave Macmillan, 2001), 8.

29. Sigmund Freud, *Three Essays on the Theory of Sexuality* (1905), in *A Case of Hysteria, Three Essays on Sexuality, and Other Works*, trans. and ed. James Strachey, vol. 7 of *The Standard Edition of the Complete Psychological Works of Sigmund Freud* (London: Hogarth, 1953).

30. Sigmund Freud, "An Outline of Psychoanalysis," in *Moses and Monotheism, An Outline of Psycho-Analysis and Other Works*, trans. and ed. James Strachey, vol. 23 of *The Standard Edition of the Complete Psychological Works of Sigmund Freud* (London: Hogarth, 1955), 52.

31. Tadej Troha, "On Ambivalence," *Problemi International* 1, no. 1 (2017): 217–44.

32. Karl Abraham, "A Short Study of the Development of the Libido, Viewed in the Light of Mental Disorders," in *Selected Papers of Karl Abraham* (New York: Basic Books, 1953), 418–501.

33. A Lacanian neologism, *hainamoration* is composed of the noun *haine* (hate) and the adjective *enamore* (enamored).

34. Jacques Lacan, *On Feminine Sexuality, the Limits of Love and Knowledge*, ed. Jacques-Alain Miller, trans. Bruce Fink, vol. 20 of The Seminar of Jacques Lacan (New York: Norton, 1999), 90–91.

35. See David Pavón-Cuéllar, *Sobre el vacío* (Mexico: Paradiso Editores, 2022).

36. Troha, "On Ambivalence," 221.

37. Jean Laplanche and J.-B. Pontalis, *Vocabulaire de la psychanalyse* (Paris: Presses Universitaires de France, 1984), 84.

38. Pierre Fédida, *Diccionario de psicoanálisis* (Madrid: Alianza, 1988), 51.

39. Sigmund Freud, *Totem and Taboo and Other Works, 1913–1914*, trans. and

ed. James Strachey, vol. 13 of *The Standard Edition of the Complete Psychological Works of Sigmund Freud* (London: Hogarth, 1958), 129.

40. André Green, *Conferencias en México*, vol. 1 (Mexico: Paradiso Editores, 2011).

41. Jacques Lacan, *The Other Side of Psychoanalysis*, ed. Jacques-Alain Miller, trans. Russell Grigg, vol. 17 of The Seminar of Jacques Lacan (New York: Norton, 2007).

42. Julia Kristeva, "Psychoanalysis and the Polis," in *The Kristeva Reader*, ed. Toril Moi (Oxford: Basil Blackwell, 1986), 301–20.

43. Lacan, *On Feminine Sexuality*, 93.

44. Jean-Claude Maleval, "Quand Preciado interpelle la psychanalyse," *Lacan Quotidien* 859 (2019): 1–4.

45. *Jouissance* "indicates the limit between a pleasure arising from the drive that can be controlled and one that cannot, thus threatening us (in our imagination) with the loss of our sense of identity." Verhaeghe, *New Studies of Old Villains*, 13.

46. Louis Althusser and Étienne Balibar, *Para leer El Capital* (Mexico: Siglo XXI, 1969).

47. Lacan, *The Ego in Freud's Theory*.

48. Immanuel Kant, *El conflicto de las facultades* (Buenos Aires: Losada, 2004).

What Is a Body?

A Question between Critical Theory and Psychoanalysis

Silvio Carneiro

What is a body? This question seeks to understand the body in terms of extimacy.[1] Following Lacan, David Pavon-Cuellar defines extimacy as that which "joins *ex-teriority* with *in-timacy*, and states explicitly the interpenetration and mutual transformation of both spheres."[2] So, the question "what *is* a body?" does not result in a definition, a limit; instead, it connects a corporeal concept with multiple relations. What is at stake in this Lacanian reading is the form of appearance of the body beyond the physiological image. The question, then, can be posed as follows: *How many relations can a singular body support?* In addition to the body as organism, there are social relations that constitute the body and its identity. Modern political philosophy uses metaphors such as "political body," which is the case when people occupy streets in demonstrations or disappear under necropolitical rules. As a result of these different relations, the body is understood as a part of ourselves as well as the social structure. These multiple relations compel questions about the body that concern both intimate and exterior constitutions in our contemporary world. In this sense, this essay assumes that the body is a boundary between inner/outer, individual/social, and, as will be demonstrated below, biological/symbolic. Consequently, the ontological question about the body demands a critical position sustained by the frontier itself, as an open relation mediated by its extremes. However, these introductory reflections pose a further question: Can we conceive the body from its boundary-position? As a frontier, the body is neither solely an individual element nor purely social; rather, it is simultaneously inner as well as outer. "What *is* a body?" assumes this extimate (dis)placement as a part of its fundamental question.

The concept of extimacy is crucial for understanding the boundaries of such relations. These two extremes—inner and outer—contact each other through a short-circuit, encapsulated by Rimbaud's formula: "I is an other" (*Je est un autre*). However, we should avoid a naive understanding of such a connection, as Lacan reminds us in his second seminar; if we interpret this motto as an equivalent identity (I = other), the extimate value will be worthless.[3] Extimacy differs from the juxtaposition of the "I" as an "other" or vice versa. Here, Lacan warns against a meaningless dialectics of abstract equivalence between "I and the other." The immediate reflection of I and the other includes everything, it is another way to say nothing about nothing. According to Lacan, such a general abstraction can be avoided by focusing on the means that mediate the other and the I. That is, extimacy does not absolutize either one of the two parts of this relationship. Neither the other nor the I are isolated parts of a relationship. On the contrary, extimacy arises when corresponding elements emerge as elements structured by the boundaries of the relations between the other and the I. In this sense, social and organic bodies involve multiple relations and their elements. In fact, the body works as a frontier that separates the other and I and brings them close. Extimacy reveals the distances and the proximities among different entities, and in this way, the body is constituted by apertures and closures; it is a dynamic structure with multiple variations, where boundaries continuously shift their positions. That is, the body is an extimate element, which disrupts reified identities and displaces fixed relations as well. This understanding of the body troubles a fundamental element of modernity: the relationship between individual identity and its representations. In fact, the ontological question about the body haunts modernity and its history.

The first two sections of this essay will examine the body as a political instrument in modernity. Rather than beginning with Lacan, however, these sections address the body through critical theory. Although working within a vastly different framework, the theorization of the body in critical theory has strong relevance for the Lacanian notion of extimacy, and in particular, for offering it a more explicit social context. The first section will turn to Adorno and Horkheimer's *Dialectic of Enlightenment*, which presents a dual view of the body in Nazism: *Leib* as a sublimated version of the body and *Körper* as its reified version. This dual vision presents the body within a history of its domination. The second section turns to Marcuse, who also maintains this historical view of domination in late capitalism, but who posits the body as capable of resisting this political trend. The second section of this essay thus examines Marcuse's *Eros and Civilization*, with a focus on the biological trends of the Freudian theory of the instincts as an important element for understanding the potential radicality of the so-called "Great Refusal," which represents a radical negation of the status quo and a possible claim for social transformation. In fact, Marcuse considers bodies in revolt to be an important aspect of contemporary political struggles. However, does he run the risk of assuming an illusory metaphysics of nature in this revolt? This question guides the third section, which focuses on Lacan's critique of biologism in psychoanalysis, as well as his psychoanalytical view of language as fundamental to the Freudian theory of the instincts. Taking into consideration these two Lacanian interventions, this section asks: Can the views of Marcuse and Lacan—and their particular "returning to Freud"—provide a way to go beyond the biological-cultural dualism of the body? In general, it would appear that the ontological question about the body can displace the apparently fixed frontier between the biological field and the symbolical field. As an extimate element, the body opens a new horizon for this apparent dualism. Certainly, the question "what *is* a body?" engages us in this short-circuit.

Körper and *Leib*: A Critical View of the Body

Although the extimate perspective on the body comes from psychoanalysis, critical theory also exposes the body as a cultural frontier between the ruler and the ruled, an important point for understanding domination as a continuous historical movement that always maintains a division between valuable and non-valuable bodies. In a philosophical fragment presented in the *Dialectic of Enlightenment* entitled "Interest for the Body," Adorno and Horkheimer consider the "love-hate for the body" that runs through the subterranean history of Europe.[4] According to them, the body is not only a sublime model of culture but also a fundamental element of the logic of domination, from the fate of the slaves in antiquity to the colonial processes of modernity.[5] Despite the different historical contexts, Adorno and Horkheimer argue that there is a continuous logic of domination, in which the body is an element of human slavery. Yet, at the same time, they also point to the development of a sublimated body that serves as a model of culture. These dual trends of culture and barbarism reproduce a dual conception of the body. On the one hand, the reified body (*Körper*) as an object that sustains domination; on the other hand, the living body (*Leib*) that sustains a self-image of the hegemonic culture and its values for the acceptable limits of civilization. Therefore, the body in this dual history of Europe corresponds to the surface of a sublime image of the body (*Leib*), and its replicate image of the reified body (*Körper*).

In a Freudian-inspired analysis, Adorno and Horkheimer term this relation as the repressive mechanism of the psyche: besides the manifest content of the known history of Europe, there are the ruins and other historical layers which run as a subterranean history of repressed elements.[6] However, Adorno and Horkheimer do not present the subterranean layer of history as the secret of civilization that ought to be disclosed; rather, they are interested in presenting what could be termed an extimate relation between the subterranean and its surface as the relation between barbarism and civilization. In this sense, fascism has a "vantage point." As Adorno and Horkheimer ironically note: "the hidden is coming to light" when the subterranean place is juxtaposed with the surface as a dual view of this historical paradox in fascism.[7] The body as *Leib* and as *Körper* respectively corresponds to the images of the Greek gods that represent Aryan people as the ethos of beauty, and the images of rats that represent Jewish people as the converse side of this established ethos. In fact, the figure of the Aryan body as *Leib* is an empty image if there are no *Körper* to oppose or even annihilate. The body is not just the reified or sublimated substance; rather, it is the aim of ambivalent "love-hate" values. *Körper* and *Leib* share an extimate position between loved and hated bodies.

Fascism makes explicit this civilizational "love-hate" towards the body. As a strategy of humiliation, the correspondence of a body reduced to *Körper* with inferior images of rats and ill people is just the first moment of this operation. There are also moral values that sustain such a view: the "inferior" body—forbidden, reified, estranged—is the opposite of something that is desired.[8] That is, *Körper*—the body in concentration camps—sustains the fantasy of the "Beauty" of the Aryan body, the "pure" Beauty that destroys the forbidden *Körper*. *Leib* remains a stereotyped image of the Aryan body while *Körper* becomes the sign of no-body. The latter is both the concentration camp inmate and the workers of a perverse system. On the one hand, the no-body *Körper* is some sort of living being that can be killed by anyone; on the other hand, the Aryan *Leib* is the image in this mirror of perversions, sustaining a pseudo-identity forged by primordial mythos and the shadow of the *Körper*. Here, the mirror-structure creates an image of the body that cannot see itself, a blocked experience of the body. In fact, this extimate perspective shows that in fascism an Aryan *Leib* is sustained by the annihilation of *Körper*, which is both limited by the sublimated body and subjugates itself to the ideal of such a superior body. In this sense, the aesthetics of aggressiveness underpins the imaginary field of fascism: from the military uniforms to the grandiose architecture of its buildings, authoritarian destruction appears as the rule of this society.[9]

In many ways, the *Dialectic of Enlightenment* seems to present an old-fashioned perspective on the body, given that the uniform picture of the body under totalitarian regimes differs in many respects from the bodies in contemporary capitalism. It is true that something has changed. But perhaps we should not abandon what has been identified as the idea of the extimate relation between *Körper* and *Leib* so quickly. Indeed, this split view of the body is central to Marcuse's effort to describe the body in late capitalism. After World War II and during the Cold War, Marcuse discussed the body of the 1950s and the technological apparatus as follows: "Without ceasing to be an instrument of labour, the body is allowed to exhibit its sexual features in the everyday work world and in work relations."[10] Marcuse's view was grounded in sociological research on the new form of capitalism that was based on an economy of services, advertisement, and mass consumerism. In this sense, the architecture of a sexualized office is occupied by pretty, helpful secretaries and handsome, virile junior executives, rather than the bureaucratic places within the totalitarian architecture of destruction. A different *Leib* emerges in this new situation: a body completely integrated into technological devices due to the functional pleasure of taking part in this reality as the only possible choice.[11] Consequently, the *aesthetics* of *Leib* joins an ethos founded on the performative development of reality. According to Marcuse, such a corporeality is sustained by an internally divided libido. On the one hand, intensified sexual energy mobilizes the social functions of sexualized workers. On the other hand, the erotic dimension is reduced to a restricted performance inside the established reality.

Moreover, the established reality subjugates *Körper* to the abstract guarantees of law and order. If an alternative to the status quo (and the erotism within it) should appear, it is a strange body that should be isolated in ghettos or even annihilated as a dysfunctional organism. Marcuse's *Eros and Civilization* records the social struggles of that time and the violence against peripheral bodies. The freedom of men and women integrated into the values of efficacy and productivity has a cost: the shadow of the sexual libido of the integrated *Leib* is the infernal place of repressed people in decolonial wars and in the ghettos of the advanced industrial society.[12] After 1950, the status quo's repression against Black movements and the new forms of imperialism against the independence in the countries of the so-called "Third World" result in a counterrevolution, which reduces political alternatives to the reified *Körper*. In other words, these peripheral bodies appear as killable bodies, living in "pockets of misery and poverty in a growing society capable of eliminating them gradually and without a catastrophe."[13] The correspondence between *Körper* and *Leib* shifts the extimate boundaries of the body. As a historical process from World War II into the period of the Cold War, the concentration camps spread to peripheral territories around the world. There is another frontier here: the sexual *Leib* in the offices that opposes the poor *Körper* living in ghettos.

However, the relation between *Körper* and *Leib* is not unilateral. The peripheral body can represent a *Körper* for the *Leib* of the body organized by the values of the integrated and hegemonic society. At first glance, *Körper* is located in a subterranean part of the body enveloped by the aesthetic and ethical rules of *Leib* in late capitalism. However, social movements in the cultural revolution of the 1960s became connected at a point where *Körper* is no longer silent. According to Marcuse, "Black is beautiful"—a slogan of the Black movement—redefined a central concept of the *Leib*, "*kalos kagathos*," and the ethos of beauty.[14] And we can see such a revolt in many different dimensions, where colonized, young, and even working bodies appear to be fighting against the established *Leib*.

In fact, we can pose the following question: Is *Körper* just a representation of the established *Leib*? Marcuse's interpretation of the aesthetic value of the Black movement for *Leib* suggests not only a reversal of the logic of domination over bodies; it also asserts a "new sensibility," which expresses new elements for emancipation: for instance, the anticolor of darkness can be seen to have symbolic value.[15] The Lacanian conception of the mirror as an extimate relation is helpful here. It is not the case of thinking this situation as simply a reversed image, replacing black with white and vice versa, but rather as a looking into the mirror from an already extimate perspective, where the image is itself split as is the body. Contrary to a naive interpretation of this proposition as an antirational deflection, we should bear in mind that from a new sensibility comes a new rationality.[16] A new sensibility from the Black movement establishes an extimate relation and questions the binary logic of modern (and white) rationality between *Körper* and *Leib*. Marcuse poses a fundamental question for philosophical beauty arising from the perspective of the Black movement. "Black is beautiful" reverses the meaning of beauty, a central concept of traditional culture, and drives this aesthetic idea to the point of an open contradiction to the white view. Black culture, in the subterranean level under the so-called "traditional" culture, emerges as a structural point of criticism and demands a new rationality to understand the relation beyond the dual perspective of a dominated and sublimated body.

In this sense, we can understand this new sensibility as part of the extimate relation, which demands a dialectical interpretation beyond dualisms such as rationality versus sensibility. By questioning the established relationship between rationality and sensibility, the Black movement creates a new position irreducible to either. Consequently, it maintains a tension between reason and sensibility rather than an erasure of one of these two elements. Marcuse notes that the Black movement expresses a new sensibility that tries to find a "rational expression" of the life instincts with the aim of social transformation.[17] However, this does not mean that there is a rational telos to sensibility. On the contrary, Marcuse seeks to delineate a new—extimate—relation between reason and sensibility. The next section turns to Marcuse's interpretation of Freudian psychoanalysis to further explore this new relation.

Back to Freud and Beyond

Marcuse's understanding of biological structures in their historical development relies on a neo-Freudian "cultural orientation" derived from Erich Fromm. As Marcuse affirms, revisionists shift "the emphasis from the organism to the personality, from the material foundations to the ideal values."[18] Consequently, revisionists claim a new anthropological view in opposition to Freud's bourgeois perspective on morality. Fromm's understanding of liberation denies Freud's theory of the instincts, according to which humanity can never set itself decisively free from the tragic alternative of destroying others or itself.[19] Consequently, Fromm considers Freudian pessimism about the impossibility of happiness in civilization as a perpetual crisis in psychoanalysis based on the idealist biological fate of the instincts. However, as Marcuse notes, in avoiding Freud's biological fate of discontent, revisionism understands the cure as self-fulfillment, as the "optimal development of a person's personalities and the realization of his individuality."[20] The context of a class-based society casts doubt on Fromm's proposition. The paradisaic "claim for happiness" of the individual contrasts with the social context where one lives.

Against Frommian revisionism, Marcuse insists on the biological basis of Freud's theory of the instincts: "It's not the conflict between instinct and reason that provides the strongest argument against the idea of a free civilization, but rather the conflict which instinct creates in itself."[21] The struggle of the instincts leads to the Marcusean defense of Freudian biologism as the "social theory" in psychoanalysis.[22] In other words, Marcuse understands the struggle of the instincts as a form of Freudian materialism, and the vital energy of the instincts expresses a historical dimension of civilization. Consequently, the body is an important piece of this social-biological puzzle. As seen before, the materiality of the body sustains not only the objective *Körper* but also the social inscriptions of *Leib*. Within a Marcusean framework, these two trends of the body could be understood as the material condition for conflicts in society; the body is part of this instinctual struggle. There is no tragedy without a body, and bodies are the first thing to be annihilated in tragedies.

Nonetheless, advocating for Freudian biologism has its risks. Understanding the body in its exclusively biological element diminishes the extimate character of the corporeal structures insisted upon throughout this essay. Thus, it is important to consider another return to Freud, a more "symbolic" one. Lacan upholds another interpretation of psychoanalysis, supporting the Freudian theory of drives as part of linguistic structures.[23] From his early analysis in "The Family Complex in the Formation of the Individual" (1938), Lacan questioned biological interpretations as "philosophical attempts" to reduce the human family either to biological phenomena or to a theoretical element of society.[24] The family is not a natural development of animal grouping or a fixed cultural ideal for humanity across the years. As an institution, the family provides order to a system of laws or rules that inscribe subjectivities inside them. Such a view was held by structural anthropology and served as a model to the early Lacan regarding the "intersection of nature and culture."[25] In other words, the family is not just a cultural development. Moreover, this institution is a structural base whose social functions are different in each culture. Here, the body arises from the multiple interferences of the social spheres. A baby does not express his/her human condition, but already relates to symbolic expectations even before speech. As the "mirror stage" shows, the noun brings a lot of conditions to the subject: it carries a constellation of meanings. Stated otherwise, institutions express relations in series, inscribing human beings in a symbolic system.

Culturalism is not a good title for this movement, and Lacan recognizes that.[26] The problem is the regress to Freudianism that relies on one exclusive cause from which all the other elements develop themselves. In such an abstraction, there is no place for constituting relationships of social structures. To reconsider Freud's theory of the instincts, as Lacan does, means to rethink the constitutive relationship beyond the cultural or biological, and beyond our usual understanding of causality. The body is not a subjective point of departure, but a knot of elements that are imaginary, symbolic, and real—the constitutive dimensions of the experiences of subjectivity.

This does not mean that there is an absence of any biological foundation, where material foundations connect with certain ideal relationships.[27] Biology is an insufficient but significant piece of human existence. The biological development of the human individual describes the regulation of biological functions, but it cannot present the multiple universes of experiences of individuals. Human bodies are branded with the symbolic function and its material interference in the body. That is, the body in pieces is a dismantled, fragmented body. However, a symbolic totality reorganizes such a fragmented body. Lacan's initial step was to take the symbolic sphere as "the totality of everything which is human. Everything is ordered in accordance with the symbols which have emerged, in accordance with the symbols once they have appeared."[28]

Lorenzo Chiesa presents the Lacanian symbolic totality as a "pseudo-environment" for the human body.[29] Different from the biological environment of the animal world, which Lacan conceives as a closed world, the pseudo-environment of the symbolic environment "presents itself as a totality only insofar as it is structurally not-all."[30] This paradox of the symbolic world follows the function of this "pseudo-environment" for the human being: on one hand, Lacan follows the anthropological thesis of the "primordial biological discord" between the human being and its environment, centered on its premature birth; on the other hand, the symbolic world presents itself as a totality despite the "primitive impotence" of human beings. According to Chiesa: "man's world remains an *open totality*, a pseudo-environment that is both animal-like and, at the same time, irreducible to an animal environment, since, differing from animals, man's very openness to his pseudo-environment makes him experience it as a totality, a meaningful uni-verse."[31] The symbolic "pseudo-environment" produces the experience of the human being in language. That is, the subjectivity constituted by the symbolic world does not result from the development of the biological individual, but rather the symbolic body appears as a machine because of its *open totality* that joins the body in pieces and, as Lacan affirms, "the machine embodies the most radical symbolic activity of man."[32] Moreover, Lacan follows this *open totality* regarding the polyvalence of the meaning of language rather than a well-made language; that is, Lacan notes the "criss-crossings" of the symbolic world where "a thousand of things correspond to each symbol, and each thing to a thousand symbols."[33]

According to Miller, another psychoanalytical category of the body results from this polyvalent symbolic world: the "speaking body" that arises from this paradoxical constitution of human beings, the body engaged with words, as well as the body whose words can escape from it.[34] Chiesa affirms that the open totality of the symbolic world has its lacks, which results in this polyvalence of the language.[35] That is the openness of the symbolic system, the totality that is structurally not-all. The body is based on an extimate relation between the symbolic and biologic dimensions, which compose an open totality instead of a one-dimensional environment. Moreover, the openness could be the language of the speaking body, which connects the symbolic world to the not-all structures, that is, to the real.

Indeed, bodies are not reduced to biological facts for Lacan. Miller notes that for Lacan Freudian biology is not biology itself, but energetics.[36] In other words, Freud was not following his contemporary biology that contains life as its object, but rather the relation between vital trends and even their conflicts. In fact, it is unclear what life really meant in biology at that time. Lacan poses this question in his second seminar, regarding how biology escapes from the ideal concept of life by vitalism. For example, Bichat's biology observes life in relation to death, avoiding a metaphysical view of life by itself.[37] However, according to Miller, "Freudian biology is first of all energetics," which presents the vital relations and their dynamics.[38] In this sense, the living body arises as the condition for these relations. The body appears as the matter of this unknown life. However, this is not to suggest a return to the metaphysics of nature and a kind of transcendental vital energy. Lacan rejects vitalism as a principle for his psychoanalysis. Indeed, Lacan here upholds an anti-vitalism. The dynamics of the vital energy of a permanent biological instability of the human body makes evident the impossibility of vital harmony. Consequently, biology cannot be reduced to adaptation. Life as an "unknown concept" renders all the elements of biology as permanent instability, resulting in a body that is an extimate element and a knot for the polyvalent meaning of language. Contrary to the transcendental body of vitalism, Lacan conceives the body as a human condition for the open totality. There are many bodies inside a body: the imaginary one, the machine, the speaking body. All of these kinds of bodies embody different aspects of Freudian biology. These multiple meanings of the body put the Marcusean concept of biology into question.

What about Biology?

In conclusion, it is worth reconsidering the fate of biology after Lacan's criticism. Marcuse may be seen as one of the most radical thinkers of his generation, because of his defense of a radical connection between social values and the biological condition. In *An Essay on Liberation*, Marcuse explicitly develops biology as a condition for revolution. An important footnote in this book discerns the meaning of this biological question: it is close to "second nature" instead of a "physiological need."[39] Therefore,

Marcuse can express the "biological need of freedom" or the "biological basis for solidarity." That is, the civilization processes of "inclinations, behavior patterns, and aspirations become vital needs which, if not satisfied, would cause dysfunction of the organism."[40] In other words, the alienation of social life in capitalism results in social and organic dysfunctions, which are diagnosed by critical theory. Marcuse's view presents an extimate frontier in which social elements are interpenetrated by biological terms and biological elements are interpenetrated by sociological terms. Freedom and solidarity are values that exist through a biological organism, and at the same time, the organic body gives rise to claims for social and historical values such as freedom and solidarity. So, Marcuse's concept of biology follows the Freudian philosophy of nature, with social suffering diagnosed as a result of a contradictory capitalism.

At first glance, biology could be understood as an illusionary fate. However, one could say that biological functions are not illusions at all. As I have argued, the presence of biology is not neglected by Lacan. For example, Johnston records that Lacan considers the biological condition of the fragmented body-in-pieces.[41] In a sense, biology could be submitted under an extimate position transgressing the frontier between nature and culture. Accordingly, Lacan can offer another view of Marcuse's concept of biology.

Surely, Marcuse does not suggest that conflicts have a natural basis. Marcuse's criticism of Nazi racist discourse shows that he is aware of the "Aryan body" as a site of domination justified biologically. He criticized the ideology of "blood and soil" as an illusionary propaganda that veils the misery of lived experience in a totalitarian society.[42] As will be noted below, Marcuse also mentions the implications of the technological apparatus in late capitalism and the apparent liberalized bodies of affluent society. In fact, he acknowledged the restricted place of a pure nature in his criticism of technological reason. Moreover, Marcuse claimed: "nature, too, awaits the revolution!"[43] Following Lacan's propositions, we could say that nature is amorphous and is the key for the topological resistance of the body, a place for multiple relations.

Marcuse presents the multiple relations of the body as a polymorphic matter, and we can consider the way in which this body revolts against the established society.[44] Marcuse names such revolt the "Great Refusal": a resistance which impels the human body to rebel against intolerable repression by throwing itself against the engines of repression.[45] "I can't breathe," said George Floyd, suffocated by a white policeman. His complaint became a slogan for the Black Lives Matter movement, which refused to take his murder as an exception. In fact, this case expressed a "usual" procedure against Black bodies. Floyd's complaint turned into a global revolt for life.[46] It echoed Marcuse's own description of such kinds of protests: "The fact that they start refusing to play the game may be the fact which marks the beginning of the end of a period."[47] The Great Refusal is an openness against the established totality, it questions the established symbolic world and its values.[48] Consequently, this negative condition of the Great Refusal conceives the social position of the body as a polymorphic possibility to change the symbolic machine of the status quo. The Great Refusal of the body against the status quo points to the radical aspects of Marcuse's concept of biology.

Joel Kovel presents a singular interpretation of these Marcusean readings of biology. According to Kovel, biology is at the center of the human dilemma: either "to *split* ourselves from nature and make it radically Other (that is, the relation with Nature in Capitalism)," or "to *differentiate* ourselves from Nature, that is, to recognize it in ourselves, as body, and to recognize ourselves in it, as those who care for the earth."[49] Does Kovel's interpretation of Marcuse's biology allow for an extimate perspective? Surely, the extimate view of the question considers the body as a critical issue: a singular element that puts our thinking in a continuous displacement. The body is not nature in the human; rather, it is a sign of an irreconcilable difference between nature and the human. The question of the body refers, then, to the concept of extimacy as an operation of differentiation. This is not the totalitarian revolution of the Terror cutting heads off but the constant exercise of criticism, the permanent revolution of critical theory seeking a non-reified relation, a Great Refusal for an emancipated society that denies false identity among bodies.

Lacan's critique of Freudian biologism challenges the Marcusean concept of radical bodies. Lacanian psychoanalysis also called into question a naive view of Freudian biologism. There are many consequences that stem from this critique, but I highlight the following ones: the body as part of the symbolic world embodies biological elements as part of the open totality based on the human condition. Consequently, the body is a knot of multiple aspects of the constitutive structures of the human being and not just determinate as a biological individual. In this sense, the body-machine relates to the symbolic world and the speaking body of the real: the language as a "pseudo-environment" is the same language that creates new horizons and the possibility of transforming social relations. So, the Lacanian view of biology produces new interpretations of Marcuse's philosophical interpretation of Freud: biology as a part of history should be part of language.

There is no opposition between the biological and the symbolical world, but a perpetual tension between these two different views. The extimate question of the body represents this possibility: neither biologism, nor culturalism, but rather a speaking body and its language. This view of the body, as a negative form of displacement, opens the possibility of enacting a Great Refusal of contemporary civilization and its discontents; of saying "no" to established identities of domination, and forming the first step toward qualitative social changes for emancipation.

Notes

1. A first version of this paper was presented in the international workshop "Extimacy: Authority, Anxiety, and the Desire for Revolution" at the American University of Beirut, 2020. I would like to express my deep sense of gratitude for the astute commentaries and reviews suggested by Prof. Surti Singh and Prof. Nadia Bou Ali, whose careful criticisms improved this paper and helped me to reframe it. This research was supported by the Andrew W. Mellon Foundation.

2. David Pavón-Cuellar, "Extimacy," in *Encyclopedia of Critical Psychology*, ed. Thomas Teo (New York: Springer, 2014), 661.

3. Jacques Lacan, *The Ego in Freud's Theory and in the Technique of Psychoanalysis (1954–1955)*, ed. Jacques Alain-Miller, trans. John Forrester, vol. 2 of The Seminar of Jacques Lacan (New York: Norton, 1988), 7.

4. Theodor Adorno and Max Horkheimer, *Dialectic of Enlightenment: Philosophical Fragments*, trans. Edmund Jephcott (Stanford, CA: Stanford University Press, 2002), 192.

5. Adorno and Horkheimer, *Dialectic of Enlightenment*, 193.

6. We can recall here Freud's analogy between the psyche and historical moments of Rome as a "spatial juxtaposition." Sigmund Freud, *Civilization and Its Discontents*, trans. James Strachey (New York: Norton, 1961), 16–18. This Freudian metaphor reflects an overdetermination of emotional and representational layers, in which the subterranean layer expresses a juxtaposition between two layers and not a sedimented layer of the surface.

7. Adorno and Horkheimer, *Dialectic of Enlightenment*, 192.

8. Adorno and Horkheimer, *Dialectic of Enlightenment*, 193.

9. See Peter Cohen's 1989 film, *Undergångens arkitektur* [The Architecture of Doom].

10. Herbert Marcuse, *One-Dimensional Man: Studies in the Ideology of Advanced Industrial Society*, 2nd ed. (London: Routledge, 1991), 77.

11. Although Marcuse does not present the question as a *Leib/Körper* problem, these two categories are helpful for understanding the question of the body in his philosophy. Moreover, Marcuse explicitly takes *Dialectic of Enlightenment* as a reference for his works.

12. Herbert Marcuse, *Eros and Civilization: A Philosophical Inquiry into Freud* (Boston: Beacon, 1966), xiii.

13. Marcuse, *Eros and Civilization*, xiii.

14. Herbert Marcuse, *An Essay on Liberation* (Boston: Beacon, 1969), 36.

15. Marcuse, *Essay on Liberation*, 36.

16. Marcuse, *Essay on Liberation*, 30.
17. Marcuse, *Essay on Liberation*, 24.
18. Marcuse, *Eros and Civilization*, 274.
19. Erich Fromm, *The Crisis of Psychoanalysis: Essays on Freud, Marx, and Social Psychology* (Open Road Distribution, 2001), 16.
20. Fromm, *The Crisis of Psychoanalysis* quoted in Marcuse, *Eros and Civilization*, 258. A note of caution is due here, since some quotations in this chapter refers to the terms "his" or "man" as denoting human beings in general. This chapter follows the original text and its terms. However, as feminism properly advises us, it is necessary to review critically the use of these terms. The question about the body troubles this male position.
21. Marcuse, *Eros and Civilization*, 86.
22. Marcuse, *Eros and Civilization*, 5.
23. In the 1950s, two "returns to Freud" put his work under critical examination, regarding the body in particular. On the one hand, there were Marcuse's efforts towards a philosophical interpretation of Freud and a biological basis for the theory of instincts. On the other hand, there were Lacan's seminars on Freud and the symbolic intervention of psychoanalysis based on the assertion that "the unconscious is structured like a language." In these two trends, there were two different returns to Freud. Marcuse's biology and Lacan's language result from different understandings of the body and the drives. Although the authors represent two apparently different Freuds, would it be possible to put them in conversation? What kind of short-circuit could that offer? Could biology and language be considered in an extimate relation? These are important questions, because Marcuse does not refute language as a critical element, nor is Lacan indifferent to biology.
24. Jacques Lacan, "Les Complexes familiaux dans la formation de l'individu: Essai d'analyse d'une fonction en psychologie," in *Autres Écrits* (Paris: Éditions du Seuil, 2001), 24.
25. Lacan, "Les Complexes familiaux," 75.
26. For example, in the limits of Erikson's culturalism for the interpretation of Irma's Dream (Lacan, *The Ego in Freud's Theory and in the Technique of Psychoanalysis*, 152).
27. Lacan, "Les Complexes familiaux," 35.
28. Lacan, *The Ego in Freud's Theory and in the Technique of Psychoanalysis*, 29.
29. Lorenzo Chiesa, "The World of Desire: Lacan between Evolutionary Biology and Psychoanalytic Theory," *Filozofski vestnik* 30, no. 2 (2010): 84.
30. Chiesa, "The World of Desire," 84.
31. Chiesa, "The World of Desire," 90.
32. Lacan, *The Ego in Freud's Theory and in the Technique of Psychoanalysis*, 74.
33. Lacan, *Freud's Papers on Technique* (1953–54), ed. Jacques Alain-Miller, trans. John Forrester, vol. 2 of *The Seminar of Jacques Lacan* (New York: Norton, 1991), 268.
34. Lacan, *Freud's Papers on Technique*, 268; Jacques Alain-Miller, "Lacanian Biology and the Event of the Body," trans. Barbara P. Fulks, *Lacanian Ink* 18 (January 2001): 15–17.

35. Chiesa, "The World of Desire," 92.
36. Miller, "Lacanian Biology," 7. Miller relates Freudian energetics to the scientific view of thermodynamics. In contrast, Zupančič conceives of psychoanalytical energetics as a question of sexuality rather than a scientific concept. According to her, Freudian energetics does not designate a quantum of energy but "the irreducible unbalance of human nature." That is, libido is a "surplus energy" and not a "kind of general energetic level involved in our lives." Alenka Zupančič, *Why Psychoanalysis? Three Interventions* (NSU Press, 2008), 9–10. A debate between Marcuse's Eros and Zupančič's sexuality could present interesting points between philosophy and psychoanalysis, a debate to be pursued hopefully in a further opportunity.
37. Lacan, *The Ego in Freud's Theory and in the Technique of Psychoanalysis*, 75.
38. Miller, "Lacanian Biology," 7.
39. Marcuse, *Essay on Liberation*, 10.
40. Marcuse, *Essay on Liberation*, 10.
41. Adrian Johnston, *A Weak Nature Alone*, vol. 2 of *A Prolegomena to Any Future Materialism* (Evanston, IL: Northwestern University Press, 2019), 213.
42. Herbert Marcuse, "The Struggle against Liberalism in the Totalitarian View of the State," in *Negations: Essays in Critical Theory*, trans. Jeremy Shapiro (London: Penguin, 1968).
43. Herbert Marcuse, *Counterrevolution and Revolt* (Boston: Beacon, 1972), 74.
44. Marcuse, *Eros and Civilization*, 49.
45. Marcuse, *Eros and Civilization*, xix, 149.
46. Charles Reitz, "Herbert Marcuse Today: On Ecological Destruction, Neofascism, White Supremacy, Hate Speech, Racist Police Killings, and the Radical Goals of Socialism," *Theory, Culture & Society* 38, no. 7–8 (2021): 87–106.
47. Herbert Marcuse, *One-Dimensional Man: Studies in the Ideology of Advanced Industrial Society* (Boston: Beacon, 1964), 257.
48. Arnold Farr and Andrew T. Lamas, "Afterword: The Great Refusal in a One-Dimensional Society," in *The Great Refusal: Herbert Marcuse and Contemporary Social Movements*, ed. Andrew T. Lamas (Philadelphia: Temple University Press, 2017), 396.
49. Joel Kovel, "Commentaries to Marcuse's *Ecology* and the *Critique of Modern Society*," in *Philosophy, Psychoanalysis, and Emancipation* by Herbert Marcuse (New York: Routledge, 2011), 217.

Hate Your Neighbor as You Hate Yourself

How to Think Psychoanalytically about Hate, Racism, and Exclusion

Patricia Gherovici

The main contention of this essay is that the Lacanian notion of *extimacy*—a neologism combining "exteriority" and "intimacy" to imply that something exterior, strange, and foreign can be at the same time the closest, most privately, deeply felt thing—allows us to both understand and rethink symptoms of hate, such as racism, discrimination, and exclusion. My point of departure is the injunction from the Old Testament to "love your neighbor as yourself." The commandment is formed by a unit of two verses that instruct the Israelites not to hate one another or take revenge or bear grudges against one another, but instead to love one another. "You shall not take vengeance or bear a grudge against any of your people, but you shall love your neighbor as yourself."[1] While in the Old Testament the mandate was limited to "your people," the commandment of universal love was later associated with one of the most fundamental requirements of Christianity.

Sigmund Freud was skeptical about a commandment that he deemed impossible to follow. In an often quoted and quite extraordinary passage in *Civilization and Its Discontents*, Freud asks us to forget everything we know about the injunction to love one's neighbor in order to address it anew. Freud writes, "Why should we do it? What good will it do us? But, above all, how shall we achieve it? How can it be possible? My love is something valuable to me which I ought not to throw away without reflection. It imposes duties on me for whose fulfilment I must be ready to make sacrifices. If I love someone, he must deserve it in some way."[2] Freud purposely leaves out any account of the "use" that the neighbor may provide, for instance as a sexual object, since this option is not considered in the commandment to love one's neighbor. Freud argues that the love for one's neighbor would be deserved only if the neighbor is "like me," a proposition that implies that the neighbor would be not just "one of us," but rather, an exterior part of oneself—an "extemious" being, if one can use this term. But if we can love ourselves in our neighbor, if our neighbor deserves it, then our neighbor becomes so much more perfect than ourselves that we end up loving the ideal of our own self in our neighbor. Only then could this "extimacy" be tolerated. Things, however, are quite different when our neighbor happens to be just a stranger "that cannot attract me by any worth"; then, Freud writes, "it will be hard for me to love him"—the exteriority prevails and intimacy dissolves.

Freud continues: "Indeed, I should be wrong to do so, for my love is valued by all my own people as a sign of my preferring them, and it is an injustice to them if I put a stranger on a par with them."[3] Or, Freud ponders, is our love so unbiased that we love our neighbor even when our neighbor may not deserve our love, even if our neighbor is a lesser being? Then our self-preservation may be compromised. Freud proposes: "But if I am to love [the neighbor] (with this universal love) merely because [the neighbor], too, is an inhabitant of this earth, like an insect, an earthworm or a grass-snake, then I fear that only a small modicum of my love will fall to his share—not by any possibility as much as, by the judgement of my reason, I am entitled to retain for myself." Not only can the neighbor be a perfect stranger, but, as Freud adds, they can be "unworthy of my love," a dehumanized, enigmatic inhabitant of this earth, not much above an insect. Then it is clear that the commandment has become even more unreasonable: "What is the point of a precept enunciated with so much solemnity if its fulfilment cannot be recommended as reasonable?" Freud continues: "I must honestly confess that [my neighbor] has more claim to my hostility and even my hatred." Freud moves away from the biblical injunction to love all others in order to discuss a general human disposition toward aggression and mutual hostility. Indeed, humans "are not gentle creatures who want to be loved, and who at the most can defend themselves if they are attacked; they are, on the contrary, creatures among whose instinctual endowments is to be reckoned a powerful share of aggressiveness."[4]

People consider their neighbor "not only a potential helper or sexual object, but also someone who tempts them to satisfy their aggressiveness on him, to exploit his capacity for work without compensation, to use him sexually without his consent, to seize his possessions, to humiliate him, to cause him pain, to torture and to kill him."[5] In the end, Freud has supplanted the commandment to love with Plautus's proverb *Homo homini lupus*, "man is a wolf to man." "Who," Freud asks, "in the face of all his experience of life and of history, will have the courage to dispute this assertion?" Both love and hatred are implied by the biblical injunction. The title of this essay simply inverts this commandment and replaces "love" with "hate." Freud has shown how the plasticity of the libido allows for permutations such as those illustrated by Schreber's paranoiac delusions of persecution, where for instance the proposition "I (a man) *love* him" becomes "I do not *love* him—I *hate* him." Soon "I hate him" is transformed into "*He hates* (persecutes) *me*, which will justify me in hating him." Freud observes that this is how an internal feeling becomes an external perception: "I do not *love* him—I *hate* him, because *He Persecutes Me*."[6]

We can find echoes of this mechanism of projection in Carl Schmitt's theory of politics, according to which everything is founded on the opposition between the friend and the enemy. Schmitt supposes a clear-cut delineation, but we know that things can become more complex and that the former friend may turn into an enemy; this is the logic of paranoia. Rather than following Jacques Derrida and Giorgio Agamben by tracing this logic of paradox and reversibility, I focus on the conflation of external and internal suggested by the notion of extimacy. This intimate exteriority that Lacan describes as the "excluded interior," the subject's inside that becomes "the first outside" and which has nothing to do with "the experience of reality" but is an exteriority around which subjects orient themselves, is a dimension already suggested by Freud's elaborations on hatred.[7]

In "Instincts and Their Vicissitudes" (1915), Freud states that "hate, as a relation to objects, is older than love."[8] For the infant, hatred is the primary manner in which the external world is perceived: "At the very beginning, it seems, the external world, objects, and what is hated, are identical."[9] In the beginning, there was hatred—the child needs to be taken care of, is powerless and overwhelmed with pressing needs that can only be satisfied by an external agency. Babies experience their needs as pain—their internal needs (hunger, cold) as well as the external world of objects (the food that is not yet there to satisfy the hunger, the caretaker who takes too long to respond and may be at a loss about how to help) are not differentiated. Internal needs and external objects both cause displeasure and hatred.[10] Freud proposes a basic paranoiac disposition: what we cannot accept is projected and expelled onto the external world. Here, Freud is following Wilhelm Stekel, who defined hate as the ground of all affects, including altruistic feelings.[11] Indeed, Freud showed that hatred is not exclusively destructive toward the object. Hatred introduces a first differentiating boundary between inside and outside; the permanence of that boundary is its constituting principle, by which reality is created as such. Hatred appears at this limit of extimacy, at a point where outside becomes inside and inside becomes outside.

Freud started exploring this fundamental relationship with the figure of the neighbor as a familiar-strange other early in his career. Before Schreber, in the 1894 "Draft H. Paranoia," Freud discusses the relationship of paranoiacs to their delusions (which can be understood as a regression from love to hate).[12] Freud talks about what could be the origin of extimacy when he refers to the *Nebensmench* (German for the next-human or adjoining person). He returns to it soon after in the 1895 *Project for a Scientific Psychology*, where he considers the fellow human as simultaneously the first satisfying object and as the first hostile object, as well as the sole helping power. Freud argues that it is in relation to this loved/hated first fellow human that the human being learns to judge and remember.

Following this speculation about the origins of subjectivity, Freud concludes that humans learn to think in the encounter with this fellow human being. This next important person is for Freud the "subject's first satisfying object and further his first hostile object, as well as his sole helping power."[13] The baby is in a state of need, fully dependent on an other for its survival. The baby experiences needs as painful; being at the mercy of the caretaker, babies are unable to fend for themselves and are fully dependent on the outside world that will supply nourishment and comfort. Freud writes that this "initial helplessness [*Hilflosigkeit*] of human beings is the *primal source* of all *moral motives*."[14] Such an early recognition of helplessness sends us in the direction of a basic ethics of the other. The other should be tolerated and not just loved or hated. The baby's awareness of its own extreme vulnerability and dependence on the caretaker, combined with the appeasing function of helping, is primordial—then hate and love can follow.

Love vs. Hate

Can love trump hate? This recent political slogan has often been misunderstood. Some people took it as a rejection of Trump, while others saw it as an endorsement of his ability to overcome obstacles and unleash our right to openly express our hatred. However, one might say that in psychoanalysis, hate is not an affect to be "trumped" or even ignored, especially in transference. While transference has often being theorized on the axis of love, one should not neglect the emergence of "hate in the counter-transference." Donald W. Winnicott goes as far as saying that analysts need to be able "to hate the patient objectively." [15] To illustrate this, Winnicott describes his experience of treating a nine-year-old boy who was in foster care at Winnicott's home for three months during World War II. This time is characterized by Winnicott as "three months of hell."

> The evolution of the boy's personality engendered hate in me. . . . Did I hit him? The answer is "No, I never hit." But I should have had to have done so if I had not known all about my hate. . . . At crises I would take him by bodily strength, and without anger or blame, and put him outside the front door, whatever the weather or the time of day or night. There was a special bell he could ring, and he knew that if he rang it he would be readmitted and no word said about the past. . . . The important thing is that each time, just as I put him outside the door, I told him something; I said that what had happened had made me hate him. This was easy because it was so true. I think these words were important from the point of view of his progress, but they were mainly important in enabling me to tolerate the situation . . . without losing my temper and every now and again murdering him.[16]

Winnicott argues that in order to be closer to the truth, one needs to recognize the hate one develops in oneself—it would be worse to try to deny it. He makes a convincing case for the expression of hate in a knowing manner. It is only if we accept our hate as psychoanalysts, within the privacy of our office, that we can start tackling the hate underpinning unconscious racism and the weight of unanalyzed white privilege.

This nuance has been missed by Frank Wilderson, who explains in *Afropessimism* that the curse of slavery has not been lifted, and that the subjugated position of African Americans prevents them from "ever being regarded as human beings." This structural exclusion, according to Wilderson, places them in a position of "social death"—a deathliness that saturates Black life.[17] For Wilderson, structural racism takes away the Black person's humanity. It may sound counterintuitive that my inversion of the biblical motto—hate your neighbor as you hate yourself—should generate hope, but it does. I argue that by acknowledging the repressed hate, we can overcome the mechanism by which we dehumanize others. If I hate my neighbor, at least my neighbor becomes a human person similar to me.

Love?

To go back to basics: we know that in the infant's evolution, hatred is initially experienced as the displeasure derived from the encounter with the "other" and the "objects" that threaten the ego's integrity. The question here is, how does the infant move from this primal stage of hatred to an ability to love? In "Instincts and Their Vicissitudes," Freud argues that love "is originally narcissistic, then passes over on to objects . . . as sources of pleasure. . . . As the first . . . we recognize the phase of incorporating or devouring—a type of love which is consistent with abolishing the object's separate existence and which may therefore be described as ambivalent." The oral stage involves incorporating and devouring the object; in the pregenital, anal-sadistic stage, "injury or annihilation of the object is a matter of indifference. Love in this form and at this preliminary stage is hardly to be distinguished from hate in its attitude towards the object."[18] Freud maintains that early in life, there is no distinction between love and hate. This definition calls up another of Lacan's punning neologisms that results from joining seeming opposites—*hainamoration* or "hate-love." Freud moves away from the claim that hatred originates from love and thus from sexual drives. Instead, hate comes into being alongside the constitution of the ego. It expresses the ego's self-preservation instincts, the will to power and the urge for mastery. Before the genital stage, the self-preservation of the ego is endangered by the encounter with the object. The later acquisition of the love/hate distinction that forms in the genital stage allows them to be linked together, bringing the whole person into being.

It is worth reconsidering Melanie Klein's elaborations on the mechanism of projection and introjection as showing the mechanism of extimacy in action: I expel and externalize what is uncomfortable and incorporate what is good. The dynamic challenges a clearly defined border since for Klein the object that is lost is "introjected"—not interior but internalized, this psychic object's existence is precarious. It will be consumed by the ego; lost again, now internally, guilt will emerge after the aggression. Following *Beyond the Pleasure Principle*, Melanie Klein sees hatred, alongside sadism, as expressions of the death drive. Like Freud, Klein gives a fundamental role to hate; love is only a provisional victory over hate. We find a similar primacy granted to hate in the writings of Donald Winnicott. Wilfred Bion too postulates both love and hatred, alongside knowledge, as "basic emotions" and basic "links" when he develops the idea of the linking of objects.

If the biblical commandment admonishes one to love one's neighbor as one loves oneself, and if this proves to be impossible, as Freud claims, we may also have to question the nature, and even the existence of self-love. I cannot love my neighbor because my neighbor is too extimate to me. Then the question is: Do you have to love your neighbor *as* you love yourself, or *like* yourself? ("As I am . . ." expresses an identity, while "like" expresses a comparison, "like me.") If your tendency is to hate your neighbor, perhaps you hate your neighbor exactly as you hate yourself. The inability to love oneself may bring someone to analysis.

The analysand will be, as often happens, both full of hate and love, which can elicit a hateful response in the analyst (or a negative countertransference). For example, Ramona, a woman from the Dominican Republic, once came to therapy flustered and upset: she complained that "dirty Blacks" had moved to her block.[19] Even though she had dark brown skin, she did not identify as Black because she spoke Spanish. Assuming herself to be a part of the amorphous Hispanic crowd, she identified with hegemonic racialized discourse that used language to construct racial difference. Unaware that she was supporting an extimate racist discourse that also segregated her, she herself became a victim of such disparaging remarks. As we know, "Hispanic" refers to a language and not a skin color. What is the race of Hispanics? Even the U.S. Census Bureau admits that Hispanics "may be of any race." Many of my barrio patients often identify themselves as belonging to "the Puerto Rican race" or to "La Raza" rather than as Hispanic or Latino. Even if we may call them, more politically correctly, "Latinx," those subjects and their experiences of oppression, like other populations belonging to so-called minorities, will continue to be negated and viewed as part of a crowd, a single undifferentiated body. Hispanics or Latinx are presented by mainstream discursive practices as a host of frozen images in which any trace of individuality and class, culture, and gender difference is erased. This oppression is perpetuated in the notion of "race" that has shaped Latinx identities.

Because racism was Ramona's symptom, I had to address it without immediately combating it or even attempting to reduce it. Ramona offered the "royal path" to overcome her stereotyping, prejudice, and bias when her new neighbors started appearing in her dreams. Like Freud, Lacan takes the dream as a metaphor of desire; that is, he holds that dreams are a compromise formation, a substitute satisfaction for an unconscious desire. Like her symptom of racism, Ramona's dreams were granting her a form of displaced satisfaction located in a place of nondistinction between interior and exterior—she hated her neighbors as much as she hated herself. A simple word association to a dream (she was at a party at the despised neighbor's house) proved revelatory.

She first thought about the saying "*mi casa es su casa*" (my house is your house), or "what's mine is yours." Surprised that the disliked neighbors were in her dream, and that they welcomed her to their home, she exclaimed "¡Ay, bendito!" (Oh blessed!), an expression equivalent to "Sweet Jesus!" in some Latin American countries. The homophony of "Ay" was, she told me later in her associations, an echo of the pronunciation of "Haiti" in Spanish (ay-tee). Another racialized other that she did not like had appeared, and it was one that exposed the prejudice, the selective interpretation of history, and the nationalism of the Dominican Republic, which were expressed in systemic xenophobia against darker-skinned Haitians. Indeed, in the Dominican Republic, Ramona's birth country, Haitians are not just second-class citizens; they are considered the "eternal enemies of the Dominican people." There, "students are, quite literally, educated to hate" Haitians, which is called *antihaitianismo*.[20] In the past, Haitians have been the victims of several mass slaughters.

Because of her skin color, on several occasions Ramona herself had been discriminated against because she was suspected of being Haitian. Under threat of being deported, she had been compelled to prove her Dominican citizenship to the authorities. So she never left her house (*casa*) without her *cédula* (an identification document detailing ethnicity, race, and immigration status.) Ramona also acknowledged that she secretly felt like an impostor. Fundamentally, she believed that all true Dominicans had lighter skin; in fact, she suspected that she was of Haitian descent. As a child, she would hear an occasional joke mocking her father, which brought up questions about his paternity—her parents and grandparents on both sides had lighter skin than Ramona. This biological quirk, the pigment of an unknown darker-skinned ancestor, was both the source of her difficulty growing up in a racist society and the source of her unstable identity.

Her work in the treatment centered on what Freud has called the narcissism of minor differences—namely, the human proclivity for aggression intertwined with the desire for distinct identity.[21] When Freud used the expression "narcissism of *minor* differences," he wanted to highlight something that we can revisit under the frame of extimacy—it is precisely the most minimal differences that generate clashes between people who are otherwise quite alike; this is the root of a perception of strangeness leading to hostility between them, once again affirming the power of extimacy in the construction of identity.

Before he mentioned the notion of minor differences in *Civilization and Its Discontents*, Freud referred to such differences in 1918 in "The Taboo of Virginity." Speculating that the origin of men's "narcissistic rejection of women" can be traced to the castration complex, Freud refers to the work of the English anthropologist Ernest Crawley: "Crawley, in language which differs only slightly from the current terminology of psycho-analysis, declares that . . . it is precisely the minor differences in people who are otherwise alike that form the basis of feelings of strangeness and hostility between them. It would be tempting to pursue this idea and to derive from this 'narcissism of minor differences' the hostility which in every human relation we see fighting successfully against feelings of fellowship and overpowering the commandment that all men should love one another." Here the narcissism of minor differences appears as a symptomatic construction, a defense against castration that also impedes the acknowledgment of sexual difference.

When Freud returns to the idea of minor differences in 1921, he addresses intimacy to show how hatred emerges at the threshold of extimacy. In *Group Psychology and the Analysis of the Ego*, he writes:

> The evidence of psycho-analysis shows that almost every intimate emotional relation between two people which lasts for some time—marriage, friendship, the relations between parents and children—contains a sediment of feelings of aversion and hostility, which only escapes perception as a result of repression. . . . The same thing happens when men come together in larger units. . . . Closely related races keep one another at arm's length; the South German cannot endure the North German, the Englishman casts every kind of aspersion upon the Scot, the Spaniard despises the Portuguese. We are no longer astonished that greater differences should lead to an almost insuperable repugnance, such as the Gallic people feel for the German, the Aryan for the Semite, and the white races for the colored.[22]

Freud shows us that the "glue" that binds the members of the crowd is the conviction that their love for the leader will unite them, creating a link (a specular, hypnotic connection) that will save them from their radical helplessness. Crowds erase difference because they crave conformity—they need a leader or master to love and to be loved by without any concern for truth. Whenever we find mass phenomena, we encounter segregation. Segregation is not a secondary consequence but a crowd's formation. Segregation is what constitutes the crowd.

Segregation is the disavowal of difference. All group formations erase difference since their constitution is based on a principle of identity, an identity constructed in alienation, in identification with an other. Any attempt at stressing differences, no matter how minimal, can be experienced by the crowd as an attack threatening its very existence. The members of the crowd love each other while they hate the outsider, the stranger, the other, who is not "like us." The narcissism of minor differences plays a central role in the creation of the "us." These differences may be "minor" but are clearly intolerable because the "other" represents a blind spot in the mirror image. The power of racism stems from the extimate primordial fascination each of us experiences facing human counterparts, the captivation by a mesmerizing image of the other in the mirror. This fascination for the other paradoxically erases it as such, since one identifies with the other's mirror image while making the other, as such, disappear. As Philippe Julien explains:

> With his invention of the mirror stage, Lacan had exposed the very source of racism . . . Indeed the power of racism is rooted in the primordial fascination of each of us with his or her counterpart, in the captivating vision of the Gestalt of the other's body in the mirror. A specific sort of beauty, silhouette, and muscle tone; the power of the body moving or at rest; the color of the skin, eyes, and hair—all this defines a phenotypic physiognomy productive of kinship along genotypic lines. On the other hand, this vision excludes the stranger, the one with whom I cannot identify lest he break my mirror.[23]

This blind spot in the mirror is also the place that conceals subjective division. We deny the "other's" sameness so as to imagine a complete other, denying our own castration, which harkens back to Freud's first introduction of "minor differences" in connection with sexual difference.

Racism is not simply intolerance of differences but intolerance of excessive sameness. If the characteristics that define this "other" get blurred, those who identified themselves as not "like them" feel their identity threatened. That is to say, the negation of the other is correlative of the self's affirmation. To see one's neighbor reflect and mirror oneself too much threatens a person's unique sense of self. As Pierre Bourdieu proposes in *Distinction*, social identity is constructed on the differences created by the things closest to oneself; these similarities represent the greatest threat, since differences are exacerbated to create an illusion of superiority.[24] Implicit in Bourdieu's text is the idea of extimacy because the external is tasked with defining the internal. In Ramona's hatred of her new Philadelphia neighbors, she was replicating the racism of which she herself had been a victim, while trying to assert an identity which denied the fact that this view was built on similarity disguised as difference. In the end, Ramona became aware of this repetition; she understood that the hatred she projected onto the neighbors was the hatred she herself had been subjected to. She unconsciously expressed her notion of extimacy with the phrase "what's mine is yours." I could not help but think about the saying that appeared in her dream, "*Mi casa es su casa*," and wonder whether Ramona could extend her hospitality to neighbors that she saw as beneath her.

I will return to the notion of hospitality; first, Ramona's situation prompts the question: how does someone become a racialized other? This is a question that Toni Morrison posed in her lectures given at Harvard University on race, fear, borders, the mass movement of peoples, and the desire for belonging, published in *The Origin of Others*.[25] Morrison's nuanced meditation is not about racial difference but about hatred, because she believes that there is only one race—we are all humans. "Race is the classification of a species, and we are the human race, period."[26] Differences between people might be constructed tangentially on genes and biological taxonomy, but most are rooted in projective fantasy. Morrison discusses the fetishization of skin color in our era of mass migration, pondering why human beings invent and reinforce categories of otherness that are dehumanizing. As the character Booker in the last of Morrison's novels, *God Help the Child,* says to Bride, the woman he loves and the novel's protagonist, "scientifically there's no such thing as race, Bride, so racism without race is a choice. Taught, of course, by those who need it, but still a choice. Folks who practice it would be nothing without it."[27] In her analysis of racism, Morrison's originality is to turn the tables, showing that racism not only objectifies its victims, who are stripped of their humanity, but that it also dehumanizes the racists themselves, who "would be nothing without it." This obsession with otherness is a strategy to obscure the fact that we are in fact strangers to ourselves. If we reject our extimate genealogy, we also reject our own human condition.

Whenever I talk about my experience conducting psychoanalytic cures with poor Puerto Ricans and other Latinos, many of whom are of Native American origin, I am met with doubt. The idea of working psychoanalytically with minorities, people of color, is often dismissed. It is as if poor people could not have an unconscious. In those situations I am confronted with a prejudice similar to the attitude of Ramona: the others are seen as too "other." Especially relevant here is my work on *ataques de nervios,* the so-called Puerto Rican syndrome (considered in the *DSM* as a culture-bound syndrome, as if "otherness" was pathological), which I argue is a curious return of the repressed racism of certain psychiatric practices in the barrio.[28]

To continue thinking through the problem of the other, let us discuss Ramona's dislike of her neighbors who she saw as "other" or "not-me"; she hated them because she saw them as having access to a form of enjoyment, a *jouissance* from which she was excluded. To understand the hatred expressed in racism, we need to understand the unconscious profit or economy of *jouissance* that is always at play in racism.²⁹ Ramona complained that her new neighbors were loud, they were always sitting outside on the steps as if they owned the sidewalk, they were unfriendly, they had too many people over, they played loud music, they barbecued on the sidewalk. In other words, she thought that they had access to some strange *jouissance* from which she needed to take distance: "They"—the neighbors—were not like "us." Not only did her neighbors seem to enjoy themselves in some alien and unfamiliar manner, but in doing so, they also spoiled Ramona's fun, because she could no longer enjoy the block where she lived as she did before.

Here is how I intervened. First, I identified the fundamental problem: Ramona created a racist fantasy in which the enjoyment of the "Other" was inversely proportional to her own. This situation was becoming increasingly intolerable, and Ramona believed that the presence of the new neighbors would force her to move somewhere else. Interestingly, Ramona told me that when she had moved to her house a few years earlier, she was surprised that she liked her block so much; curiously, there was a disturbing intensity in the pleasure associated with living where she lived, north of Roosevelt Boulevard, an avenue that functions as an invisible boundary and marker of upward social mobility in the barrio. Everything was great for Ramona, until "these people," "*esos prietos*" (those Blacks), moved to her block.

Ramona claimed that her new neighbors did not belong there, but in fact it was Ramona herself who felt she did not belong. A few years earlier, when she made it to the other side of Roosevelt Boulevard, Ramona was concerned about not fitting into what she thought was a better-off area; she projected that same feeling of not belonging onto the new neighbors. The despised neighbors became a manifestation of her old fears, of her own experience of being an outsider. Above all, she hated the neighbors because they looked at ease, comfortable and happy in their new surroundings, enjoying themselves "too much." This disruptive excess was in fact her own but was disavowed, because like them, she had moved from a less desirable area to this better section of the barrio and liked it a lot. Her access to her own enjoyment became regulated from the outside by the hated neighbors, an "Other," who enjoyed in excess and as a result diminished her own enjoyment. Ramona's racist projection was a fantasy that allowed her to regulate her own *jouissance* by reinstating balance in a situation that was experienced as overwhelming.

Fantasy, according to psychoanalysis, is a construction with a void at its center. Ramona's racist fantasy was a screen with nothing behind it, and it was only a matter of time before she would arrive at the root of her true problem. Facing this kernel of nothing, Ramona deflected her anxiety by blaming the neighbors for forcing her to consider moving and thus having to leave a block that was so desirable, so "full of nice people," "just perfect." Insofar as Ramona was able to fantasize that the neighbors were stealing her enjoyment, that the block was perfect until the new neighbors arrived, she could construct the block as an ideal (lost) space. The neighborhood could then be imagined as the most beautiful one, a place from which she is excluded by the others she excludes.

"If the *prietos* would not be there," Ramona pondered, "the block would be great again." This inner dialogue is quite stereotypical in all forms of racism. If we could only get rid of the "other" (the immigrants who take our jobs, the Jews, the Blacks, gays, atheists, and so on), everything would be perfect. The logic of exclusion requires a problematic "other," an embodiment of imperfection. Ramona identified this necessary, extimate "other" in the Black neighbors; she needed them in order to maintain the fantasy of a perfect situation of an ideal block, a perfectly harmonious neighborhood where all neighbors like each other, a fantasy that was predicated on her own exclusion from it, projected onto the neighbors. With this fantasy intact, Ramona avoided the personal upheaval that *jouissance* entailed for her.

Humor in the analytic session introduced a shift for Ramona. The space that laughter opened allowed her to separate from her own racist prejudices. For Ramona, to accept the neighbors, to tolerate them and not move, was to simultaneously accept a measure of dissatisfaction without her racist fantasy as a placeholder for an impossible ideal. I wanted Ramona to recognize that the excess she projected onto the "other" concealed the truth of her own failed enjoyment. It was only when she accepted this inconvenient and limiting dynamic that she could achieve some agency. Through treatment, a yielding of *jouissance* took place and she finally achieved a modicum of freedom from this symptom. A silly joke that elicited her laughter during a session lifted the racist paranoid mechanism, pointing to the fact that her hate would hide and reveal at the same time the minor differences that are exacerbated into major hurdles to create a sense of identity. In the joke, Ramona constructed a meaning where it never was. Rather than exacerbating minor differences, she was eventually able to sympathize with the strangers who had moved to her block, the neighbors that she had previously racialized and dehumanized, and she was able to overcome the fear she had of becoming a stranger herself, a dark-skinned foreigner, a Haitian who could in turn be racialized and dehumanized.

The body in psychoanalysis has a special status that we may also call "extimate," as revealed by language—we "are" not bodies, but rather we "have" a body, evincing that embodiment is a process of becoming in which one needs to *assume* a body. In certain situations, such as with anorexia and what is called body dysmorphia (when someone experiences intrusive thoughts about a bodily flaw that is not noticed by others), the whole body reveals itself as extimate. When Freud abandoned hypnosis to teach himself a new language, which was psychoanalysis, in order to listen to the unconscious, he worked under the assumption that the body spoke by way of symptoms. He believed that this extimate discourse could be reclaimed by the subject who could then overcome the deadly cycle of repetition. Freud approached the body through the mediation of speech, limiting the treatment to an invitation to the analysand to say whatever came to mind. He tried to overcome patients' resistance by using transference to push the analysis forward. Transference helped make symptoms intelligible and evoke in the analysand a desire to separate from their symptoms. Even if an analysis begins by consulting the analyst's supposed doctor-like expertise that will cure the analysand's ailments, the dynamics of the analysis itself eventually push the analysand further through their desire for knowledge. In this process, the analyst will sooner or later move away from their role as knowledge-keeper, and a new desire will emerge, a desire for difference. Insofar as psychoanalysis offered Ramona a place where she was not an object but a subject, it gave her the space for transformation, a space with emancipatory potential, a space that not only "tolerates" difference but desires it.

In my progression so far, I have explored how psychoanalysis can help us understand the role of racism in the construction of identity. I am trying to comprehend why we choose to hate, why so many patients fear the theft of their "extimate" enjoyment, why trauma re-creates the violence that had generated it earlier, all of which structure the subjectivity of an oppressed other. I will conclude by hoping that we can start thinking psychoanalytically about symptoms of hate like racism, discrimination, and exclusion. After the COVID-19 pandemic and the growing awareness of class inequality, violent discrimination, structural racism, and the impact of the Black Lives Matter movement, it seems that no analyst can be immune to the cultural context in which we work. It seems unavoidable to take a position, since our practice is affected by the current sociopolitical context. Psychoanalysis is not outside of history. We need, for instance, to start addressing the seemingly unspeakable whiteness of psychoanalysis. It is crucial to take race into account, given the weight of hate it carries with it. Moreover, such hate cannot be subsumed under the concept of ambivalence.

As for whiteness, Adrienne Harris is prescriptive in her plea to abandon any attachment to white privilege; aware of the losses entailed for those in a privileged position, she writes: "White people must go through a loss of identity. Yet, as I have to acknowledge, even the identity of colonial thief and oppressor is too necessary, too integral to be given up."[30] If the analyst's desire is not a pure desire but a desire to obtain absolute difference, as Lacan argues,[31] then a first step is to acknowledge that the hate we experience for the other, the neighbor, the stranger, the foreigner, is related to the possibility of *being* an other, as Julia Kristeva has shown.[32] We are strangers to ourselves. It is not a matter of a humanist respect for an other, but rather the awareness that we are often alienated from ourselves, that we are foreigners within. As extimacy suggests, we have an "other" within while the hatred for the other is our own.

Class, whiteness, and heteronormativity should not impede the treatment. I would like to define my practice as predicated upon an unconditional welcome, or in other words, full hospitality, like opening one's *casa* to all others, as Ramona might have implied. However, as Jacques Derrida pointed out, the etymology of "hospitality" sends us back to the "host" who accepts all the "guests" who can be invited, but it also contains a *"hostis,"* a Latin term meaning "enemy." How does this new awareness affect our ideal of neutrality? Is it enough to be aware of our unconscious racism and prejudice like heterosexism or gender normativity? How can we help psychoanalysis develop and thrive in our currently conflicted situation? I would argue that the answer is not to bracket off hate—after all, as the Latin motto went, *qui bene amat bene castigat* (who loves well punishes a lot). Or, to love well is to hate well.

Freud points out that hatred is a strategy of separation that demarcates a boundary between an inside and an outside that ensures the permanence of both. Can hate not only destroy the Other but also make it exist? Winnicott suggests that an analyzed hatred allows the Other to survive the aggression it generates, to exist as such. Hatred is a precursor to a separation that gives security to the connection. Winnicott and Freud agree: hate is at the origin of thought, without hate there is no separation, and without separation there is no construction of the body and the psyche.

We have seen that the Lacanian neologism "extimacy" has the main function of superseding the inside-outside opposition. It implies that the most intimate can exist outside of ourselves and that the most private and personal will be at the same time external, extraneous, foreign. This idea derives from Freud's description of the unconscious as the "other scene," from G. T. Fechner's *eine andere Schauplatz*. The paradox of an exteriority of inner life, of the intimate as foreign body, is at play in Freud's concept of the ego as a mental projection of the physical body. We saw that extimacy was at the origin of subjectivity, as illustrated in Lacan's mirror stage. This dialectical progression in which children identify with their mirror image is a decisive turning point in the infant's ego formation. Once they identify with the mirror image, there is a joyful moment of triumphant, illusory mastery over the body. This crucial movement takes the infant "precipitously from insufficiency to anticipation."[33] The reflection is both intimate and external to the child. Outside becomes inside, and vice versa. The ego starts with a misrecognition in which the "extimate" determines the beginning of subjective constitution. Extimacy appears not as the opposite of the intimacy, but rather as its external-internal manifestation. As the racialized other is a stranger who is like us, if we become aware of our extimate condition, then we may hate more responsibly, and perhaps even ethically.

Notes

1. Leviticus 19:18.

2. Sigmund Freud, *Civilization and Its Discontents* (1930), in *The Future of an Illusion, Civilization and Its Discontents, and Other Works (1927–1931)*, trans. and ed. James Strachey, vol. 21 of *The Standard Edition of the Complete Psychological Works of Sigmund Freud* (London: Hogarth, 1961), 109.

3. Freud, *Civilization and Its Discontents*, 110.

4. Freud, *Civilization and Its Discontents*, 110.

5. Freud, *Civilization and Its Discontents*, 111.

6. Sigmund Freud, "Psycho-Analytic Notes on an Autobiographical Account of a Case of Paranoia (Dementia Paranoides)" (1911), in *The Case of Schreber, Papers on Technique and Other Works (1911–1913)*, trans. and ed. James Strachey, vol. 12 of *The Standard Edition of the Complete Psychological Works of Sigmund Freud* (London: Hogarth, 1958), 63.

7. Jacques Lacan, *The Ethics of Psychoanalysis*, ed. Jacques-Alain Miller, trans. Dennis Porte, vol. 7 of The Seminar of Jacques Lacan (New York: Norton, 1997), 139, 52, 52.

8. Sigmund Freud, "Instincts and Their Vicissitudes" (1915), in *On the History of the Psycho-Analytic Movement, Papers on Metapsychology and Other Works (1914–1916)*, trans. and ed. James Strachey, vol. 14 of *The Standard Edition of the Complete Psychological Works of Sigmund Freud* (London: Hogarth, 1957), 139.

9. Freud, "Instincts and Their Vicissitudes," 136.

10. Freud, "Instincts and Their Vicissitudes," 134 note 2.

11. See W. Stekel, *Die Sprache des Traumes: Eine Dartsellung der Symbolik und Deutung des Traumes in ihren Deziehungen zur kranken und gesunden Seele* (Wiesbaden: Verlag von J. F. Bergmann, 1911), 536.

12. Sigmund Freud, "Draft H. Paranoia" (1894), in *The Complete Letters of Sigmund Freud to Wilhelm Fliess: 1887–1904*, trans. and ed. Jeffrey Moussaieff Masson (Cambridge, MA: Belknap Press of Harvard University Press, 1985), 107–112.

13. Sigmund Freud, *Project for a Scientific Psychology* (1895), in *Pre-Psycho-Analytic Publications and Unpublished Drafts (1886–1889)*, trans. and ed. James Strachey, vol. 1 of *The Standard Edition of the Complete Psychological Works of Sigmund Freud* (London: Hogarth, 1950), 331.

14. Freud, *Project for a Scientific Psychology*, 411.

15. D. W. Winnicott, "Hate in the Counter-Transference," *International Journal of Psychoanalysis* 30 (1958): 69–74.

16. Winnicott, "Hate in the Counter-Transference," 73.

17. Frank Wilderson, *Afropessimism* (New York: Norton, 2020), 95.

18. Freud, "Instincts and Their Vicissitudes," 139.

19. For another discussion of this case, see Patricia Gherovici, "The Lost Souls of the Barrio: Lacanian Psychoanalysis in the Ghetto," in *Lacan and Race: Racism, Identity and Psychoanalytic Theory*, ed. Sheldon George and Derek Hook (Routledge: New York, 2021), 188–90.

20. See Shari K. Hall, "Antihaitianismo: Systemic Xenophobia and Racism in the Dominican Republic," Council on Hemispheric Affairs, https://www.coha.org/antihaitianismo-systemic-xenophobia-and-racism-in-the-dominican-republic/.

21. Freud, *Civilization and Its Discontents*, 57–146.

22. Sigmund Freud, *Group Psychology and the Analysis of the Ego (1921)*, in *Beyond the Pleasure Principle, Group Psychology and Other Works (1920–1922)*, trans. and ed. James Strachey, vol. 28 of *The Standard Edition of the Complete Psychological Works of Sigmund Freud* (London: Hogarth, 1955), 65–144.

23. Philippe Julien, *Jacques Lacan's Return to Freud: The Real, the Symbolic, and the Imaginary* (New York: NYU Press, 1994), 28.

24. Pierre Bourdieu, *Distinction: A Social Critique of the Judgement of Taste*, trans. Richard Nice (London: Routledge, 1984).

25. Toni Morrison, *The Origin of Others* (Cambridge, MA: Harvard University Press, 2017).

26. Morrison, *The Origin of Others*, 15.

27. Toni Morrison, *God Help the Child* (New York: Vintage, 2016), 143.

28. See Patricia Gherovici, *The Puerto Rican Syndrome* (New York: Other Press, 2003).

29. To see a similar analysis of racism inspired by Slavoj Žižek's analysis of racism as theft of *jouissance*, see Patricia Gherovici, "Laughing about Nothing: Democritus and Lacan," in *Lacan, Psychoanalysis and Comedy*, ed. Patricia Gherovici and Manya Steinkoler (Cambridge: Cambridge University Press, 2016); and Patricia Gherovici, "The Lost Souls of the Barrio: Lacanian Psychoanalysis in the Ghetto," in *Lacan and Racism*, ed. Derek Hook and Sheldon George (London: Routledge, 2021).

30. Adrienne Harris, "The Perverse Pact: Racism and White Privilege," *American Imago* 76, no. 3 (2019): 326.

31. Jacques Lacan, *The Four Fundamental Concepts of Psychoanalysis*, ed. Jacques-Alain Miller, trans. Alan Sheridan, vol. 11 of The Seminar of Jacques Lacan (New York: Norton, 1998), 276.

32. Julia Kristeva, *Strangers to Ourselves*, trans. Leon S. Roudiez (New York: Columbia University Press, 1991).

33. Jacques Lacan, *Ecrits: The First Complete Edition in English*, trans. Bruce Fink (New York: Norton, 2007), 78.

Objet a and the Possibilities of Political Resistance

Extimacy, Anxiety, and Political Action

Andreja Zevnik

The discourse of direct political action often mythologizes the 1968 Paris student protests. In the midst of those protests, Jacques Lacan voiced a rather provocative statement, which students met with some dismay. "What you aspire to as revolutionaries is a new master. You will get one."[1] While Lacan was supportive of the protests, he was not blind to what he called the *jouissance* attained through the act of resistance to authority. In what was later called the "discourse of the hysteric," Lacan explained how the desire to change the system, to start a revolution, can turn against itself, because those participating in political actions are seduced by the enjoyment derived from their refusal to recognize authority. In political resistance, which is the primary concern of this essay, political action is reduced to a negative form. That is, those taking actions know what they do not want, but they are unclear about what they would replace the existing authority with. While this is not uncommon, in the context of revolutions, Lacan found this somewhat problematic. His work suggests that protests based on a refusal to recognize authority will not lead to the desired outcome—a change of the system. Rather than just finding a "new master," political action needs to alter the structure of the institution itself. In an attempt to think such a change of structure, James Martel returns to the Althusserian idea of interpellation, where the subject is hailed into the social and symbolic order.[2] The subject's response to the call, its recognition in the call, allocates the subject its imaginary place in the social order.[3] But what happens when a person who responds to a call is not the one for whom the call was intended? Considering the example of the Haitian Revolution and the emergence of the first free Black republic, Martel shows how formerly enslaved free Haitians identified with the slogans of the French Revolution and built their struggle on political foundations that were not "meant for them."[4] Through this misrecognition (or misinterpellation, in the words of Martel), formerly enslaved free Haitians used revolutionary political ideas of the time for their gain. They challenged and subverted the structure in a way that even Lacan might see as political resistance.

While similar examples might be hard to find in contemporary politics, the old Althusserian concept of interpellation (and misinterpellation) points to an important structural moment. Lacan locates the "truth" of the structure in what he calls *objet a* (an unobtainable lost object of desire), and it is precisely this object that, as Mladen Dolar reminds us, exceeds interpellation, resists ideology.[5] In this essay, I aim to tease out the significance of *objet a* for political resistance. While *objet a* as a (social) bond of non-relation is commonly discussed in the context of the four discourses, I would like to suggest that we place it in the context of interpellation and subject-formation. There are three separate and yet interconnected moments in which *objet a* is particularly significant: the context of interpellation and misinterpellation that introduces the excess of *object a*; extimacy, which emphasizes the proximity of the *objet a* to the subject; and anxiety, where *objet a* can lead to two different modes of political action (acting out and *passage à l'acte*). Finally, I conclude by drawing together *objet a* and contemporary struggles for racial justice such as the Black Lives Matter movement, and point to where or how contemporary political resistance challenges the structure of interpellation.

The Failure of Interpellation

In "The Subversion of the Subject and the Dialectics of Desire," Lacan developed a four-stage analytical framework that explains how an individual turns into a social being (a subject) through the process of signification (being inscribed in language), by being placed in relation to the Other (a form of authority or mastery) and "castrated" (deprived of drives and primordial desires) to fit social norms.[6] It is through this four-fold process that the subject becomes socially and politically recognized. This process carries a particular political significance. The central political premise in all this is the subject's struggle for recognition: the subject wishes to appear to the other in the image it thinks the other wants them to appear (it poses the question "*che vuoi?*" to the other).

Starting from the Saussurean theory of signifiers, Lacan based his understanding of the subject on the process of signification and meaning production.[7] In this process of signification, the subject is born retroactively, which makes the signifier the cause of the subject and the subject's submission to the signifier inevitable.[8] Or, as Lacan's famous definition of the subject goes: "a signifier represents a subject to another signifier"—through which the subject is an effect of language and is represented by a signifier for another signifier.[9] This definition of the subject implies retroactivity in that the political subject emerges when the master signifier recognizes this subject in a chain of signification.[10] In the modern Western liberal order, the master signifier stands for liberal values such as equality, universalism, and human rights but also what are "acceptable" ways of protest, political action, or political sacrifice. Such universalist logics are also underpinned by the notion of whiteness that is implicit in modern liberal ideas of rights, equality, and forms of acceptable political action, as theorists who bring together Lacanian psychoanalysis and critical race theory have argued.[11] Secondly, these master signifiers are foundational for society-wide social fantasies and work as one of the subject's defense mechanisms against the "returned of the repressed." In other words, these master signifiers facilitate "community-building"—they bring together political subjects who share common values and exclude those who are deemed to be disruptive to the unity or the cohesion of the group, community, or nation. Finally, the retroaction is hidden in the moment in which the subject (unconsciously) seeks out the desire of the other: the image, the form in which the subject should appear to the Other. As the subject is always in a subordinate relation to the signifier, it seeks *recognition* from that signifier.[12] Thus, to achieve political recognition, the subject must give up on that which distinguishes it from others, that which it has "in excess." The subject starts to resemble or imitate a trait in the other whose authority the subject recognizes; it begins to identify with the same values or pursue and defend the same political goals. However, this imitation, as Philippe Van Haute writes, never results in the eradication of differences between the subject and the other, between a political recognition a subject wants to achieve and a political recognition a subject can achieve; and furthermore, this imitation will not eradicate the difference between subjects themselves.[13]

The quest for political recognition can be paired with Althusser's theory of interpellation, which is foundational for understanding how ideology works on subjects. Althusser gives an example of a police officer who calls out, "Hey, you!" and the subject who hears the call turns and responds "who, me?"[14] This rather simplistic exchange represents an exchange of recognition: an individual has been interpellated into a subject who was meant to hear the call and respond to it. However, this perceived smooth transition into a political subject (or a subject of ideology) is not nearly as neat as Althusser himself might have suggested.

The call to which the subject responds might be misunderstood or—and this is particularly crucial for the argument developed here—what the signifier "catches" might not be the entirety of the subject.[15] There is something—*object a*—that Althusser cannot account for, something that transcends ideology.[16] The failures of interpellation are significant for thinking political resistance.

In his work *The Misinterpellated Subject*, Martel introduces the idea of misinterpellation to show how revolutionary emancipatory action can take place within the Althusserian logic of recognition. Drawing on the works of Frantz Fanon, Martel locates his discussion of misinterpellation in the Haitian Revolution.[17] For Martel (and others), that revolution is a prime example of a subversive political action, because a group of people responded to the call embodied in the ideals of the French Revolution and French Enlightenment even though these ideals were not meant for them. In Haiti, the enslaved population in the country rose up to fight French colonial powers. As one of the leaders of the revolution maintained, the uprising took place at least partly as a direct response to the freedoms and ideals of the French Revolution and the 1789 Declaration of the Rights of Man and of the Citizen.[18] However, the declaration was never intended for the enslaved, and yet in the context of Haiti, it was the enslaved who answered the call. It was the enslaved in Haiti who inspired the working class and made the French Revolution into a world-changing event. "The hallmarks of misinterpellation, the refusal or inability to hear the siren call of global powers in the ways that were intended, the fact of showing up when unwelcomed, of hearing oneself as being called when one hasn't been, and of refusing to leave once the mistake becomes clear, lead to resistance, radicality, and subversion, sometimes on a massive scale."[19] Martel's practice of misinterpellation suggests that there are always some people who turn up unexpectedly and unannounced and who remind us that political recognition and sovereign authority are not as stable, coherent, and impenetrable as we often imagine.

In contrast to misinterpellation, which operates within an Althusserian framework of interpellation, Dolar's challenge shows its incompleteness. In other words, it shows how interpellation into ideology (or subject-formation) misses out on an important element; and what is more, it shows why this element—*object a*—evades the structure of interpellation. Dolar's psychoanalytic challenge to Althusserian theory exposes the fantasmatic structure of interpellation in that the process assumes a complete/imminent transition between a pre-subjectivized (pre-ideological) individual and a subject; and a clear division between the external, or material, conditions and interiority, or subjectivity, created in the process of interpellation. Althusser's insistence on the completeness of interpellation rests on the assumptions that "the subject makes ideology work."[20] The subject produces and reproduces its meaning. In other words, the subject recognizes itself in ideology—or for the purposes of this paper gets attached to the master signifier—as always already within or belonging. This effortless transition from a pre-ideological to an ideological subject is essential for Althusser; it constitutes the exteriority, or the outside, and the interiority, or the inside, and ensures the continuity of meaning production.

Following Lacan, the subject's attachment to the symbolic order and signification is never complete. There is always a remainder or an excess that defies signification. The excess remains invisible to Althusserian interpellation even though it is internal to this process.[21] Dolar further writes: "The remainder . . . is the point of exteriority in the very kernel of interiority, the point where the innermost touches the outermost, where materiality is the most intimate. It is around this intimate external kernel that subjectivity is constructed. Lacan [named it]: extimacy."[22] This "third extimate space" opens up what is otherwise a closed-up process of interpellation. It questions the "authority" of the master signifier (acknowledging the lack in the Other), the completeness of the subject's attachment to the signifier, and its bond to the remainder that signification and interpellation leave behind.

The emergence of this gap in the production of subjectivity is problematic because it reveals inconsistencies in the symbolic order and the master signifier. It is not only the subject who is lacking; the Other and the master signifier are lacking as well. Dolar resorts to the idea of love as a force which can sustain and cover up the passage from the inner to the outer.[23] It is through blind love for the other that the subject gives itself to cover the lack. In psychoanalysis, for example, this suggests that there is no "call" to which the subject is to respond. However, that doesn't mean that there is no Other. In fact, the Other here is even more present, as the subject has to construct its presence. First, the subject has to make the Other exist through the subject's own belief in it, and second, the subject has to recognize itself as its addressee. Psychoanalysis demystifies the Other as a bearer of knowledge that is external and outside the subject (signifying) relation. Further, Dolar shows how even for Althusser, the Other is not some external pre-ideological material reality through which interpellation is triggered. Rather, for him, the Other has to be supplied by the subject. In a similar process of retroactive recognition of the subject's position within it, the Althusserian subject creates the Other through its ritualized belief in it.[24] Such an Other is reliant on symbolic codifications. This final observation allows Dolar to say that the subject and meaning do not emerge from materiality devoid of any meaning, but from the symbolic that regulates it. In this way, the subject is only an "empty space" in the chain of signification to which meaning is attached and, as such, there is something that transcends the process even after meaning, or ideology, is produced. Žižek identifies this "something" as the pre-ideological kernel of enjoyment.[25] This is the final support for the subject's interpellation into ideology; it is what transcends interpellation and also what supports it. This remainder—the *object a*—is the sacrifice the subject has to pay for its recognition within a social field, but it is also the ultimate object of desire. Situated in the extimate space, *objet a* both constructs and disrupts signification and can never be filled successfully. It is a moment where the structure lacks. Or as Dolar points out, "the structural problem of ideology is ultimately that this [*jouissance*/remainder] fuel cannot be integrated into the edifice, so it turns out to be at the same time its explosive force."[26]

If the notion of misinterpellation outlined by Martel illustrates how resistance can take place within the process of interpellation, assuming that it comes from groups for whom the call wasn't meant, Dolar's critique opens up the structure of interpellation to show its incompleteness (its blindness to that which exceeds interpellation) and its structural reliance on that very excess. With the introduction of the remainder (*object a*) and its distinct, neither inside nor outside, location, a new spatiality has been introduced—the *extimate*. When put in relation to the *object a*, the extimate opens up a potentiality for resistance by either refusing (being unable) to attach itself to master signifiers or by challenging those signifiers from the extimate space. I now turn to the extimate and extimacy to explore their political power.

Extimacy and the Excess in the Other

"Extimacy," as Jacques-Alain Miller writes, describes the presence of the exterior in the interior, the foreign in what is deemed to be an intimate space.[27] Extimacy is not in opposition to intimacy; rather, "the intimate is Other—like a foreign body, a parasite."[28] In his text on the "Extimate," Miller elaborates on Lacan's references to and different uses of extimacy. He highlights two relationships in particular—the relationship between the subject and the Other and between the Other and *object a*. These two relationships will help us understand the structural impossibilities of complete interpellation, the potentiality and the role of the excess (*object a*) in creating an illusion of complete signification.

Lacan states that the extimacy of the subject is the Other, suggesting that at the heart of the most intimate part of the subject we find an attachment to the Other. In the process of subject-formation, it is the desire of the other though which the subject is formed. Lacan nevertheless reminds us that we wish to appear for the Other in the way we think the Other wants us to appear. Thus, "at the heart of my identity to myself, it is the Other who stirs me—where the extimacy of the Other is tied to the vacillation of the subject's identity to himself."[29] Extimacy is thus structural in that it is something that the process of subjectivization (or identity formation) relies upon.[30] It is a way in which the subject becomes. If interpellation was about the emergence of the subject in ideology and its symbolic field, subjectivization is—in psychoanalysis—the emergence of the subject in the field of the Other/signification. With extimacy, Lacan emphasizes the presence of the external object in this very process of formation.

The second "relationship of extimacy" that Lacan exposes is the one between the Other and the *object a*. If the purpose of the relationship between the subject and the Other was an exposure of the external object, the task of this second relationship is similar. There is something in the Other that is foreign to it. In other words, *objet a* is what we can find at the center of the Other. Such a piercing of the Other signifies another structural moment in the process of subjectivization. The Other to whom the subject refers and in relation to which the subject is created is not whole. Extimacy thus locates alterity in the concept of the Other, or asks a question of why the Other is really other.[31] Miller proposes two answers to this question—one is that the Other of the Other is law.[32] It is that which is common, universal, and that which conforms. In contrast, and this is the line Lacan follows, when there is no Other of the Other, alterity is bound to *jouissance*. Miller states: "It is in relation to jouissance that the Other is really Other. This means that none can ground the alterity of the Other from the Signifier, since the very law of the signifier implies that one can always be substituted for the other and vice versa."[33] The master signifiers that determine the other are interchangeable. They can signify universality, human rights, and universal humanity, but these universal ideals mask a struggle—alterity—internal to the Other.

The violence of *jouissance* marks the internal struggle of the Other.[34] Lacan in *Television*, for example, explains how conflict between the Other and *jouissance* turns into racism.[35] Racism is a product of hatred towards the *jouissance* that the subject sees in the Other. Racism calls into play, as Miller writes, "a hatred which goes precisely towards what grounds the other's alterity, in other words its jouissance."[36] No master signifier representing universal, shared, or common humanity can counter this. While the extimate relation of the *objet a* to the Other is structural, what is attached to *objet a* depends on the subject and the *jouissance* the subject locates in the Other. It depends on the subject's assumption that the Other enjoys in a way that is prohibited to the subject. And further, it is the closeness between the subject and that Other which "exacerbates racism."[37] Thus, for Lacan, racist violence arises from the assumptions the subject makes about the other's enjoyment. The Other enjoys too much. Thus, the true intolerance is the intolerance of the Other's *jouissance*. Of course "races exist, but they exist insofar as they are, in Lacan's words, races of discourse, i.e., traditions of subjective positions."[38] In contemporary politics, such differing traditions of subjective positions are the Others, they can act as *objet a* which structurally exist beyond signification—that is, beyond what the signifiers of humanity, universality, and equality are supposed to stand for. Furthermore, as Seshadri-Crooks points out, such different traditions of subjective position are structurally prevented equal access to social capital even if and when the master signifiers allude to their inclusion.[39] How, then, can resistance or political action from such structurally *extimate* positions—where even interpellation fails or comes in excess—bring about political change?

Something in a Place Where There Should Be *Nothing*

If earlier the concern was about locating the *extimate* and putting it in relation to the object of desire, *object a*, then now the question is what happens when something emerges in the place where there should be nothing, when lack is no longer lacking. This emphasis continues to explore the type of violence that exists between the Other and *jouissance* and the significance of extimacy for thinking this relation. When the lack is no longer lacking or when the subject gains something too much, or is too close to the object, as Dolar writes, that is the moment of anxiety. "What one loses with anxiety is precisely the loss—the loss that made it possible to deal with a coherent reality."[40] Anxiety makes signification fall, it exposes the incompleteness and fragility of the symbolic order, not because the subject lost something but because they gained something too much, something too much in a space of loss.

In his tenth seminar, *Anxiety*, Jacques Lacan introduces anxiety as the most profound affect.[41] It is an affect that relates to the body and the structure. While Lacan did not discuss anxiety in political terms, its political applicability is vast. For Burgess, "anxiety is the fundamental antagonism of underlying forces cast together in an unresolved economy of struggle. . . . It is the core of violence, the meaning of violence."[42] What is the violence referred to here? The violence of anxiety concerns again the very institution of the subject and its relation to the Other. One becomes a (political) subject in the moment when one becomes a speaking being.[43] But in this moment of the subject's inception, something is lost, and the loss of this object determines the subject's political and social existence. It is this *object a*, which the subject pursues in hope of returning to the (unattainable) state of completeness, totality, or unity. *Objet a* constructs the subject as a desiring subject, a subject permanently seeking its completeness.

The loss of completeness can be described in more political terms as the experience of alienation. Alenka Zupančič states that it is with alienation that the subject gains awareness of itself. She writes: "This fundamental loss or 'alienation' is the condition of the thinking subject, the subject who has thoughts and representations. It is this loss that opens up the 'objective reality' and allows the subject to conceive himself as subject."[44] This foundational loss or alienation from its "primary" existence also creates the conditions for anxiety, not as an object-driven experience but as a structural condition of the subject's existence. When Lacan says that anxiety is not without an object, what he has in mind is that the object of anxiety is the "ultimate" object of desire, the object of primary loss—*object a*.

Lacan further states that anxiety can only be experienced through representation. However, the representation tells us nothing about the object that triggered a response. Instead, as Zupančič writes, it tells us more about "the window of fantasy in the frame of which a certain object appears as terrifying."[45] In other words, it tells us more about what the subject imagines or creates as terrifying. Anxiety emerges when the object of desire comes too close to the subject and threatens the disappearance of alienation.

Politically, fantasies also work as narratives that reassure belonging to a community for some but also exclusion for others. Often those who do not belong (figures such as a migrant, a figure of a Muslim person, or a homeless person) are represented as possessing something that those who "belong" had to give up. Belonging to the community comes "at a price" and can be experienced as a sacrifice or—in psychoanalytic terms—castration. Belonging is experienced as "a trade-off"—giving up on something in exchange for the feeling of safety. Fantasies surround these castrating experiences. They cover up the fundamental lack (sacrifice) and create a story, a perspective which gives life consistency and stability.[46] Anxiety, then, emerges when the fantasies protecting subjects' rationale for belonging fall or are perceived in danger of falling. As Salecl writes: "anxiety emerges when at the place of the lack one encounters a certain object, which perturbs the fantasy frame through which the subject assessed reality."[47] Objects or figures of fear are invented at the level of fantasy.[48] They either endanger or destroy fantasies of "harmonious life," or they become objects of our fantasies. These objects do not become objects of fear because there is something in them which makes "us" afraid of them. Instead, they tell us more about our relation to the self, to authority, and to our fantasy than they do about themselves. Žižek explains this well when he states that fantasy is a destabilizing dimension, the elementary form of which is envy, jealousy, and loathing.[49] Fantasy becomes a collection of things that irritate us about others who need to be changed or eliminated because they, as Hirvonen writes, "are threatening our being, destroying our cultural heritage, invading our harmonious communities, intruding into our existence."[50] The presence of these others can be read as the filling of the lack. It is as if these "outsiders" fooled the Other (the master signifier) and avoided the sacrifice of *jouissance* that underpins belonging (to the master signifier). The *extimate* object that exists in the Other is here presented as the outsider who can enjoy limitlessly and who avoids castration. The other is the one "who enjoys at the subject's expense: he commits acts that one wouldn't dare to commit, he indulges in one's repressed desires and makes sure that the blame falls on the subject."[51]

In these conditions, anxiety can trigger action. Most often, political action arising from anxiety is one which attempts to eradicate the other—those who emerged in the subject's field and disturbed its sense of reality. These logics align with white supremacy and alt-right ideologies. An example of a slightly different form of anxiety-triggered action would also be the case of political mobilization and the emergence of the Black Lives Matter movement. As I have written elsewhere, the context of a post-racial fantasy that dominated U.S. politics during Obama's administration created a distinct political moment which challenged white liberals who saw the election of President Obama as the final confirmation of a long-awaited coming of racial equality.[52] The widespread mobilization against the shooting of Black men and claims for justice and equality came as a shock to these liberal groups. The collapse of the fantasy led parts of the white community to join the protest and call for equality, while other parts reverted to conservative racist logics which challenged the rightfulness of these protests. If the first response acknowledges the fall of the fantasy and attempts to construct a different fantasy, the second persists in the correctness of the post-racial fantasy, blames individual failures for lack of progress, and in doing so aims to reinstate the (racist) post-racial order. There is, however, another way to think about political action in the context of anxiety. This is the way that starts from the *extimate* space that determines the structure of both the subject and the Other. Thus, we can ask, what might political action look like if it was to come from the remainder, the excess that fantasies and master signifiers cannot account for? In Dolar's words, what is the political action that comes from the space beyond interpellation?

Anxious Politics: Acting from the Place of Extimacy

In Lacanian theory there are two forms of action: *acting out* and *passage à l'acte*. These two strategies of action against the authority or master signifier derive from the experience of anxiety, which pushes the subject to make the ultimate shift in its symbolic order. In *acting out* the subject performs what Lacan would call a hysteric move of opposition to authority, which can derail the symbolic order, but ultimately it reinstitutes it in the same or in a somewhat different yet similar form.[53] It is this act that Lacan described in his talk to the students at Vincennes in 1968 as "resist, but all you will get is a new master."[54] In contrast, *passage à l'acte* stands for a transgression of the symbolic order. It stands for a break with the symbolizing logic, with the way in which the subject has been interpellated and recognized as a political subject. It is a moment when the subject escapes the symbolic network and dissolves its social bond. In effect this action also marks an end to the subject—it stands for the symbolic death of the subject, its refusal to participate in the network of symbolic power relations and in the reinstatement of symbolic authority. *Passage à l'acte*, as I intend to show, is what offers a different way of thinking about political action. While the disruption to signification, interpellation, and symbolic order that comes with this act suggests that it is often materialized in grand political events such as revolutions, the same effect can be achieved if and when action comes from a particular *extimate* place/group.

Where, how, and what might be the conditions that question the structure of the existing political order? Martel's idea of misinterpellation and Dolar's beyond interpellation allow us to start from a position where the act of resistance does not present a complete rejection of liberal universalism, with the rights, privileges, and duties that it stands for. In misinterpellation, the act of resistance is created within the apparatus of ideology and stands for a dysfunction of the system. For example, "in refusing not to be the subjects of the call, the Haitian revolutionaries did not show that the liberal universal was capacious enough to contain everyone after all. . . . Rather they showed that liberal universalism's . . . principles could be grounds for their subversion and ruination, producing a completely different political outcome and process."[55] The internal act of subversion is what makes misinterpellation politically powerful. The act itself makes two interrelated points: its exposes the inner logic of dominant ideologies and in doing so presents it as flawed; and it denies the sovereign the power to complete an act of interpellation, which on the one hand reproduces a subject that was not meant to exist, and on the other hand questions the authority of the sovereign. In the moments when the subject refuses to hear the sovereign in the intended way, a political space opens up, offering the subject a chance to assert itself as "being an entirely different kind of subject than what is usually produced through the process of interpellation."[56]

Although the act of interpellation is never complete, it is grounded in the assumption that it is such. Working within the principles of liberalism, universalism, and human rights, the idea of beyond interpellation not only exposes the false nature of these principles or their potentiality for subversion; it also shows how that which falls beyond interpellation (the excess, reminder, *object a*) in fact allows us to think universality of rights or common humanity in a way that subverts the dominant ideology. Beyond interpellation shows how there is an other (as a subject or space) which upholds that very liberal order and yet does not fully belong to it. Such excluded inclusion is the site of extimacy where we might begin to think political action anew. Drawing on beyond interpellation and extimacy, I now briefly turn to the recent mobilization for racial justice in order to explore how such resistance presents a challenge to contemporary political imaginaries.

For many centrist liberals, the emergence of the Black Lives Matter movement in the aftermath of police shootings of unarmed African American boys and young men in the United States came as a surprise.[57] With President Obama well into his second term in office and enjoying high popularity among the American people, a campaign with a strong racial undertone was not expected. This unpreparedness of the majority population for a political and social movement of such proportions, however, can only be accounted for if the assumption (a fantasy) of the existence of a post-racial society in the United States is taken seriously. Many scholars of African American protest movements, civil rights, and critical race theory write about the ideological undertone that took over the country with Obama's presidency.[58] That ideological undertone can only be described in a self-congratulatory way as overcoming a final hurdle in becoming a post-racial society. That undertone, however, was not experienced in the same way by everyone. If white liberals celebrated a long-awaited victory, the African American communities largely saw it as a moment of political opportunity to fight for what white liberals thought their fellow African American citizens already had.[59] The tension between what one is thought to be and what one actually is in relation to the existing political order opens a possibility for action.

In the situation of post-racial society, where post-racial equality operates as a social fantasy upheld by a master signifier of a white liberal subject, the double interpellation of those who were historically unequal, and whose rights are deemed protected by the liberal order, is played out in a peculiar way. This double interpellation can also be linked to an idea of double-consciousness developed by W. E. B. Du Bois and Frantz Fanon. If the desire of the subject is to shape itself in the image of the other, or appear in the way the subject thinks the other desires them to appear, then how, in the condition of double-consciousness, does the subject relate to mastery and interpellation? For Black Americans, as Du Bois argues, the master in relation to whom "one wants to appear likeable" is not singular. He writes: "It is a peculiar sensation, this double-consciousness, this sense of always looking at one's self through the eyes of others. . . . One feels his two-ness—an American, a black man; two souls, two thoughts, two unreconciled strivings."[60]

In these powerful words, Du Bois outlines where the unovercomeable alterity resides. Whiteness is interpellated into a political subject despite the difference, whereas Blackness never fully becomes such. It remains in the space of otherness in relation to which liberal universalist ideals gain meaning. At the moment of interpellation, the "Black subject" doesn't fit well in the sociopolitical order. It creates an excess which cannot fit into the form of a subject as a political being. If in misinterpellation resisting subjects need to act as if they belong, in beyond interpellation their action is different. They are deemed to be inside, and yet their demands testify to their lack or exclusion. Such positioning acknowledges their extimate position. And it is this positioning that is powerful, for they are deemed to belong. Equally, it is from the extimate space that they make claims for justice and equality. They appeal to the liberal signifiers of justice and equality, but because these claims derive from the extimate space, those appeals—if heard—remove the foundations from the liberal order (master signifier) that instigates change.

It is the banality of claims such as "I too am American" or the chants of "Black lives matter" that does away with the fantasy of the post-racial order and shows the falseness of political claims of their belonging. Barnor Hesse writes about white sovereignty and authority and strategies of acting politically.[61] He gives pertinence to the performativity of power over the law. It is indeed the case that all men are equal (as liberal ideology proclaims) and that racism is prohibited by law, but it is the performativity of power embedded in white structures that determines the future of Black political capital. Thus, acting from the place of extimacy in the context of Black Lives Matter and racial struggles for equality can be, first, to insist on the letter of the law that is deemed legitimate and, second, to continue to expose how the performativity of that legal (or personal) authority departs from the law and continues to exclude, harm, and kill.

Such a demand for something that is already in place (and yet unattainable) introduces a modification in *passage à l'acte*. Instead of breaking with a symbolic order, a demand insists on it to the letter. This is a flip side to Martel's interpretation of the Haitian Revolution when the slaves recognized themselves in a call that was not meant for them. In this modification, the identification with the call is not one of misinterpellation, but one which assumes that interpellation can be complete; where the *objet a* no longer exceeds the call. In the contemporary context of racial struggles for justice, the call a political subject racialized as Black is responding to is a call that the sociopolitical context cannot recognize, because it assumes it is already there—secured in legal equality and antiracist discourse. And yet, despite, or precisely because of the laws and political correctness, such political subjects raise and demand what the liberal order assumes they already have. The impossibility of their demand does not lie in its radicality but in its performativity. A demand coming from the position of extimacy destabilizes the foundation of signification—and in contemporary politics that is the liberal order. Thus the state cannot respond to or embrace those demands for justice and equality without recognizing that the organization of the sociopolitical order to which they are central is not only racist but dependent on the existence of extimate spaces and groups whose demands can never be heard. It is not actions of epochal proportions that challenge and alter the political space, but internal subversive demands coming from the remainders of interpellation: these groups and spaces expose the inner logics of exclusion and the inequality reproduced by liberal ideologies.

Notes

1. Jacques Lacan, "L'Impromptu de Vincennes," *Le Magazine Littéraire* 121 (February 1977): 24.
2. James Martel, "When the Call Is Not Meant for You: Misinterpellation, Subjectivity, and the Law," *Philosophy and Rhetoric* 48, no. 4 (2015): 494–515.

3. Here it has to be noted that interpellation into one's place is an imaginary act. One is hailed into a subject if one recognizes oneself in the call. However, Lacan introduces what we might call a symbolic interpellation in which the subject's interpellation remains incomplete, and the overlap between the imaginary and the symbolic interpellation is a failure. See Mladen Dolar, "Beyond Interpellation," *Qui Parle* 6, no. 2 (1993): 75–96.

4. James Martel, *The Misinterpellated Subject* (Durham, NC: Duke University Press, 2017).

5. Dolar, "Beyond Interpellation."

6. Jacques Lacan, "The Subversion of the Subject and the Dialectics of Desire," in *Écrits: The First Complete Edition in English*, trans. Bruce Fink (New York: Norton, 2006), 671–702.

7. Lacan, "The Subversion of the Subject," 681–82.

8. Lacan, "The Subversion of the Subject," 682.

9. Lacan, "The Subversion of the Subject," 713.

10. See Andreja Zevnik, "*Post-Racial* Society as Social Fantasy: *Black Communities* Trapped between Racism and a Struggle for Political Recognition," *Political Psychology* 38, no. 4 (2017): 621–35.

11. See Kaplana Seshadri-Crooks, *Desiring Whiteness: A Lacanian Analysis of Race* (London: Routledge: 2000), 4–5; and Juliet Flower MacCannell, "The Post-Colonial Unconscious of the White Man's Thing," *Journal for the Psychoanalysis of Culture and Society* 1 (1996): 28–30.

12. Flower MacCannell, "The Post-Colonial Unconscious," 27–28.

13. Philippe Van Haute, *Against Adaptation: Lacan's "Subversion of the Subject"* (New York: Other Press, 2002), 95–96.

14. Louis Althusser, "Ideology and the State," in *Lenin and Philosophy and Other Essays* (New York: Monthly Review, 2001), 116–20.

15. Martel, *Misinterpellated Subject*.

16. Dolar, "Beyond Interpellation."

17. Martel, "When the Call Is Not Meant for You"; Martel, *Misinterpellated Subject*.

18. Martel, "When the Call Is Not Meant for You," 498.

19. Martel, "When the Call Is Not Meant for You," 497.

20. Dolar, "Beyond Interpellation," 78.

21. Dolar, "Beyond Interpellation," 78.

22. Dolar, "Beyond Interpellation," 78.

23. Dolar, "Beyond Interpellation," 82–89.

24. Dolar, "Beyond Interpellation," 90–91.

25. Slavoj Žižek, *The Sublime Object of Ideology* (London: Verso, 1992), 124.

26. Dolar, "Beyond Interpellation," 93.

27. Jacques-Alain Miller, "Extimit," *Prose Studies* 11, no. 3 (1998): 122.

28. Miller, "Extimit," 123.

29. Miller, "Extimit," 123.

30. Miller, "Extimit," 124.

31. Miller, "Extimit," 124.

32. Miller, "Extimit," 125.
33. Miller, "Extimit," 125.
34. In Lacanian psychoanalysis, *jouissance* and violence are inextricably linked. The social or symbolic order guards the subject from the violence of *jouissance*. This is a vast topic that cannot be discussed here. For more, see Slavoj Žižek, *Enjoy Your Symptom: Jacques Lacan in Hollywood and Out* (London: Verso, 2001); Slavoj Žižek, *Violence: Six Sideway Reflections* (London: Profile Books, 2009); and Alenka Zupančič, "When Surplus Enjoyment Meets Surplus Value," in *Jacques Lacan and the Other Side of Psychoanalysis: Reflections on Seminar XVII*, ed. Justin Clemens and Russell Grigg (Durham, NC: Duke University Press, 2006), 155–78.
35. Jacques Lacan, *Television: A Challenge to the Psychoanalytic Establishment*, ed. Joan Copjec (New York: Norton, 1990).
36. Miller, "Extimit," 125.
37. Miller, "Extimit," 125.
38. Miller, "Extimit," 126.
39. Seshadri-Crooks, *Desiring Whiteness*.
40. Mladen Dolar, "'I Shall Be with You on Your Wedding Night': Lacan and the Uncanny," in "Rendering the Real," ed. Parveen Adams, special issue, *October* 58 (Autumn, 1991): 13.
41. Jacques Lacan, *Anxiety*, ed. Jacques-Alain Miller, trans. A. R. Price, vol. 10 of The Seminar of Jacques Lacan (Cambridge: Polity, 2014).
42. Peter, J. Burgess, "For Want or Not: Lacan's Conception of Anxiety," in *The Politics of Anxiety*, ed. Emmy Eklundh, Andreja Zevnik, and Emmanuel-Pierre Guittet (London: Rowman and Littlefield, 2017), 20–21.
43. Žižek, *Sublime Object*, 111.
44. Alenka Zupančič, "The Subject of the Law," in *Cogito and the Unconscious*, ed. Slavoj Žižek (Durham, NC: Duke University Press, 1998), 66.
45. Zupančič, "The Subject of the Law," 67.
46. Renata Salecl, *On Anxiety* (London: Routledge, 2004).
47. Salecl, *On Anxiety*, 24.
48. Ari Hirvonen, "Fear and Anxiety: The Nationalist and Racist Politics of Fantasy," *Law and Critique* 28, no. 3 (2017): 258.
49. Žižek, *Sublime Object*, 192.
50. Hirvonen, "Fear and Anxiety," 258.
51. Dolar, "I Shall Be with You," 14.
52. Zevnik, "*Post-Racial* Society as Social Fantasy," 630–33.
53. Jacques Lacan, *The Other Side of Psychoanalysis*, ed. Jacques-Alain Miller, trans. Russell Grigg, vol. 17 of The Seminar of Jacques Lacan (New York: Norton, 2007).
54. Lacan, "L'Impromptu de Vincennes."
55. Martel, "When the Call Is Not Meant for You," 499.
56. Martel, "When the Call Is Not Meant for You," 499.
57. Juliet Hooker, "Black Lives Matter and the Paradoxes of U.S. Black Politics: From Democratic Sacrifice to Democratic Repair," *Political Theory* 44 (2016): 448–69.

58. Michael J. Dawson, *Not in Our Lifetime: The Future of Black Politics* (Chicago: University of Chicago Press, 2011).

59. Dawson, *Not in Our Lifetime*.

60. W. E. B. Du Bois. *The Souls of Black Folk* (New York: Bantam Classics, 2005), 3.

61. Barnor Hesse, "White Sovereignty (...), Black Life Politics: 'The N****t They Couldn't Kill," *South Atlantic Quarterly* 116, no. 3 (2017): 581–604.

Transference and Its Discontents

Lacan and the Extimate Place of Politics

Vladimir Safatle

In 1967 Lacan presented a text on psychoanalysis and politics titled "Proposition of 9 October 1967 on the Analyst of the School" ("Proposition du Octobre sur le psychanalyste de l'Ecole"). Faced with the need to justify the function of the Freudian School of Psychoanalysis, an institution that he himself had founded, Lacan described the structure of transference as a site of politics. Specifically, he suggested that transference has real consequences for reflecting on emancipatory processes and that all possible emancipation must take the form of a liquidation of transference. This link between emancipation and liquidation of transference is a way to understand how extimacy arises in the clinic; that is, extimacy as a mode of relating, or a relationship, that emerges in the psychoanalytic clinic at the end of analysis. The end of an analytic process is characterized by the liquidation of transference during "subjective destitution." Liquidation of transference occurs when the analysand acknowledges that they no longer need the analyst, when they fall out of "love" with the authority of the analyst. Thus, the end of analysis affirms that the relation between analysand and analyst, one forged in the space of the clinic, is nothing other than subjectivity coming to terms with Otherness via a missing object, a position that the analyst occupies at the end of analysis. This extimate relation between the subject and the object arises when the analysand overcomes that fantasy of the analyst as a subject supposed to know, when the analyst is demoted to the status of a useless object, thereby losing their "authority."

A distinction between power and domination, insofar as they presuppose processes of identification, must be drawn here. Identification shows how social relations are necessarily power relations instituted through repetition. In identifying with something or someone, I assume an implicit development proper to what I have identified with—that is, the structures of my psychic life and its developments will be the reproduction of what I have identified with. In the mirror stage, Lacan argued that to identify with an image is to internalize the history it represents.[1] That is, all identification is an exercise of power. However, not all power relations are relations of domination. We can recall here that what sustains identification is ultimately given neither by the I nor the other, and both are incapable of mastering it; it is extimate to both. There is an extimate kernel circulating in identification processes that cannot be understood as an exercise of domination. That is, identification occurs on the basis of something that surpasses the will of the subject, and which Lacan thematizes through his theory of *object a*—something that always insists within the relations of power and which makes these relations unsteady, always ready to reverse, to drift off. Allow me to insist on one fundamental point: a relationship of domination is the expression of the submission of my will to the will of the Other, but there is something in identification that produces bonds without being the expression of my will or the will of the Other. Rather, it is the expression of unconscious dynamics or affects. Power circulates by expropriating something that can depose it. Consider, for example, the consequences of a statement such as this: "Thus functions the i(a) with which the ego and his narcissism imagines himself, by making a chasuble of that object *a* which makes the misery of the subject. This because the (a), cause of desire, for being at the mercy of the Other, anxiety then on occasion, dresses itself contraphobically with the autonomy of the self, as does the hermit crab with any old shell."[2] Lacan is saying here that the ego ideal, i(a), which is responsible for the imaginary constitution of the self through narcissistic relations, sustains itself by relying on the *objet a* to strengthen the discourse of autonomy. The autonomy of the will appears as a defensive discourse against the phobia resulting from the discovery that what constitutes us in our very identity—the images that constitute us—is sustained by something that could bring forth their own dissolution. This is why we can say that what sustains the material reproduction of psychic life, what allows the constitutive exercise of power relations, can at the same time dissolve the power relations themselves. And if power can control the circulation of these objects that destitute us, it is because it "knows" that the recognition of itself in these objects distresses us.

Power "knows" that freedom distresses us at the same time that it attracts us. If subjects accept servitude, it is because they fear the anxiety that freedom produces, and one of the fundamental things that analysis can provide concerning the exercise of freedom is to lead the subject to put down its counterphobic defenses. The anxiety of freedom does not arise from the transcendent possibility of doing and desiring everything, but from the realization that we are acted upon by external causalities which, as Lacan said, are something in us that are more than ourselves, they are extimate. This Lacanian theme of self-recognition in the object aims to expose the subject to the anguish of knowing that it is moved by causalities that decenter it, causalities deeply rooted in the uncontrolled history of our desires. If freedom were not of such a dramatic nature, the urge to avoid it would not be so constant.

The function of the Freudian School of Psychoanalysis, as Lacan understood it, was basically to recognize subjects who pass through the liquidation of the transference. This entails leaving behind a form of subjection expressed not only in the supposition of knowledge of the Other, but also in the supposition of a knowledge that is constitutive, that would define the modes of self-relation: control, autonomy, deliberation. For this reason, such a recognition is not only the guarantee for the constitution of social bonds that are no longer haunted by relations of subjection; it also holds the possibility of the emergence of bonds that are capable of transforming subjects.

After all, Lacan understood perfectly well that if one goes into analysis, it is because there is an assumption that one can know the truth of one's desire. This assumption of knowledge is not only a cognitive curiosity, a desire to know oneself better; it is an expectation of reconfiguring the structure of practice and care based on self-knowledge. However, this supposed knowledge falters, not by the simple observation of the analyst's ignorance or by the ineffectiveness of the analytic discourse, but by the emergence of an object that sustained the relationship to the Other and which was hitherto veiled. This explains why, in the analyst's discourse, the object occupies the place of an agent. In the analyst's discourse, what is revealed is how the subject's connection with the supposition of knowing was, in fact, a link to an object that caused this subject. Analytical knowledge is realized by its own self-destitution.

To illustrate this point, we can refer to the Lacanian reading of the dialogue between Alcibiades and Socrates in the *Symposium*. In a certain sense, Lacan's reading makes Socrates into the first analyst, just as he makes Socrates's response to Alcibiades's desire the first instance of a lesson on managing transference. In Plato's dialogue, Alcibiades is not just someone who does not know how to govern himself, who is not a master of his own desire. He is also someone who hopes to govern the polis, to govern others.[3] Socrates tries to show Alcibiades that he will not be able to govern the polis before he can govern himself. However, in this context, self-government is not, for Lacan, self-domination through the dynamics of control and self-regulation. In fact, governing oneself is inseparable from the capacity to recognize the remainder which, as determining the division of the subject, "brings about his fall from his fantasy and makes him destitute as subject."[4] Socrates shows Alcibiades how there will be no self-government if he is unable to confront the object that causes his desire, a confrontation that produces a traversal of fantasy and a destitution of the subject.

For this reason, Lacan emphasizes the way Socrates says that Alcibiades is wrong about his desire, because it is not exactly Socrates whom Alcibiades desires, but the *agalma* that Socrates wears. Socrates thus makes an operation of separation insofar as he tries to show Alcibiades the distance between the ego ideal and the object that supports it. By exposing this distance, Socrates produces a kind of short-circuit in the identification system that has supported Alcibiades's position, since the ego ideal no longer appears, as it appeared before, as the point of transcendence compared to imaginary objects. It appears as an article of clothing that supports the subject by preventing it from confronting an object without place that nevertheless causes it, acts in it, and constitutes it.

For this reason, it is necessary to insist that if knowledge in transference is a supposed knowledge about my desire and what causes it, the analytic process aims to extract the object that causes my desire from the paths of knowledge. Socrates denies knowing anything about matters of love, which doesn't mean that he does not know what to do with such matters. It only means that his action is not oriented by deliberation or shared knowledge, which fits within a symbolic structure. His actions are a form of openness that presupposes a destitution of domination, that is, an extimacy, or a form of recognition of an external causality against which it is useless to seek to defend oneself. Lacan then speaks of an operation of "confronting the truth" that is distinct from the operation of the exercise of knowledge. Here, the distinction between knowledge and truth is fundamental.

Lacan himself acknowledges that this initially seems to mean the impossibility of constituting any form of social bond. As he puts it: "Subjective destitution is written on the entry ticket." And he continues: "Isn't this to provoke horror, indignation, panic or even outrage, in any case give pretext for an objection in principle?"[5] For what could be a bond constituted from a liquidation of the transference that seems to preclude all symbolic identification, which can no longer mobilize any phantasmatic production? A type of bond which makes Lacan affirm that: "In this change of tack where the subject sees the assurance he gets from this fantasy, in which each person's window onto the real is constituted, capsize, what can be perceived is that the foothold of desire is nothing but that of a *désêtre*, disbeing. In this *désêtre* what is inessential in the supposed subject of knowledge is unveiled, from which the psychoanalyst to come dedicates him- or herself to the *agalma* of the essence of desire, ready to pay for it through reducing himself, himself and his name, to any given signifier."[6] This is how Lacan describes the process of the liquidation of transference. Let us first note how it is a question of breaking down the security provided by fantasy as a window onto the real—that is, by fantasy's framing of the real over a certain distance and in a certain operation. There is a temporality to fantasy, a temporality marked by repetition and the modular updating of the original experiences. What happens at the end of transference is that the subject approaches the real, experiencing a temporality outside of the structure. When the security produced by the fantasy falters, desire reveals itself as nothing more than a *désêtre*. This is not exactly a form that re-registers the subject into the ontological security of a being thought through normativity, as a necessity, but rather is a drifting off, a dispossession. Desire, then, is shown to be precisely this drifting off, and in this sense, the time of the real appears adrift. This shift from being to *désêtre* is characteristic of the destitution of the analyst's knowledge.[7] That is to say, in analysis the analyst goes through a *désêtre*, which presupposes anguish, and the analysand goes through a subjective destitution, which implies a certain helplessness.

This destitution can be described as a change in the structure of recognition processes because what occurs is not a self-recognition in another subject but in an object. Such recognition is made by reducing the name of the subject to any signifier. That is to say, the name, which establishes relations of filiation and transmission, and bears the mark of the subject's inscription in the horizon of a family constellation, becomes any signifier, in the sense of a purely contingent inscription, without place in a chain of needs.[8] The symbolic reinscription that the analytic interpretation produces through the mobilization of the frames of relation specific to the Oedipus complex and its normative horizon are destitute in such a way that the name appears as any signifier.

But a central question remains: Why is this process of the liquidation of transference not simply a depressive process, the dead time of melancholia? What makes it a process, on the contrary, of affirming emancipation?

Transference and Emancipation

To answer these questions, let us begin by asking how to finish a transferential process. Of course, this question can only be answered on a generic level, since the paths of an analysis are always unique. However, this does not mean that the generic level is devoid of importance and interest or that it does not reveal structural traces. We will say, then, that the transfer is liquidated when what Lacan calls the "analytical act" occurs—an act that can answer the general question of emancipation.

Let us first recall some considerations about emancipation as a normative horizon for political struggles. The traditional tendency is to derive discussions about emancipation from the regulatory notion of maturity by generalizing the consequences of the distinction between minority and adulthood. In this understanding, political struggles that are driven by expectations of emancipation are struggles to realize forms of development of an individual capable of self-deliberation and self-affirmation.

However, we must insist that this way of thinking does not allow us to distinguish between emancipation and subjection to disciplinary patterns that are socially required for a conformity to social roles. Exiting the "minority" can be understood as a result of the internalization of systems of judgment and socially accepted actions that are proper to those subjects who are held imputable and responsible. In this context, there is a risk that we will no longer be able to draw minimally operative distinctions between emancipation and mere social adaptation to legal patterns of imputability, or even between recognition, as the establishment of hitherto unpredicated modes of existence, and acknowledgment, as confirmation of potentialities achieved by the current mode of existence. From this arises the problem: a condition of socialization that is historically defined and legally organized turns into an ontologically stable horizon for regulating forms of life. In contradistinction to this, the notion of the analytic act allows us to see emancipation appearing as a possibility for the subject to emerge as a normative power capable of producing singularizations. But in order to do so, a structural change in the notion of agency needs to occur.

In this regard, let us remember how Lacan states that the analytic act would be grounded on a "paradoxical structure arising from the fact that the object is active and the subject is subverted," a subversion that is an inscription of the position of the subject in the real.[9] We return to this point because this idea of an act capable of inscribing the subject in the real is central. It implies that in producing an act, subjects act from a position that collapses the symbolic order. Therefore, they lose their previous inscription in the symbolic order and the order of knowledge that constituted them. This is why, from a clinical point of view, the concept of the analytic act reconfigures the processes of analytical intervention by putting in second place the mechanisms of symbolization through the significant inscription produced by interpretation. From now on, the analysis will not seek, through interpretation, to provide subjects with inscriptions within a regulated framework of conflicts and affiliations. It will confront the subjects with an act that deprives them of such a place.

This explains why, in the device of the analytic act, a force of dissolution and an operation of establishment are linked, and the complexity lies precisely in the understanding of this double movement. It is not possible to think about processes of establishment without answering the question of how dissolutions are carried out. For there are dissolutions that are only degradations of the previous order, or if we wish, which are a mere passage to the act, a mere fascination with annihilation that removes from the act every possibility of recognition. For this reason, the classic forms of the *passage à l'acte* are linked to suicide.

However, there are dissolutions and landslides that result from the pressures of new orientations. Is one of the fundamental questions that concerns political action not how to make orders collapse?[10] Considering what the experience of revolutions in the twentieth century has shown us, orders can be perpetuated even after they fall, or rather, they can be perpetuated exactly because they have fallen and have become an implicit mode of existence rather than an explicit one. They may then resurface as a recurrence that reappears when we least expect it, or they may continue to operate in an underground extimate stratum, gradually eroding the new order until it becomes unrecognizable.[11] For this reason, the question of the political act as a process of dissolution is of paramount importance.

A Kind of Revolution

This discussion brings us to the power of negation proper to every act. At various times, Lacan brings the analytic act closer to a possible reading of the political concept of revolution. However, a distinction must be made here. In multiple instances, Lacan insisted that "revolution" means, in relation to what we know about astronomical movements, "to return to the same place." In commenting on the Copernican revolution, so often used as a metaphor for epistemic change in philosophy (Kant and criticism as a Copernican revolution) and even in psychoanalysis (Freud and the Copernican revolution of the unconscious), Lacan wondered: "What is revolutionary about refocusing the solar world around the sun?"[12] Because there was no change in the hierarchy, unity, and centrality represented by the notion of spherical motion as a perfect celestial form, the true revolution was in the advent of elliptical movement—that is, the notion of two centers as the form of celestial movements. Hence, if revolution is not the wish to return to the same place, it cannot be separated from a change in the entire structure of knowledge. Revolution is not limited to transformations of the place that each element occupies within a given structure, nor to the placeholders of knowledge and power.

Lacan appeals to poetry in order to consider the revolution that an analytic experience really entails. In this respect, let us remember a poem dear to him, which he considered an expression of the "general formula of the act,"[13] Arthur Rimbaud's "À une raison":

> A tap of your finger on the drum releases all sounds and initiates the new harmony.
> A step of yours is the conscription of the new men and their marching orders.
> You look away: the new love!
> You look back—the new love!
> "Change our fates, shoot down the plagues, beginning with time," the children sing to you. "Build wherever you can the substance of our fortunes and our wishes," they beg you.
> Arriving from always, you'll go away everywhere.[14]

First, it is noteworthy that the general formula of the analytic act is given by a poem—that is, approaching the act and the emergence of another regime of language expressed in the form of the poem. If language appears here in a fundamental position, it is because it decides the form of the experience, the dynamics of our grammars of affects, and the structure of our sensibilities. There is no real revolution without a transformation in the capacity of the enunciation of language.

Second, let's remember the title of the poem, "To a Reason." The general formula of the act is linked to a poem entitled "To a Reason." What is most obvious here is the idea of "*a* reason" and not "*the* reason," as if it were to say, "everyone has their reason." But a sentence of this nature generally seems to mean: "there is no reason, because everyone has their own," "there is no truth, because everyone has their own reason." If there is no reason, then there is no ratio, not only in the sense that there is no common measure, but specifically in the sense that there is no generic implication, which is the ground of truth. Every process of truth is a process able to produce a generic implication or universal recognition. If there is no reason, it seems that nothing involves us generically, nothing gives us a common field. There seems to be only one word, one word and then another word. However, the poem expresses exactly the opposite idea. It is as though the singularity of the experience that produces the body in which a reason bursts through is an experience that can be recognized by everyone. As if what was unveiled was only the opening of a common space that transcends the world.

It is clear that the poem begins with a horizon of war and music, as if the real war was the transformation of language into music. It begins with a drumbeat, announcing creation by breaking the silence with a sound, usually dry, without resonance. But now this absence of resonance is the advent of a new harmony produced by all sounds.

I would like to note, however, an important point here. All sounds played together can only produce a cluster of sounds, they never provide a new harmony. A touch that liberates all sounds can actually be perceived as a sound capable of producing harmony, much like the substance of our fortune and our desires which can be cultivated anywhere. That is to say, we are talking about a relation (because harmony is necessarily a relation) without restriction and without loss, which can potentially operate in a time and space that is now devoid of finite determinations. And as the outbreak of war is transmuted into music, the poem produces the eruption of new men and a new love. This is a new love that needs to be repeated, which is not just said once, but makes us turn our heads back once more. It is as if love is what must be repeated, as if love would really be the scene of a repetition, or as if love would be what allows repetition to exist in its transformative power.

Like reason, love is a question of a relationship and existence in the relationship. Reason is, among other things, a decision about the logical structures of order, identity, difference, and unity—that is, the relation and compatibility between determinations. There is always a ratio resonating in reason. As Rimbaud writes in another poem, "Genie": "love, perfect and reinvented measurement, wonderful and unforeseen reason."[15] For there is a time peculiar to love and the dispersion of its act. This time of love founds another reason, as Lacan clearly understood "To a Reason": "Love is in this text the sign, pointed as such, of the change of reason."[16] In producing this repetition that denounces the desire for duration, the poem opens to a song. The children not only sing, they pray, because they feel the urgency of the desires that are cultivated in a place out of place—that is, in a place foreign to the grammar that we utilize for describing the current state of things, in an "anywhere" out of the world as it is now composed and divided.

An act is always the triggering of another time and another space. That is its function: to allow desire to be cultivated in another time and another space, breaking the hierarchy of places that desacralize distances. In this sense, it is not by chance that Lacan chose Rimbaud to provide a general formula for the analytic act. He is the poet who speaks of a time of revolutions, who writes poems on popular emancipation battles, and who leaves the verse poem behind and makes language into a colorful system through phonetic work with vowels. That is to say, Rimbaud produces a new *aisthesis* in language and expression by exploring significant dimensions elaborated beyond the purely semantic modes of determination. A "systematic derangement of the senses," as Rimbaud himself says, which is the advent of new constructive principles. Recall that "To a Reason" was written between 1872 and 1873, just after the Commune. This gives a very concrete expression to who the new men are, those who rise and live in a new harmony.

This must be kept in mind when Lacan says: "the act takes place in a saying and it modifies the subject," or "the act destitutes in its end the very subject which it establishes."[17] This demonstrates how the analytic act, instead of merely externalizing the subject, modifies it in a paradoxical movement between instauration and destitution. This paradoxical position may explain why "the act is best accomplished by failure," which does not mean that every act is a failure. There is a kind of failure that results from the pressure of the productivity of desire towards new forms. The failed act expresses the failure of the determining force of ordinary language, where one must feel that ordinary language fails, confesses its powerlessness, and transmutes its categories. Or as Lacan said: "My proof only touches on being [*à l'être*] to give it birth from the flaw the being [*l'étant*] produces from being said [*de se dire*]."[18]

We can now understand the political implications of the concept of the analytic act. It allows us to think the political notion of revolution beyond its submission to a merely restorative dynamic. The act shows us more clearly the true dimension of transformation that a revolutionary action must produce, and it shows how it is related to the modification of the structure of knowledge/power. However, and this is a decisive point, the act does not simply push the knowledge previously assumed by the Other towards a knowledge now present in the consciousness of the subject. It does not imply the reappropriation of knowledge. Reappropriation would only be the reiteration of the same regime of knowledge and action, which has now become available to consciousness. It is useless to praise the praxis if this praxis still depends on the same grammar of knowledge that we have already been subjected to. A grammar composed of the ideals of autonomy, deliberation, choice, and decision necessarily refers to the mode of representation of consciousness. It doesn't matter who actually acts—that is, if one always acts from the same grammar. In any case, it is the grammar that acts, it is the system of rules that acts. An emancipated practice is not the result of the transfer of knowledge. That is, emancipation is not a transfer of knowledge that would allow us to recover the enunciation of knowledge, and which in turn would allow us to better deliberate. Let's remember an important statement: "Thus the being of desire reunites with the being of knowledge and is thereby reborn, in their being bound together in a one-sided strip on which a single lack is inscribed, the one that the agalma sustains."[19] Desire and knowledge meet as two sides of a Möbius strip. They pass into each other, in a passage that occurs only under the condition of assuming a torsion. This passage is the inscription of a lack, which is not a lack that is simply related to incompleteness or to the subjectivation of castration, understood as the assumption of finitude, but rather is the emergence of an object that is not reduced to what a signifying chain represents. When a knowledge of desire is possible, it is only by a torsion that, from the point of view of the present configuration of knowledge, is a lack.

But I would like to insist on a fundamental point. If something is lacking, it is because I do not have it. If the articulation between desire and knowledge inscribes a structural lack, it is because such an articulation points to something that I can never have, which will never be under the sign of my possession, and this is exactly one of the main features of *agalmata*: subjects do not have them, but they support them, which is a totally different matter.[20] This is a way of saying that the destitution of knowledge, the condition for the liquidation of the transfer, has the assumption of another word, another relation to language: a language that does not seem to be exactly mine, a knowledge that does not strengthen the illusion of my propriety and domain. Hence statements such as: "Everything that is unconscious only plays on language effects. It is something that is said, without the subject representing himself or saying it—or knowing what he is saying."[21] More than being structured as a language, the unconscious is a discourse that lays down the very speech of the subject. It is the emergence of a language that no longer appears as mine. Not only because the subject's utterances are ruled by the involuntary, but mainly because it is no longer the language of meaning and the restoration of properties produced by the dynamics of meaning. This is the language of a truth event.

It should also be noted that, with this, we have said nothing about revolutionary processes in their concrete dimension of unfolding and in their historically situated causality. But what I would insist on is that psychoanalysis can say nothing about them, since they are the objects of history and politics. It can, however, talk about what was once called "the subjects' revolutionary becoming,"[22] that is, the psychic rooting of a desire for revolution that involves the effective transformation of forms of agency. Not only are there historical bases for such a desire, there are also bases for it in the drive. The concrete existence of such a becoming is the necessary opening up of potentialities within social life.

The Religion of Meaning

Following the previous discussion of language and revolution, it is important to engage with Lacan's notion of meaning. Lacan's theory of the subject hinges on the moment of enunciation (of truth) that is extimate to the given language of meaning. It is there that Lacan locates the subject of the unconscious. Among the different ways of discussing this complex problem, let us insist on the one that exposes the political dimension of this debate. Here, we can recapitulate Lacan's account of the political act that is the dissolution of an institution which he himself had created: "The International, since such is its name, is no more than the symptom of what Freud expected of it. But it is not what weighs in the balance. It's the Church, the true one, which supports Marxism by giving it new blood . . . with a renewed meaning. Why not psychoanalysis when it turns into meaning? I'm not saying that for a vain joke. The stability of religion comes from the fact that the meaning is always religious."[23] This is the Lacanian way of saying that the real political problem we face is the resurgence of the theological-political dimension of power.[24] Religion is a means of supporting social bonds through the reduction of political demands to demands for protection, through the constitution of authority by figures of pastoral power. So, to say that meaning is always religious means to say that psychoanalysis cannot be reduced to a discourse of confession because it is not thinkable within the relationships of necessity, of confirmation of the original destiny, or of the substantial unity of redemption. Lacan isn't afraid to speak here of religion, of a type of Marxism and of the bureaucratization of social ties by an international (in this case, the IPA), which is maintained only out of the fear of the analytic act.

It should also be noted that the ground of religious experience is based on the circulation of a particular notion of time—the time of providence, of redemption. In this context, meaning can only appear as a relation of necessity guaranteed by a ground that is originally situated. Meaning restores what has been lost, it heals us by returning us to an original ground. Thus, the main contrast is between meaning and event, meaning and truth. If Lacan criticized Marxism, it is because he understood its theory of revolution from a historical eschatology in which the proletariat appears as a finally reconciled subject-object. In this eschatology, every event is canceled under the weight of a time that is none other than the projection of an irresistible realization of progress. This is not the only reading possible of Marx's theory of revolution, but this is how Lacan understands it. Contrary to redemptive time, analysis plays on the destituting time of *the cut* and of a revolution which can appear as a real space for the event.

But what can psychoanalysis offer to the critique of religion, utopian politics, and the rise of bureaucracy? If we return to the question of how we know that we are not dealing with the "stylization" of a depressive position, we must insist on the relation between act and *jouissance*. For what leads to an act of this nature, an act beyond sense, is the displacement and depersonalization that the experience of *jouissance* necessarily produces. There is always a relation between act and the attempt to transform the impossible of *jouissance* into the figure of a form of future relation, giving body to the impossible. Thus, in transference, it would not be possible for the subject not to be driven by the emergence of *jouissance* beyond the forms of the symbolic inscription of desire. This is exactly what allows the liquidation of transference, its non-consolidation in a simple relationship of suggestion and dependence.

We can conclude, then, that in transference, the extimate character of *jouissance* is on display, whereby *jouissance* itself is ultimately shown to be out of place.[25] We see this, for example, in the oral enjoyment of Ernst Kris's patient, haunted by his desire for plagiarism and his decomposition of the illusions of being an author; and the example of the enjoyment of the Rat Man before the description of Chinese torture. Transference, in its destitution of knowledge, must allow the emergence of such an enjoyment, as distressing as it is. It must allow the emergence of an enjoyment that does not function to reassure the subject, but to show that there is no place for enjoyment in the administration of life as it happens in the current situation. In fact, psychoanalysis tries to show how the extimate character of this *jouissance* brings with it a political truth—namely, the fact that the conditions of the material reproduction of the life to which the subject is submitted are only sustained through a desire to not know about this enjoyment. With this enjoyment, it is impossible to do anything, and it is necessary to ruin it and forget it. That is to say, the real nature of this *jouissance* entails transformations and singular productions and relies on the subject assuming and producing an act which has the form of a non-inscription. In this sense, we can understand the importance of a statement such as "enjoyment is what truth finds in resistance to knowledge."[26] If truth is what resists knowledge in the name of enjoyment, then the action of truth will always be a destitution in the name of an impossible situation to come.

The Paradoxes of the Pass

The subjective destitution discussed above is crucial for understanding the processes of recognition that unfold in the end of transference, as a universal procedure. Lacan discusses this in his account of the pass or the watershed moment of the end of analysis. Such discussions lead us to specific problems of organization and transmission, problems that will prove unsolvable within the Lacanian horizon. This leads Lacan to dissolve his own institution.

Let us remember how the Freudian School of Psychoanalysis sustains an ultimate belief in the return to recognition processes based on the assumption of a certain form of "communication." In this sense, the school should be the place where the liquidation of transfer would be "communicated." "This experience cannot be eluded, its results must be communicated," says Lacan.[27] If the results are to be communicated, it is because the unveiling of the homelessness of *jouissance* that comes from the dejection of the analyst and their supposed knowledge does not lead us to a position of simple isolation. Lacan will say: "What does this step, of being made alone, have to do with the one alone that one thinks oneself to be by following him? Did I not trust myself to the analytical experience, that is to say that which has happened to me from the one who sorted things out alone? Should I believe myself to be the only one to have it; so, for whom would I speak?"[28] In this context, Lacan speaks of the founding act of the École Freudienne as the representative of the analytic act. This act is carried out alone, but it can nevertheless constitute a bond presupposed by the demand for "communication." And there must be an extreme tension between enjoyment and communication, a tension that may not really be resolved, which can only end in the dissolution of the space of communication, which is another way of understanding the question of the dissolution of the school. But the dissolution of the space of communication will be, paradoxically, the last wager on the institutional possibility of politics. An institution organized as a field and whirlwind.

Recall here what was at stake in the notion of the pass. Under the pass procedure, an end of analysis allows the analysand to "give an account of his analysis" to passers who will then pass it to a jury. The first question concerning this procedure lies in the notion of "give an account." At other times, Lacan will speak of an act that can be "readable" by all. But what kind of speech and full readability is this? What counts here? And for what form of common space? Here lies the full weight of the problem. There is something transmissible at the end of an analysis, but as Lacan will say: "How can one recognize a legal status to an experience that one cannot even respond to?"[29] How can one recognize a *jouissance* that language does not want and seems to know nothing about? Lacan bets on a possible transmission and describes what is fully transmissible—namely, a *matheme*, a term inspired by Lévi-Strauss to describe minimal units of formal articulation of the relations presupposed by myths. That is, the speech about analysis should be the constitution of a *matheme* capable of passing on two levels of transmission. The analytic act seems to take place in the constitution of a *matheme*.

In fact, there is communication only if we can talk in two levels of transmission. If I tell someone something and that person cannot tell it to a third person, there is no communication, for there is no guarantee that the initial statement was, in fact, understood. The communication demonstrates that meaning is the perpetuation of reference beyond the modification of its enunciators.

However, the inscription of the act in a transmission should not be its submission to sense, and at this point lies the complexity of the procedure. We may even wonder if this would not necessarily invalidate all communication. Lacan believes that this irreducibility of the act to meaning is the only way to guarantee that we will not return to a "group effect." What underlies the group is the possibility of the unity of reference, and the sharing of modes of interpretation of statements and practices. The group is the ultimate expression of belief in a common grammar and a reference that does not change in the modification of its utterers.

For this reason, we may in fact ask ourselves if the experience of the pass could have a destination other than failure. If the analytical act changes the relationship between subject and language, it is not possible to try to recover communication levels after the liquidation of transference. This experience does not communicate, it drives language beyond communication. For the requirement of communication can only be accomplished by adjusting the report of analysis to the previously shared grammatical and coding expectations. This means necessarily the reiteration of the code. This will necessarily reproduce stereotypes of reports and only confirm the singularities of the *jouissance* of the enunciator, whose proper name guarantees the identifying support of the bond produced by the school, whether this proper name is "Freud" or "Lacan." For a theory that links emancipation with subjective destitution, a "Freudian" school is a contradiction *in adjecto*, just as a "Freudian" or a "Lacanian" field will be a contradiction.

What drives Lacan to this wager? Lacan's appeal at this moment to readability and communication is his way of saying: there is something in the act that has the force of implication; it "de-supposes" knowledge, but it does not abolish the social relationship. Lacan's answer through the pass can only lead to a stalemate, as he himself will eventually realize by arguing at the end for the dissolution of the school.

However, this impasse has positive political consequences. If the process of political emancipation is a process in which clinical experience in its own way is part of and requires the recognition of the "de-supposition" of knowledge and the advent of new subjects and new relationships enunciated in the singular, then it isn't the place of psychoanalytic theory to talk about how the relations-to-come will be. The theoretical anticipation of reconciliation is an attempt at reconciliation itself. What theory can do is defend the need for subjective transformations that allow subjects to have the power to revolutionize processes in forms of life. But it cannot anticipate the form and direction of the organizations and practices that will be born out of such transformations. That is, theory can articulate the forms of emergence of new subjects, subjects that are extimate to structures, but it cannot specify the way they will organize after their emergence—that is, if it wishes to avoid the risk of making the future a mere image of the realization of possibilities immanent to the present. At this point, theory must stop in order to allow praxis to take place in its multiple and innumerable contextual configurations. Theory becomes normative if it imposes its image on praxis.

The transformation of theory into normativity is a reminder of the need for dynamic organizations that are capable of constituting and destituting themselves in a continuous process that requires the recognition of the different forms of enjoyment, that is, the knowledges and discourses, with which they are confronted. The act of liquidating transference takes its distinguishing character from the very social forms which it inhabits. For this reason, Alain Badiou is correct in appointing Lacan as heir to the "destitute operations" of revolutionary processes. But it would still be necessary to remember the importance of thinking about how to integrate these destitutions into the normal functioning of institutions, instead of settling for "anarchist leftism" or "tyrannical anarchism."[30] This is perhaps the meaning of Lacan's ultimate abandonment of the school-form and his assumption of a field-form based on concepts such as the transience of the group's existence, the randomness of relationships between participants, lability, the limitation of bureaucratic functioning processes, and the absence of hierarchy. No one ever said that such tasks are simple. However, they remain fundamental tasks for thinking about the contemporary political field.

Notes

1. See Jacques Lacan, *Écrits* (Paris: Seuil, 1966), 93–101. English translations are my own unless indicated otherwise.

2. Jacques Lacan, *Autres écrits* (Paris: Seuil, 2001), 262; translated into English as "Speech to the École freudienne de Paris," Freud2Lacan, https://freud2lacan.b-cdn.net/Discours_a_l'Ecole_freudienne_de_Paris.pdf. Hereafter cited with the French and then the English pagination.

3. See Plato, *Charmides, Alcibiades I and II, Hipparchus, The Lovers, Theages, Minos, Epinomis*, trans. W. R. M. Lamb, Loeb Classical Library 201 (Cambridge, MA: Harvard University Press, 1927).

4. Lacan, *Autres écrits*, 252, 8.

5. Lacan, *Autres écrits*, 252, 8.

6. Lacan, *Autres écrits*, 252, 9.

7. See Serge Cotter, *Freud et le désir du psychanalyste* (Paris: Seuil, 1996), 187–94.

8. For the relationship between transference and contingence, see Monique David-Ménard; *Éloge des hasards dans la vie sexuelle* (Paris: Hermann, 2011), 199–233.

9. Lacan, *Autres écrits*, 332.

10. See Vladimir Lenin, "On the State and Revolution," in *The Lenin Anthology* (New York: Norton, 1975), 130–54.

11. See Sigmund Freud, "Moses and Monotheism," in *The Origin of Religion*, trans. James Strachey, ed. Albert Dickson (New York: Penguin, 1990), 35–76.

12. Lacan, *Autres écrits*, 420.

13. Jacques Lacan, *Séminaire XV*, séance du 10/01/68 (mimeo). About the notion of act, see Eric Porge, "Clinique de l'acte analytique," *La Clinique Lacanienne* (January 2013): 35–50.

14. Arthur Rimbaud, "To a Reason," in *Illuminations*, trans. John Ashbery (New York: W.W. Norton, 2011), 55.

15. Arthur Rimbaud, "Genie," in *Illuminations*, trans. John Ashbery, 163.

16. Jacques Lacan; *Seminaire XX* (Paris: Seuil, 1973), 26.

17. Lacan, *Seminaire XX*, 375.

18. Lacan, *Seminaire XX*, 426 ("Radiophonie," Freud2Lacan, https://freud2lacan.b-cdn.net/Radiophonie_bilingual_IV.pdf).

19. Lacan, *Seminaire XX*, 254.

20. See Louis Gernet, *Anthropologie de la Grèce antique* (Paris: Flammarion, 1982).

21. Lacan, *Autres écrits*, 334.

22. Gilles Deleuze, *Pourparlers* (Paris: Minuit, 2003).

23. Lacan, *Autres écrits*, 318.

24. See also Jacques Lacan, *The Triumph of Religion*, trans. Bruce Fink (London: Polity, 2015).

25. Serge Leclaire understands this point when he asks about transference: "Que va-t-on chercher? On l'a dit. Dans l'essence même de la parole

qu'est l'articulation littérale, *comment celui qui dit se débat avec sa jouissance?*" Serge Leclaire, *Psychanalyser* (Paris: Seuil, 1968), 174.

    26. Lacan, *Autres écrits*, 358.
    27. Lacan, *Autres écrits*, 255.
    28. Lacan, *Autres écrits*, 263.
    29. Lacan, *Autres écrits*, 262.
    30. Alain Badiou, *Lacan: L'Anti-Philosophie* (Paris: Fayard, 2013), 153.

Contributors

Richard Boothby is a professor of philosophy at Loyola University Maryland. He is the author of *Death and Desire: Psychoanalytic Theory in Lacan's Return to Freud*; *Freud as Philosopher: Metapsychology after Lacan*; *Sex on the Couch: What Freud Still Has to Teach Us about Sex*; and the memoir *Blown Away: Refinding Life after My Son's Suicide.* Most recently he published *Embracing the Void: Rethinking the Origin of the Sacred* (Northwestern University Press, 2023).

Nadia Bou Ali is a psychoanalyst and an associate professor at the American University of Beirut. She is the author of *Hall of Mirrors: Psychoanalysis and the Love of Arabic.*

Silvio Carneiro is a professor at the Federal University of ABC (UFABC) in Brazil and a member of the board of directors of the International Herbert Marcuse Society, as well as the coordinator of the research group Utopia and Criticism: Subjectivity, Democracy and Social Transformation.

Alejandro Cerda-Rueda is a psychoanalyst practicing in Mexico City and the senior editor for Paradiso editores. He is a postgraduate professor at the Universidad Iberoamericana (UIA) as well as a visiting professor at the Sociedad Freudiana de la Ciudad de México (SFCM). He has published a book, *En la penumbra del sujeto,* and was a recipient of a Mellon Foundation grant to participate in the international research program Extimacies: Critical Theory from the Global South (2019–2022).

Mladen Dolar is a professor and senior research fellow in the Department of Philosophy, University of Ljubljana. His principal areas of research are psychoanalysis, modern French philosophy, German idealism, and art theory. Apart from fourteen books in Slovene, his books include *A Voice and Nothing More*, which has been translated into ten languages, and *Opera's Second Death*, with Slavoj Žižek. He is one of the founders of what has become known as the Ljubljana Lacanian school.

CONTRIBUTORS

Patricia Gherovici is a psychoanalyst, analytic supervisor, and recipient of the Sigourney Award for her clinical and scholarly work with Latinx and gender variant communities. She is a trustee at Pulsion: The International Institute of Psychoanalysis and Psychoanalytic Psychosomatics, New York. Gherovici is the author of *The Puerto Rican Syndrome*, *Please Select Your Gender: From the Invention of Hysteria to the Democratizing of Transgenderism*, and *Transgender Psychoanalysis: A Lacanian Perspective on Sexual Difference*; the coauthor of *Psychoanalysis in the Barrios: Race, Class, and the Unconscious* (with Chris Christian); and the coeditor of *Lacan on Madness: Madness Yes You Can't*, *Lacan, Psychoanalysis and Comedy* and *Psychoanalysis, Gender and Sexualities: From Feminism to Trans** (all with Manya Steinkoler).

Amanda Holmes teaches in the philosophy department at the University of Applied Arts, Vienna. Her research is situated at the intersection of psychoanalysis and philosophy, and she works on questions of desire, language, and being. She has published work in numerous journals and edited volumes.

Vladimir Safatle is a professor in the Department of Philosophy and the Institute of Psychology (Universidade de São Paulo) and the author of several books, including *Le circuit des affects: corps politiques, détresse et la fin de l'individu*; *Maneras de transformar Mundos:Lacan, emancipation, politica*; *Grand Hotel Abyss: desire, recognition and the restoration of the subject*; and *La passion du négatif: Lacan et la dialectique*.

Surti Singh is an associate professor and director of graduate studies in the philosophy department at Villanova University. She is a coeditor of the *Oxford Handbook of the Frankfurt School* and of the series Psychoanalytic Acts.

Samo Tomšič is a professor of philosophy and aesthetics at the University of Fine Arts Dresden and a research associate at the Humboldt University Berlin. His research areas comprise theoretical psychoanalysis, structuralism and poststructuralism, political philosophy, and aesthetics. His books include *The Capitalist Unconscious: Marx and Lacan* and *The Labour of Enjoyment: Toward a Critique of Libidinal Economy*.

Andreja Zevnik is a senior lecturer in politics at the University of Manchester, UK. Her research is inspired by psychoanalysis, continental philosophy, and critical race theory and focuses on the production of subjectivities and different political imaginaries in acts of resistance among various marginalized groups. She is the author of *Lacan, Deleuze and World Politics: Re-Thinking the Ontology of the Political Subject*, and the coauthor of *Jacques Lacan between Psychoanalysis and Politics* (with Tomšič), *Lacan and Deleuze: A Disjunctive Synthesis* (with Nedoh), and *Politics of Anxiety* (with Eklund and Guittet).

Alenka Zupančič conducts research at the Institute of Philosophy, Scientific Research Center of the Slovene Academy of Sciences, Ljubljana. She is also a professor at the European Graduate School in Switzerland. Notable for her work on the intersection of philosophy and psychoanalysis, she is the author of numerous articles and many books, including *Ethics of the Real: Kant and Lacan*; *Why Psychoanalysis?*; *What Is Sex?*; *Let Them Rot: Antigone's Parallax*; and *Disavowal*.